"*Basic Christian* provides us windows into some of the reasons and ways Stott's life and ministry have had such global impact. I am moved again with deep gratitude for John Stott and the faithfulness and wisdom, courage and humility with which he has lived and communicated the gospel of our Lord Jesus Christ."

MARK LABBERTON, Ogilvie Associate Professor of Preaching, and director, Ogilvie Institute of Preaching, Fuller Theological Seminary

"A young boy perched on a church balcony, dropping paper pellets into the hats of the ladies beneath him, grows into the greatest Anglican of the last hundred years—with warmth, perception and sympathy, Roger Steer describes the lifelong journey of John Stott. Scrupulously researched, vividly written, this book lights up the character of the man with the longest shadow in the modern church."

JEREMY VINE, BBC

"In this engaging, splendid and admirably readable biography, Roger Steer offers compelling details of Uncle John's life journey, the man of all continents, a unique humble and faithful servant of God with a phenomenal achievement. It is impossible to read it without learning a lot, being inspired, touched and renewed. Uncle John's biography displays a force and a resonance that will challenge and impact the younger generations who have to resist the pressure of the postmodern era."

DANIEL BOURDANNÉ, General Secretary, International Fellowship of Evangelical Students

"This is a fascinating story told well of a man described in the pages of this book as one of the most influential Christians of the twentieth century. It documents a life well lived and worthy of imitation, but it also charts some landmark moments in the history of worldwide evangelicalism. This is a valuable record of both a man and a movement. Roger Steer paints a compelling portrait packed with lessons for any who would aspire to be servant leaders in Christ's church."

REV. IAN COFFEY, Moorlands College, England

"This account of John Stott's life and ministry not only helps us understand so much of recent evangelical history but also provides us with a wonderful model of humble Christ-centeredness. We should take every opportunity to learn from the example of this great man of God."

VAUGHAN ROBERTS, author of *God's Big Picture*

"Loved by the African poor and called to advise British royalty, living simply and listed amongst *Time* magazine's most influential people, here is the story of a remarkable man. This engaging biography provides some unexpected insights, whether coping with family opposition, caring for London's underprivileged, or experiencing the pain of criticism and disagreement. It demonstrates why a world-famous writer and Bible teacher is known for the Christlike quality of humility, and not only introduces us to one of the great Christian leaders of our time but points us to the Lord whom he has served so faithfully."

JONATHAN LAMB, director of Langham Preaching, Langham Partnership International

BASIC CHRISTIAN

BASIC
CHRISTIAN

The Inside Story of JOHN STOTT

ROGER STEER

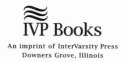

IVP Books

An imprint of InterVarsity Press
Downers Grove, Illinois

InterVarsity Press
P.O. Box 1400, Downers Grove, IL 60515-1426
Internet: www.ivpress.com
E-mail: email@ivpress.com

InterVarsity Press® is the book-publishing division of InterVarsity Christian Fellowship/USA®, a movement of students and faculty active on campus at hundreds of universities, colleges and schools of nursing in the United States of America, and a member movement of the International Fellowship of Evangelical Students. For information about local and regional activities, write Public Relations Dept., InterVarsity Christian Fellowship/USA, 6400 Schroeder Rd., P.O. Box 7895, Madison, WI 53707-7895, or visit the IVCF website at <www.intervarsity.org>.

ISBN 978-0-8308-3846-2

Printed in the United States of America

 InterVarsity Press is committed to protecting the environment and to the responsible use of natural resources. As a member of Green Press Initiative we use recycled paper whenever possible. To learn more about the Green Press Initiative, visit <www.greenpressinitiative.org>.

Library of Congress Cataloging-in-Publication Data

Steer, Roger, 1945-
  Basic Christian: the inside story of John Stott / Roger Steer.
    p. cm.
  Includes bibliographical references.
  ISBN 978-0-8308-3846-2 (pbk.: alk. paper)
  1. Stott, John R. W. 2. Church of England—Clergy—Biography. 3.
Anglican Communion—England—Clergy—Biography. 4.
Evangelicalism—Church of England—Biography. I. Title.
  BX5199.S8344S74 2009
  283.092—dc22

  [B]

                                                              2009042063

P   21   20   19   18   17   16   15   14   13   12   11   10   9   8   7   6   5   4   3   2   1

Y   28   27   26   25   24   23   22   21   20   19   18   17   16   15   14   13   12   11   10

CONTENTS AND TIMELINE

FOREWORD

In Romans 10:18, Saint Paul applies what Psalm 19 says about the starry heavens to the apostles' preaching: "Their voice has gone out into all the earth, their words to the ends of the world." Taking that same hermeneutical license, we might apply those words to the ministry of John R. W. Stott. Through doors opened by the International Fellowship of Evangelical Students, the Lausanne Movement and the Langham Partnership (known in the United States as John Stott Ministries), he has personally affected and encouraged Christian leaders of all continents.

Author, preacher, parish minister, mentor, educator of developing world leaders, architect of national and global movements—John Stott has exercised a ministry that is incredibly broad in scope. He has done so by tightly focusing on well-chosen goals.

Credit that paradoxical combination of broad scope and tight focus in part to Dr. Stott's sensitivity to God's leading, saying yes to only those invitations and challenges to which he sensed a clear call. Credit much of the achievement to his famous self-discipline, which wisely included the practice of an after-lunch "horizontal half hour."

His discernment and discipline served his congregation at All Souls Langham Place well. His decisions to say no to good things to which he did not sense a clear call (a bishopric, a chance for marriage) helped him keep his focus. As you read these pages, you will see discipline and commitment repeatedly shine through the personal glimpses offered by those who know him intimately.

One particular achievement of Dr. Stott's interests me: his efforts to energize and renew a fragmented evangelical movement. In the United States in the 1940s and 1950s, Billy Graham and Harold John Ockenga had built a movement by creating organizations such as the National Association of Evangelicals, *Christianity Today* and Fuller Theological Seminary. In England in the 1960s and 1970s, Dr. Stott worked to revive a movement that was a century older but had grown intellectually moribund and isolated from the modern world. At the 1966 National Assembly of Evangelicals where he famously clashed with D. Martyn Lloyd-Jones, at the 1967 National Evangelical Anglican Congress at Keele, and then at the second NEAC ten years later in Nottingham, Dr. Stott worked to hold together a movement that was challenged by neofundamentalist separatism and charismatic excess. Similarly, at the Lausanne Congress in 1974 he led many who feared that social ministry would undermine evangelism to see that social justice and gospel witness are inseparable in Christian mission. Beyond such public forums, he built networks of relationships that would provide the glue for an international evangelical movement.

John Stott's father, Sir Arnold Stott, disapproved of his son's call to Christian ministry. He had hoped instead for greater things: that his son, with his wit, charm and gift for languages, would find a diplomatic career in the foreign service. Instead, young John seemed to narrow his world by joining the staff of the neighborhood parish in which he had grown up. But with the benefit of hindsight, it is hard to conceive of John R. W. Stott having achieved a more global influence through diplomacy than he has had through gospel ministry. His voice has indeed "gone out into all the earth."

David Neff
Editor in Chief
Christianity Today

PREFACE

You are about to join me on a remarkable journey: it will last for nearly ninety years and take us to every continent. Like every biography we shall see how John Stott capitalised on the pluses and coped with the minuses of his birth and upbringing. As well as a story which unfolds through time and place it will also be a journey across cultural boundaries and into self-discovery, insight and understanding.

In his own Foreword to the first volume of his biography of John, Timothy Dudley-Smith expressed the hope that authors of future biographies would find that his book would 'prove a quarry from which a few of their building blocks may come'. Rarely can a hope have been more truly fulfilled. I am hugely in his debt and gladly take this opportunity to thank him for the years of patient and perceptive research on which I was able to draw through having his volumes at my side.

I also want to thank Richard Palmer and Clare Brown at Lambeth Palace library for their help in easing my way around the Stott papers of which they are now custodians. Sarah Duffield, archivist at the Church of England Record Centre, helped me with my enquiries about Harold Earnshaw-Smith, John's predecessor as Rector of All Souls. Marla Fogelman, of PubMed Central, made available to me information about Sir Arnold Stott from the *British Medical Journal*.

Over and over again as I have conducted my research, people have talked to me about John's gift for friendship, and one of the joys of writing this book has been to meet many of his friends in Britain, Africa and America and to get to know others through email exchanges and telephone conversations.

My thanks go to Aggrey Mugisha who welcomed me to Kampala Evangelical School of Theology (KEST), Uganda, and discussed with me John's impact on East Africa, to Grace Erisa Sentongo and David Zac Niringiye, Bishop of Kampala, who talked to me at the offices of the Anglican diocese of Kampala. Grace recalled John's lectures on the New Testament in Kampala and Zac shared memories of his friendship with John over many years. Zac was anxious that I should capture something of the way that John had changed over the years and I hope he will feel that I have had some success in meeting his wish. Ian Wardle, who lives in Uganda and leads the charity Youthworx East Africa, made the arrangements for me to visit both KEST and Bishop Zac and I am grateful to him for this and for taking my wife Sheila and me on an unforgettable tour of the pearl of Africa.

In Paoli, at their home near Philadelphia, John and Alysia Yates entertained us royally. We shall never forget the stimulating conversation about John over an extended meal with them and Steve Beck, reminiscing, laughing and reflecting about the remarkable man who will for them remain for ever 'Uncle John'. Over on the Californian coast Ken Perez, President of John Stott Ministries (JSM), and his wife Janet welcomed us to their home and to the Menlo Park headquarters of JSM – not only talking freely about John and the work he established but also introducing us to the delights of San Francisco bay. We add our thanks to Merritt Sawyer for charming us with her recollections of her years as International Programme Director for Scholars in the Langham Partnership. David Virtue, who regularly reminds the world of John's insights in his VirtueOnline Weekly News Digest, kindly put me in touch with many of John's friends on his side of the Atlantic. John Akers, David Bruce and Pat Turpin readily answered my queries about John's friendship with Billy Graham.

Mark Labberton, now Senior Pastor of First Presbyterian Church of Berkeley, met Sheila and me for lunch at the magnificently situated Claremont Hotel and entertained us with stories about John, all but collapsing at times with helpless laughter as he recalled his years as John's study assistant.

Roy McCloughry, the first in the long line of John's study assistants, talked to me at length, as did Alister Chapman who has written his PhD thesis on John. My thanks to you both.

I spent five of the most memorable days of my life at The Hookses in March 2008 with John and his friends: John and Anna Smith, Ted and Antoinette Schroder, Neil and Jenny Woodward, Julian and Claire Charley, Sara Thomson, Richard Bewes and Frances Whitehead. We had a marvellous week talking to and about John, eating together, and getting out onto the beautiful Pembrokeshire coastline which has meant so much to John over the years. What I wrote about John and All Souls in the late 1960s draws heavily on conversations I had with Ted Schroder, and in the 1980s and 90s with Richard Bewes.

Frances Whitehead looked after my every need, not only during that week at The Hookses but also on my visits to John at the College of St Barnabas, taking me to see the 12 Weymouth Street Rectory and promptly answering my many queries. Frances has played a massive part in the John Stott story over nearly sixty years, as my book has demonstrated, and no words of mine can adequately thank her for immeasurably aiding my task.

Michael Baughen told me the story of how he succeeded John at All Souls and the major programme of rebuilding which happened while he was vicar.

John's cousin, Tamara Dewdney, talked to me about her time living with the Stott family in the 1920s and 30s. Clark Bedford provided me with wonderful memories of his years as organist at All Souls in the 1960s. My account of John's visits to East Africa in 2000 and Asia in 2002 draws heavily on Corey Widmer's vivid journals. I am most grateful.

David Turner, John Wyatt and Chris Wright, intimate friends of John and long-standing members of All Souls, all contributed material which I used extensively, checked my manuscript and offered valuable suggestions for improvement.

A special word of thanks to James Catford who first suggested I should write a biography of John Stott way back in the early 1990s, and talked to me about the project and its subject when I eventually embarked on the task.

Julia Cameron, who has edited previous books of mine and is now Director of External Relations for the Lausanne Movement's Third

Congress on World Evangelization in Cape Town 2010, went through my whole manuscript and made many helpful and encouraging suggestions.

Brian Wilson, Eleanor Trotter, Sally Ormesher, Peter Anderson and the team at IVP publishers were unfailingly patient, helpful and encouraging throughout the process of bringing this biography to birth. Colin Duriez and Bryony Bénier used their previous experience of the subject of this book, and all their editorial skills, to enhance the final result.

Way back in 1990, when John reluctantly agreed that biographies might be written about him, he told Timothy Dudley-Smith, his first biographer, that the story of his life should be told 'warts and all'. He has adopted exactly the same attitude with me and has also encouraged me at every stage of the work by answering all my questions, giving me full access to his papers, and introducing me to his wide circle of friends at home and abroad. What followed has been both an honour and a delightfully rewarding experience.

My wife Sheila not only came with me to East Africa and the United States and shared in my conversations with those whose lives have been impacted by John, but also read the whole manuscript of this book and made many suggestions for improvement. With this, and with every book I have written, she has been both indispensable critic and encourager.

Roger Steer
Down St Mary
July 2009

1. FIRST STEPS ON THE STAGE

On 27 April 1921, to Arnold and Lily Stott's delight, their first and only son was born. They called him John Robert Walmsley. Joanna, aged nine, and Joy, two, were intrigued to have a baby brother. Arnold was thirty-six and, with Lily now aged forty-one, John was to be their last child.

On returning to civilian life after serving as a major in the Royal Army Medical Corps in the First World War, Arnold had established his own department of electrocardiography at the Westminster Hospital. He was highly regarded as a teacher. Although his students were wary of his critical and sometimes caustic comments, they recognised that his instruction at the bedside gave them a valuable introduction to clinical medicine.

In 1911, Arnold had married Emily Holland, whom he had met as a student. Emily was always known in the family as Lily and had been born in Antwerp. A month after John's arrival, the Stott family moved from West Kensington to 58 Harley Street, where Arnold established his own consulting rooms. Harley Street had been the medical heart of London for over a hundred years. The house, which still stands almost on the corner where Harley Street crosses New Cavendish Street, is imposing, with bow-fronted rooms on three of its six floors. But Lily wasn't sure that her husband had made a wise choice.

'The house is too small and inconvenient,' she complained. 'If I hadn't been recovering from John's birth, I would never have agreed to Arnold buying the place. There are too many stairs and our dining room has to double as a patient waiting room.'

Arnold's consulting room was on the first floor at the back of the house, separated from the drawing room by a glass door. His secretary-receptionist worked in the drawing room so no one in the family was allowed to use it in the afternoons. The main bedrooms were on the second floor, the nurseries on the third. The servants lived in the attic.

A number of nannies came and went, but at last one came who stayed. Nanny Golden was a cheerful Christian who taught John and his sister Joy to sing hymns and choruses. She took them along Harley Street to Park Square Gardens, and beyond into Regent's Park with its Rose Garden and famous zoo, giving them glimpses of giraffes or elephants. In the winter the frozen lake attracted skaters, while in the summer they sometimes saw the little princesses, Elizabeth (later to become Queen Elizabeth II) and Margaret Rose, driving in the inner circle.

When Nanny took the children for a picnic on a farm in the country, a cockerel showed an interest in the Stott family party. John toddled towards it with his hand outstretched to give the bird some bread. With unforgivable ingratitude the cockerel attacked John, leaving him with a scar beneath his eye.

Lily, whose mother was German, had imbibed Lutheran piety. She taught Joanna, Joy and John to go to church, read the Bible and say their prayers. But Arnold wasn't religious. A scientific humanist, he was committed to trying to make the world a better place. He believed passionately in the value of education and in the power of reason to right the world's wrongs. A keen naturalist, Arnold also loved music, stamp collecting, fly fishing and wine.

John never took to stamp collecting or developed much of a taste for alcohol, but he did inherit his father's love of music. He learnt to play the cello, accompanying his mother on the grand piano in the drawing room, and later played in his school orchestra. But Arnold's greatest success was to inspire John to take an interest in the world of nature, especially birds.

During the summer holidays, Arnold took John 'sugaring' on warm nights.

'Shut your mouth,' Arnold would say to John, 'and open your eyes and ears!'

Together they brewed a sticky concoction, based on beer laced with treacle. Then, in the garden where they were staying, they painted a band, three or four inches wide, round the trunk of every tree. Around midnight, Arnold would wake his son. They crept out into the garden and switched on a torch. In the beam of light, they could see moths and butterflies that had been attracted by the sweetness, inebriated by the beer, and now had fallen to the foot of the tree. Quickly they slipped the rarer specimens – hawk moths, yellow or red underwings – into a killing bottle and later transferred them to their growing collection.

Lily chose their local parish church, All Souls, Langham Place, as the family's place of worship – though Arnold only turned up there two or three times a year. John Nash, who designed the church in 1820, also oversaw the rebuilding of Buckingham Palace (the former Buckingham House) and planned Regent's Park and its surrounding fine terraces.

Nash's vision for All Souls, with its distinctive colonnaded portico and fluted cone spire, was that it should fit the chosen site where the upper end of Regent Street curved gently at Langham Place to meet the lower end of Portland Street. He thought that the portico and spire would offer a pleasant vista as you looked north from Oxford Circus. Since All Souls is a 'crown living' church, the royal coat of arms hangs over the entrance door. It is Nash's only surviving London church, and few who have ventured inside forget the striking painting above the communion table. George IV presented Richard Westall's *Ecce Homo* to the church at its opening in 1824. It shows Christ, handcuffed in a purple cloak and wearing a crown of thorns. Round his head are the hands of jeering priests with soldiers looking and pointing at him.

When the Stott family began to attend All Souls, the church had a new Rector, Arthur Buxton, who cultivated friends from the world of theatre and invited them to his church. John and Joy were usually separated and made to sit one on each side of Nanny Golden to keep them in order. But this didn't prevent John making little pellets from used bus tickets and dropping them from his seat in the gallery on to the hats of the ladies sitting below. When he scored a direct hit, he would duck down so that he wasn't identified.

The BBC was founded in 1922 and, four years later, John Logie Baird invented television, although the first TV programmes were not broadcast until 1936. In 1928, builders began to demolish houses to the north of All Souls to make way for Broadcasting House. Arthur Buxton was quick to form a strong link between his church and the BBC, giving regular broadcast talks on Sunday evenings.

Harley Street was only five minutes' walk from Oxford Street and Regent Street, the heart of London's West End. At Christmas, the big shops like Selfridges competed to present the best illuminations and the most sumptuous window displays. On Christmas Day itself Arnold agreed to attend the service at All Souls before returning home for the family get-together in the drawing room. Arnold took to his hands and knees under the Christmas tree and distributed the presents one at a time. When John was eleven, the family listened to King George V making the first Christmas Day broadcast to the people of the British Empire.

At Christmas, too, Arnold took the children with him to the old Westminster Hospital opposite Westminster Abbey, on the site of the present Queen Elizabeth II Conference Centre. Arnold stood with a junior doctor at a heart patient's bedside. Both the younger man and the patient looked anxious.

'What,' Arnold asked, turning to the doctor, 'should he be given to eat?'

'A little fish, perhaps?'

Arnold snorted. 'Do you mean a sardine or a sprat?'

The trainee doctor made a mental note to remember that his boss was a stickler for accuracy in the use of language.

But where was Stott junior? Arnold ordered a search and at last they found him flat on his back on the floor of the dispensary, his mouth open beneath the tap of a huge jar of cod liver oil and malt, the contents slowly trickling into his mouth.

Back at 58 Harley Street, John's cousin Tamara often stayed for long periods with the Stott family while her own parents were abroad. She was daughter of Lily's sister Ella who had married the famous conductor Albert Coates. 'John was always fighting with his sister Joy,' she recalled, 'but would never fight with me, although I wished he would!'

Tamara also remembered Arnold as rather resenting her presence, and his habit of firing unkind remarks in her direction.

When John was eight, Arnold and Lily decided to send him away to preparatory school as a boarder. They chose Oakley Hall, near Cirencester in Gloucestershire. When John arrived at the school in September 1929, the Stotts' chauffeur parked the big Chrysler in the shadow of an ivy-covered building of Cotswold stone. With a butterfly net protruding from his luggage, John climbed out of the car and surveyed the scene: a flower garden, neatly cut lawns, gravel paths with trimmed edges, flowering shrubs, a lily-pond and fountain. Beyond, he saw a tennis court and cricket pitch. Major Letts, who had recently taken over as head teacher, greeted John and four other new boys before handing them to the care of his wife.

Mrs Letts prided herself on a large conservatory with vines and exotic plants. She showed the new boys into their dormitory, where John saw eight iron-frame beds covered with eiderdowns and a row of eight china wash basins. John soon discovered that Major Letts ran his school on military lines, with every day carefully ordered. He attached importance to academic work, hoping that his boys would gain entrance to one of the main public schools. But he thought that games were important too, in the afternoons, with soccer and rugby in winter and cricket in summer.

Lily was relieved, after a week or so, to get a letter from Mrs Letts explaining that John had settled in well. He was eating heartily. The cold he arrived with had gone. He was enjoying games. His first half-term report noted that his spelling was excellent and that the teaching in French he had received from French governesses at home, and from King Arthur's school, had served him well. When winter came, John found that the dormitory was virtually unheated and ice formed on his wash basin.

An ex-army sergeant in charge of the gym taught John to box in a proper ring, wearing gloves. Major Letts reported that John's behaviour was by no means perfect but added, reassuringly, that 'he is perfectly straight-forward and such trouble as he gives is certainly no more than might be expected from a healthy boy of his age with a good deal of energy to work off. I think he has the makings of a first-class boy.'

One morning, a teacher told John, 'Your mother is in the head teacher's study and would like to see you.'

An assistant escorted John to the study. He saw Lily standing there with Major Letts and his wife. Unable to decide how to behave in this situation, John advanced towards his mother and stretched out his hand to shake hers.

'How do you do, Mrs Stott?' he asked.

Mrs Letts burst out laughing, but Lily played along with her son.

'How do you do, Johnnie!' she said.

A few weeks later, in a letter home, John honestly reported that he had been beaten six times, receiving twenty-five strokes of the cane since he had been at the school. Anxiously, Lily wrote back asking what he had done to be punished so.

'I honestly don't know why I get caned such a lot,' he replied.

On his first summer holidays from Oakley Hall, Arnold presented John with a leather-bound notebook, inscribed, 'Johnnie from Daddy, 19th August 1930, Burton Bradstock, Dorset.' Burton Bradstock was a favourite holiday destination for the family.

At the start of his final year, the school put on a performance of *Scenes from Julius Caesar*. The drama teacher needed someone with a keen sense of the theatrical to play the part of Mark Antony. He chose John to star in one of the most dramatic moments in any of Shakespeare's plays, when Mark Anthony enters a packed forum in Rome bearing the body of the murdered Caesar. John rose to the occasion:

> Friends, Romans, countrymen, lend me your ears;
> I come to bury Caesar, not to praise him.
> The evil that men do lives after them;
> The good is oft interred with their bones:
> So let it be with Caesar . . .

John knew that this was high drama. He recognised that, in this speech, words were beautifully used and crafted by the world's greatest master of language. Although the school magazine reported that he was 'inclined to overact,' the account concluded that overall John Stott's 'performance can rarely have been equalled in this school'.

A new teacher arrived at the school, Robbie Bickersteth, having just graduated from Eton College. He lacked teaching qualifications but was a keen bird watcher. In the distant corner of the main playing field, a common whitethroat had built her fragile nest in a bed of nettles. Robbie and John constructed a ramshackle hide out of old sacking, and erected it within photographic range of the nest. They didn't have to wait long before the eggs hatched and the parents were busy feeding their chicks. With a camera his father had given him, John took a picture of a parent carrying an insect to the nest – it won the school photographic competition.

During his last few months at the school, in 1934, Major Letts made John head prefect. Then, in November, he sat the scholarship examination for Rugby, the school where Arnold had been a pupil from 1898 to 1904. A few days later a telegram arrived at Oakley Hall addressed to John.

23 NOVEMBER 1934: HEARTIEST CONGRATULATIONS ON GETTING AMONG THE FIRST THREE LOVE MUMMY AND DADDY.

In his final school report, Major Letts wrote that John 'has made an excellent Head Prefect. I am very sorry to lose him and wish him every success at Rugby.'

Rugby School, in Warwickshire, had long been a household word through rugby football, invented in a moment in 1823 when William Webb Ellis, ignoring the rules of soccer as it had always been played, picked up the ball and ran with it. From then the distinctive feature of the game of rugby as it is played throughout the world came into being. The name and reputation of the school's most famous headmaster, Thomas Arnold, lingered. Arnold had put character before brains as the aim of education, and made the senior boys his colleagues in securing it. At Rugby they made everyone work. The school's fame was perpetuated through Thomas Hughes' book,

Tom Brown's Schooldays. School House still displayed, as it does today, the original fireplace where Tom Brown was 'roasted' as part of his initiation into Rugby life.

In 1935, when John arrived, Rugby had become more civilised than in the days of Tom Brown. He discovered that the long tradition of 'fagging' remained, however: new and younger boys had to do chores for the senior boys in the house. When the cry of 'fag' rang out, John had to race along the long corridor. If he was last to arrive, he had to do the fagging – perhaps fetch something from the school shop, clean some shoes, carry some books or polish some brass buttons on the school military uniform.

Arnold Stott wrote to John regularly and made no secret of his pride when his son began to demonstrate that he had unusual abilities: 'You are already a form higher, at least, than I was at your age, and nothing in the world will please me more than you beating me at *anything*...'

Arnold and Lily had never found No. 58 Harley Street large enough to contain all that went on there. So when, in 1936, No. 65, just across the road, came on the market, Lily persuaded Arnold to buy it. The house was six stories high, with steps leading to a stone porch under a high semi-circular roof, supported by elegant columns. There was a mews for the chauffeur and doctor's car.

Twice a year, Arnold arranged formal dinner parties for the doctors in his departments at the Westminster and Royal Chest hospitals. The young men were careful to be on their best behaviour, calling Arnold 'Sir' while Lily did her best to put them at their ease.

Small, grave and determined, with half-moon spectacles, Arnold acted and spoke with great precision. At dinner he prefered the doctors training under him to think before they spoke, and then to express what they had to say as concisely as possible. But while his trainees found him an awe-inspiring figure, Arnold's colleagues thought of him as a charming dinner companion. One said of him that 'his appreciation of good food and wine, his pretty wit, his lively anecdotes, and his sound common sense make him the happiest of companions and the most agreeable of men'.

One evening during the summer holidays of 1936, Lily was driving John on the South Carriage Drive through Hyde Park. It was getting dark, the lighting was poor, and Lily failed to spot a bollard in the middle of the road: there was a mighty crash as she drove straight into it. John was catapulted forward, putting his chin through the windscreen, and landing on the pavement.

Lily thought for a long moment she had killed her son. He lost consciousness and only came to in Westminster Hospital, where he spent a few days before emerging with a scar beneath his chin, just inches from his jugular vein.

When John recovered, the family took a holiday in County Galway on the west coast of Ireland, staying at a small hotel near Moyard in what later became Connemara National Park. They enjoyed the view of the mountains, expanses of bogs, heaths, woodlands and coastal inlets washed by the Atlantic. Arnold introduced John to the joys of fly fishing, taking him in a boat on Lakes Ballynakill and Fee, accompanied by a gillie.

There was something else to delight fifteen-year-old John: he fell in love. His first girlfriend was the same age as he, the daughter of another doctor and staying in the same hotel. He thought her very beautiful. Riding behind her on the same pony, he put his arms around her waist – his first awakening to sexual desire. Nothing came of the encounter except that a friend of Arnold's, a radiologist with them on the holiday, teased John.

'You have an eye for the girls!' he told him.

Since it seemed clear that his academic strength was to be modern languages, Arnold arranged for his son to make yet one further trip away that summer – a few weeks in Germany, staying in a small hotel at a beautiful spot near where the Rhine and Moselle rivers meet at Koblenz. John went bird-watching, entering his sightings in his notebook. When he saw a cello he fancied, he persuaded a music teacher to give him a second opinion.

'It's a splendid instrument,' the expert told him, 'and good value for money.'

John bought the cello and prepared to take it home with him to England.

Some miles to the south-west of Koblenz, in that area of Germany bordering Belgium, Luxemburg and France called the Rhineland, Adolf

Hitler alleged that the French were planning to encircle Germany and ordered German troops to take up positions in the demilitarised zone. Preoccupied with a crisis over Abyssinia, the British and French governments contented themselves with protests and did little more.

The British government had its own crisis to deal with. Following the death of George V, Edward VIII had become King. But he was infatuated with Mrs Wallis Simpson, an American with one divorced husband still living and another she hoped to divorce. It was the talk of the world's press, but by a voluntary agreement the British newspapers avoided all mention of it. However, Prime Minister Stanley Baldwin tackled the new King about it. Edward was adamant that he wanted to marry Mrs Simpson and suggested a morganatic marriage, by which Wallis would be his wife but not queen. Baldwin wouldn't hear of it.

A few weeks after John's return from Germany, the Stott family listened to the radio as the King told the nation that, faced with the choice of the throne or 'the woman I love', he had chosen to abdicate.

Edward's successor was his brother Albert, Duke of York, who took the title George VI. On 12 May 1937 he and Queen Elizabeth were crowned in Westminster Abbey. A weary Baldwin retired and Neville Chamberlain became Prime Minister. Mussolini and Hitler dominated Europe.

Arnold Stott was now eminent in his profession and the new royal household appointed him their physician – to be called in when a member of Buckingham Palace staff needed medical attention. Hearing the news, John sent his father a telegram from Rugby:

HEARTIEST CONGRATULATIONS SIMPLY GRAND BRAVO – JOHN

In February 1938, Anthony Eden resigned as foreign secretary in protest against Chamberlain's policy of appeasement, and a month later Hitler annexed Austria, bringing closer the prospect of a second world war in the twentieth century.

At Rugby, John made good use of the cello he had bought in Germany. He joined a singing sextet and every week, from Monday to Friday, as soon as classes were over he ran to the music department to practise with the other boys. He also sang solo, as a baritone, in performances in the school chapel.

John was also developing a social conscience. Outraged when he saw 'tramps' who were both unemployed and homeless, he founded a society to help them, called ABC or Association for the Benefit of the Community.

His thoughts turning to what his son was going to do with his life, Arnold Stott arranged for John to be assessed by the National Institute of Industrial Psychology. The institute gave its opinion that the soon-to-be-seventeen-year-old's intelligence was 'distinctly good though not exceptional'. They recognised a flair for languages. As to his character, the institute described John as friendly and open, markedly sociable, emotional and sensitive, particularly over the question of social relationships. They spoke of 'some initiative and driving power and considerable perseverance' and of 'promising qualities of leadership'.

The institute suggested that the civil service or the Foreign Office or hospital administration might be suitable as a career – but added that, since John's education was likely to be prolonged, it would be unwise to make a definite decision at this stage. His interests and aims might change as he grew older.

2. OPENING THE DOOR

Religion played a substantial part in the life of Rugby School. In John's time, the school day included a chapel service conducted by one of the three chaplains, house prayers each evening led by the housemaster, and a time of silence in the dormitories when it was intended that the boys said their prayers. They celebrated Holy Communion on Sundays and one of the chaplains supervised an informal Bible study group. After a series of six classes, John was confirmed in the autumn term in 1936 by Mervyn Haigh, Bishop of Coventry.

In his mid-teens John was vaguely aware of two things about himself. 'First,' as he put it later, 'if there was a God, I was estranged from him. I tried to find him, but he seemed to be enveloped in a fog I could not penetrate. Secondly, I was defeated. I knew the kind of person I was, and also the kind of person I longed to be. Between the ideal and the reality there was a great gulf fixed. I had high ideals but a weak will. I fell far short of the person I wanted to be.'

On half-holiday afternoons, John had a habit of creeping into the Memorial Chapel on his own. Next to the lofty school chapel, the smaller but impressive Memorial Chapel had four huge windows portraying the passion, crucifixion, resurrection and ascension of Christ. Sitting there in the quietness and half-light from the stained glass windows, John often perused the little devotional books put there by the chaplains for the boys to read, and absorbed the atmosphere of mystery.

Every Wednesday or Thursday evening, the chaplains held a voluntary service for about half an hour. John nearly always went but was disappointed to find that, although he could work up some sort of religious feeling, he couldn't achieve a meaningful relationship with God. He said his prayers but God seemed shrouded in mists, unapproachable, remote and aloof.

John Bridger was a year older than John, a talented sportsman who played cricket for the school at the age of fifteen. In the spring term at Rugby in 1938, Bridger approached John with an invitation.

'Would you like to come with me to the meeting? We meet in a classroom on Sunday afternoons straight after lunch.'

The 'meeting' he referred to would today be known as a Christian Union. Two years earlier, Bridger had decided to become a Christian at a holiday run by an evangelical organisation, the Scripture Union.

Sometimes visiting speakers addressed the group, including one in particular, Eric Nash, or 'Bash' as he was always known. Eric Nash, now in his forties, had graduated at Trinity College, Cambridge, and done his theological training at Ridley Hall. Six years earlier he had been appointed by the Scripture Union to work among public school boys. He was soon to establish summer camps in the little Dorset village of Iwerne Minster and to plant the name *Iwerne* in Christian vocabulary for a generation of young people.

Bash was neither athletic, nor (despite being a Cambridge graduate) particularly academic. But he had had a vision in a railway carriage that he was to win Britain for Christ. His strategy was to work and pray for the conversion of the future leaders of the country while they were still at one of the boys' public schools. Nothing would deflect him from this vision he believed God had given him. Speaking to a group of sixth formers or undergraduates, he would use his personal charm to gain their attention and a fair hearing. Without pretending to be a profound theological thinker, he spoke with relevance about what he saw as the greatest issues in life.

Accepting John Bridger's invitation, John Stott turned up at the meeting on Sunday 13 February 1938, a few weeks before his seventeenth birthday.

He listened as Bash focused his talk around Pilate's question, 'What shall I do, then, with Jesus who is called Christ?'

It had never occurred to John that he needed to *do* anything with Jesus. Hadn't Jesus done what needed to be done? Here was Eric Nash insisting, quietly but powerfully, that everybody had to do something about Jesus. Nobody could remain neutral.

'Either you copy Pilate and weakly reject Jesus,' said Bash, 'or you accept him personally and follow him.'

At the end of the meeting, John approached the speaker with some questions. When Bash took him for a drive in his car, John told him a good deal about himself. 'If there is a God,' he said to Bash, 'and I believe there is, I don't know him. I know the kind of person that I want to be. But I feel defeated. I fall short of my own ideals.'

To John's surprise, Bash answered his questions and explained what he called the 'way of salvation' in a manner which uncannily met his two needs – his feelings of alienation from God and defeat in his life. He pointed John to the verse in the Book of Revelation in which the risen Lord Jesus, in the last of the letters to the seven churches, pictured himself knocking at the door of the human heart: 'Here I am! I stand at the door and knock. If anyone hears my voice and opens the door, I will come in and eat with him, and he with me.'

Bash didn't press John to make an immediate decision.

That night, when the Rugby dormitory lights were out, John knelt beside his bed and said a prayer 'opening the door' to Christ. He was aware of nothing spectacular happening and had no emotional experience. He got into bed and went to sleep.

John wrote to Bash telling him that he had opened the door of his heart to Christ and, in return, Bash began to write to him. For five years, Bash sent him letters once a week. Often they were long, parts of which were heavily theological, for example unravelling the doctrine of the atonement. Other sections were ethical, outlining principles of morality and behaviour – including practical advice such as the importance of getting ten hours sleep a night. Yet others gave John tips on how to read the Bible, or pray, or practise the presence of Christ so that he 'becomes as real on the rugger field as in chapel'. He gave advice on how to encourage others who were new in the Christian faith. Bash always ended his letters with a 'best thought', usually a text from the Bible, and then a joke to lighten the mood.

Bash had high expectations of the young men he had 'led to Christ' and his letters to John often included some form of rebuke. At one period, Bash's ticking-offs were so frequent that, whenever John saw the familiar handwriting on an envelope, he braced himself for half an hour before he could face opening it.

Walking down a street in Rugby, John had a new feeling that he was in love with everyone and the world seemed to smile back. 'I had,' he wrote, 'no enemies left.'

He was now coming towards the end of his first year in the sixth form, and in the Easter holidays he turned seventeen. He ran regularly for the school in cross-country events, once played rugby for a school XV, and continued his interest in acting. When the dramatic society performed a new farce by J. B. Priestley, *Bees on the Boat Deck*, John played the part of Hilda Jackson and, according to the *New Rugbeian Supplement*, managed to give a 'distinctively feminine performance', despite being too tall for the part.

John began his summer holidays in 1938 with a month on the continent of Europe working on his language skills. On his return in the second half of August, he attended one of Bash's 'camps' – actually a schoolboys' holiday at Beachborough Park, near Folkestone in Kent. John arrived at the event late in the evening, hotfoot from France, and ran up the stairs clutching a bottle of wine – a gift for Bash, not yet realising that Eric Nash was a strict teetotaller.

During his second year in the sixth form, the school made John head boy – a position which carried with it the task of editing the school journal, *The Meteor*. This job resulted in his entering into an exchange of letters with a former old boy of the school, William Temple, then Archbishop of York and soon to be Archbishop of Canterbury. As Chairman of Governors, William Temple often visited the school, and a few times John dined with him in the headmaster's house. He was struck by his geniality and 'quite extraordinary laugh which was like a cataract'.

Listening to Temple preach in the school chapel, John began to grasp his emphasis that sin equals self, and this thought remained with him all his life. In later years he often quoted Temple in his preaching and writing.

'My thoughts are now firmly fixed on ordination to ministry in the Church of England,' John told his headmaster.

Soon after John's eighteenth birthday in 1939, the producer of the school play chose him for the title role in Shakespeare's *Richard II*. 'Be prepared for the ghastly sight of your son in a rich auburn wig,' John wrote to his parents.

Here was another opportunity for him to appreciate the treasures of the English language. In rehearsals, he listened entranced to the dying John of Gaunt's description of the land where John of London was born –

> This royal throne of kings, this scept'red isle . . .
> This other Eden . . .
> This happy breed of men, this little world,
> This precious stone set in the silver sea . . .
> This blessed plot, this earth, this realm, this England.

John well understood his responsibility to do justice to the demanding part of King Richard. He worked hard to learn his lines so that all would go well on the first night:

> I'll give my jewels for a set of beads,
> My gorgeous palace for a hermitage . . .
> And my large kingdom for a little grave,
> A little little grave, an obscure grave . . .

In the event, the local newspaper report enthused that it was 'probably the finest Shakespearean show ever produced in the school . . . J. R. W. Stott's characterisation is one which is head and shoulders above even the efficient company the school provides.' The *New Rugbeian Supplement* reported that John held the audience's interest with subtle inflexions of his pleasant voice.

When John joined Bash and two hundred others for the annual holiday at Beachborough in August, Britain was just days away from declaring war on Germany. The War Office notified Arnold Stott, who had returned from the First World War as Major, that they were recalling him to the Royal Artillery Medical Corps with the rank of Colonel.

Summer brought the customary dinner party in Harley Street for Arnold's housemen.

'What does your son plan to do in life when he leaves school?' a young doctor asked his boss.

There was a pause.

'He wants to go into the *church*,' Arnold replied. The young man never forgot Dr Stott's reply and the disdainful emphasis he put on the last word.

A few weeks later, the family sold the house in Harley Street, never to return, and rented Woodlands Farm House, between Cobham and Leatherhead in Surrey. They said goodbye to the cook, maids and chauffeur they had enjoyed in London.

Britain declared war on Germany on 3 September 1939. Back at Rugby for his final year, and sitting his Cambridge scholarship, they issued John with his gas mask. Teams of men were building air raid shelters, and the area was full of sandbags, wardens' posts and static water tanks. Britain soon had 150,000 men in France, and German U-boats had begun to attack allied ships. Rugbeians who had left school the previous term were already in uniform.

Five or six weeks after the outbreak of the war, the school arranged for John and a group of senior boys to attend an army recruiting office in Birmingham in order for them to have a medical examination and enlist as potential soldiers.

'You will not be called on to report for duty until you turn twenty,' the military men told the boys. 'But when you do join the army it is likely that you will soon attain commissioned rank. We see your service in Rugby's Officers' Training Corps as good preparation.'

John, however, was beginning to take a distinctly pacifist position. He now read the Sermon on the Mount through Christian eyes. As Jesus spoke of turning the other cheek and loving our enemies, he couldn't begin to understand how you could be a Christian and fight. At this stage of his life he was, in his own words, an 'instinctive pacifist'. Nobody introduced him to arguments about the 'just war' or helped him to balance the biblical statements.

As long as his thoughts were set on ordination to the Anglican ministry, John was entitled to exemption from military service without having formally to appear before a tribunal as a conscientious objector. At the start of the January term in 1940, he wrote to Mervyn Haigh, Bishop of Coventry. Haigh replied by offering to see him with a view to arranging his provisional acceptance for ordination in his diocese. The bishop noted, however, that there was 'the moral problem whether a young fellow who had not begun his training for ordination ought to regard himself as justified in not doing military service at a time like this and in a struggle like the present'.

To this John replied that, although he fully understood what the bishop meant about the moral problem, he had received a very definite call to the ministry, and therefore he felt he should go ahead with preparation for that. He believed that in the long run he could serve his country better in this way.

On the afternoon of 7 February 1940, Bishop Mervyn called at the house of the headmaster of Rugby and interviewed John. Next day, the bishop's secretary wrote to John and told him that Haigh wanted to be in touch with his mother since his father was out of the country on active war service. Haigh then wrote to Lily telling her that he had seen John, and was fully prepared to accept him as an ordination candidate; this would leave open the possibility of her son changing his mind while he was at university. The bishop however added, 'Before writing to him formally in this sense, I naturally should wish to know that I have your good-will and concurrence in so doing? He assured me that I should have, but I ought to have it from you personally as his mother; and I should be grateful if you could tell me that you can safely speak on behalf of his father. I should be writing to his father but I know that he is in France. I understand from the boy himself that his father is, not unnaturally, a little uncertain and possibly rather disappointed about the way his inclination is tending, but I gather he would take no exception to my doing what I propose to do?'

'A little uncertain' was of course an under-statement. Arnold Stott was bitterly disappointed that his son wanted to be ordained. The high hopes he had cherished for him would come to nothing. With John distinguishing himself as head boy at Rugby and showing himself gifted in foreign languages, he could surely enjoy a glittering career in the foreign service of his country.

Lily was faced with the delicate task of replying to the bishop's letter. She explained that both she and Arnold believed that John should keep an open mind about his career until he had taken his university degree. With his flair for modern languages they had hoped for a diplomatic career. Her son had a great urge for service and high standards of Christian duties – but he was young, very impressionable and more than usually sensitive.

Meanwhile, at the headquarters of the British Expeditionary Force in Dieppe, Arnold received the bishop's letter forwarded by Lily. He lost no time in writing forcefully both to John and the bishop.

'I am in entire agreement with my wife's letter to you,' Arnold told Mervyn Haigh, 'and my wish is that you do not accept my son provision-ally as a candidate for Holy Orders at the present time. I am most anxious that he should take no step with regard to his future career until he has taken his degree at Cambridge.'

To his son he wrote a letter beginning 'My dearest Johnnie' but which went on to tell him that he felt strongly that it would be a mistake for him to be accepted now as a candidate for ordination. He didn't want him to make a decision about his future while still a schoolboy. There was no need for any decision now. John had great character, grand talents, and wonderful possibilities of being useful to his fellow men. Even if he had been whole-heartedly in favour of him entering the church, Arnold said that he would still be very much against him beginning theology in the second year. He would make a better clergyman, or schoolmaster, or both, if he had the longest possible general education first, giving him an opportunity to develop a broad outlook and knowledge of the world.

The bishop wrote to John at Rugby telling him that, in the light of his father's refusal to agree, he could not consent to register him as a candidate for Holy Orders.

John reflected on his father's letter and, on Easter Sunday 1940, sat down in his room at Rugby and wrote to his father in (as he put it) 'some trepidation'. He told Arnold that he saw the need of the world and that it was his great ambition to serve his fellow men and women in some way and to meet their need. He felt daily more convinced that it was by ordination that he could best fulfil God's purpose for his life. He wanted his father to trust him and his judgment enough to let him have his name put on the list of provisional ordination candidates straight away. After all, his desire to be ordained was just like the wish his father had had at the same age to be a doctor. He hated being treated like a child and felt 'dreadfully thwarted'.

For her part, Lily was anxious about her husband's safety in France. 'I feel a bit worried about Daddy,' she told John in a letter in May. 'The enemy seems to be so near Dieppe . . . I hope we shall hear from him soon.' Unknown to her, the retreat to Dunkirk had already been ordered and by the end of the month the troops on the coast were totally encircled.

Lily was concerned both about John's adamant determination to be ordained and his doubts about whether he could in conscience fight for his country. 'I feel you must have some talks with men who are in the church,' she told him. 'Talk to men of culture and wide views who would explain that many sayings of our Lord uttered two thousand years ago cannot be quite literally taken. There is a duty to the community as well as to ourselves and very often it has to be put first for the sake of the good of the majority. Daddy and I don't mind the conscientious objector so much in theory but in your case we feel you have not sufficiently explored the pros and cons. All the churches pray for the fighting forces and countenance taking up the sword in a good cause. Unsullied consecration is rather isolationist isn't it? I agree with Daddy that you ought not definitely decide to be an ordinand until you are 21 and have a good basis at Cambridge of a not absolutely theological education.'

With the capitulation of the Belgian army to the north of Dunkirk and the thrust of German tank forces to the south, the British Expeditionary Force and the French First Army were cut off. At the end of May and the beginning of June 1940, over 200,000 British were evacuated from Dunkirk. More than 850 vessels took part in the evacuation, half of them small craft hurriedly sent across from England. To Lily and the family's great relief, Arnold Stott was aboard that last ship back to England from St Nazaire at the fall of France.

3. CAMBRIDGE BATTLES

In the summer and autumn of 1940, Britain faced the threat of invasion as it hadn't done since Napoleon's Grand Army camped on the French coast a hundred and forty years earlier. But the invasion never came. The RAF took to the air for the Battle of Britain and the navy kept control of the Channel. Beginning on 10 July, the Germans, with an initial force of over 1,350 bombers and 1,200 fighters, launched a series of attacks, first against British ships, then against airfields, and finally against the towns.

The British Hurricane and Spitfire fighters were outnumbered three to one by the enemy. The climax of the 'Battle of Britain' came on 15 September when British pilots shot down 56 German planes. During twelve weeks 1,733 German aircraft were destroyed for the loss of 915 British fighter planes. Britain had survived the fall of France and, led by Winston Churchill, obstinately committed itself as a nation to nothing short of victory. As the Germans now resorted to indiscriminate bombing of the larger cities, especially London, it seemed like an impossible goal.

Such was the state of the country when John Stott arrived as a nineteen-year-old undergraduate at Cambridge in October 1940. During his final term at Rugby, he had successfully passed the modern language scholarship exam for Trinity College. Twelve thousand evacuees had arrived in

Cambridge, and the town quickly filled with mothers and children from the East End of London, various fighting units, fighter pilots training at nearby airfields, and students from a variety of London colleges which had hurriedly relocated to Cambridge.

Although some people thought that Cambridge would become a principal target for enemy air raids, bombing proved to be only slight. John found that the blackout meant that after dark you could see very little: no street lamps or lighted windows, but sometimes enough welcome moonlight to reveal the paths across the cobbled courts and shadowed doorways.

Every college had made elaborate air raid precautions with shifts of fire-watchers patrolling roofs against incendiary bombs. John came across air raid shelters and static water tanks in the most unlikely places. He found cement mixers and piles of gravel outside Trinity Great Gate, and concrete defences replacing sandbags around the Porters' Lodge. They had taken the beautiful stained glass windows out of King's College chapel and replaced them with either plain glass or boarding.

Trinity College, Cambridge, had been established by King Henry VIII. It was then (as it remains) the largest and wealthiest college in either Oxford or Cambridge. The Chapel, gatehouse, Hall, Master's Lodge and rows of staircases looked much as they did in Tudor times. However, the war was taking its toll. Food was rationed so that you were only allowed a tiny weekly portion of butter. All colleges abolished their customary feasts and cut out courses from dinner.

But even in war time, the view of Wren's great library by the river, with its cool colonnades and slender arches, the Backs, Trinity Bridge, the Avenue and Fellows' Garden, lifted John's heart. His own rooms were across Trinity Street in F4 Whewell's Court, a Gothic style building erected in the 1860s. Climbing to the first floor of a small block, he eagerly inspected the accommodation which, as a scholar, he would be able to retain for the whole of his four years at Trinity.

He found a bedroom and sitting room, with a tiny kitchen and was at first alarmed by the dark and drab atmosphere, with doors, window frames and skirting all painted black. John used all the charm he could muster to persuade the college clerk of works to provide him with a sofa, bookcase, carpet, standard lamp, curtains, dressing table mirror and armchairs.

In those early days at Trinity, John adopted the habit of early rising which stayed with him all his life. He set his alarm for 6.00 a.m. (later in life it became 5 a.m.), and allocated an hour and a half for a time of Bible study and prayer before crossing Trinity Street and Great Court for breakfast in hall at eight. After breakfast he made his way through the Court to the library, striding purposefully, as a contemporary remembered, with his gown flowing behind him.

Some Trinity undergraduates volunteered to do war work – fire fighting or first aid or as staircase marshals, roof watchers or messengers. John joined the college first aid squad as a dresser and attended a stretcher-bearer practice given by a St John's Ambulance sergeant. 'He's very comic,' John told his parents, 'a dapper little man with a chocolate coloured moustache. He gave us a long lecture on the structure of the human body – blood circulation, digestive system etc and my mind is a chaos of capillaries, gut, kidneys, plasma etc.'

Just over fifty miles to the south in Central London, late in the evening of 8 December 1940, a defence officer sat fire-watching on the roof of Broadcasting House. He watched in horror as a huge land mine, attached to an enormous dark parachute, as wide as the street, floated silently down into Portland Place. He immediately reported the presence of the bomb. Then, a few minutes later at 10.55 p.m., it exploded.

The bomb wrecked all the offices on the west side of Broadcasting House, destroyed the Queen's Hall just south of All Souls, and badly damaged the Langham Hotel, together with all the houses and properties on the west side between Portland Place and Duchess Street, Seymour Place and Harrowby Street. It destroyed water and gas mains and caused serious flooding at the BBC. Two people were killed and many needed hospital treatment.

A Church Army Sister, Phoebe Jordan, for many years a well-known member of the congregation at All Souls, was on night-duty in a nearby air raid shelter. As dawn broke on 9 December she made her way to All Souls. She found that every door in the church house had been blown off and window frames were hanging loose. Inside the church she and the Rector, Harold Earnshaw-Smith, discovered a chaotic scene. As the light improved they began to collect books, hassocks, curtains and carpets as best they could. And then the surveyor arrived.

'I cannot allow you to carry on,' he told them, 'unless you wear your helmets. Pieces of the church are falling and will continue to fall.'

'It was amusing to see the Rector,' Sister Jordan told friends, 'who was always so spick and span, looking more like a sweep than anything, with his flannels tucked into his gum boots and his face and hair as black as coal. I hardly liked to tell him – and then later found that my face was just as bad!'

The blast had so damaged All Souls' famous steeple that thirty feet of it had to be taken down. The whole roof of the church had lifted and then dropped, bringing the ceiling down and some of the main beams. Tons of falling plaster had damaged pews and choir stalls.

Next Sunday, Sister Jordan arrived early at the shattered church to meet members of the congregation who hadn't heard the news. She walked with them to St Peter's, Vere Street, for morning prayer.

Harold Earnshaw-Smith was already acting as priest-in-charge at St Peter's. And so St Peter's, Vere Street, became the new home of the All Souls congregation throughout the war and for six years beyond – although they held the remaining wartime winter evening services in a hall in the Regent Street Polytechnic (now the University of Westminster) since St Peter's couldn't be blacked out.

Four days after the bomb damaged All Souls, and now back at the new family home, Woodlands Farm House, John Stott wrote another letter to the Bishop of Coventry. He told him that, after much thought and discussion, he had decided to apply for exemption from military service, 'being honestly convinced that I can, in the long run serve my country better in this way'. He claimed that his father had consented to this and was willing to give him a free hand although, he added, 'he does not altogether agree with my decision'.

The Principal of Ridley Hall theological college had offered to send John's name to the Bishop of Manchester as long as he could provide evidence of his sincerity. On John's behalf, Mervyn Haigh, Bishop of Coventry, wrote to the Bishop of Manchester enclosing evidence from the headmaster of Rugby, John's former school chaplain, Patrick Duff his tutor at Trinity, and from Bash, confirming his suitability for ordination and, crucially, stating that he had expressed this intention before war had broken out.

The result was that, since he was training for ordination, the British government gave John exemption from military service and he never needed to go before a tribunal as a conscientious objector. However, if he thought (as he implied in his letter to the Bishop of Coventry) that his father would acquiesce in his decision, he was gravely mistaken.

Soon after the start of term, in January 1941 in his room at Trinity, John opened a letter from his mother. It contained the devastating news that Arnold was so angry about John's pacifism that he had decided not to pay his university expenses after his first year and as long as the war lasted.

'You seem to be in the soup now Johnnie,' Lily told him, 'and it worries me thinking of what you may be planning to do. I'm afraid that I do agree with Daddy that you should give service to your country when you are called up – if you don't hold with actual fighting – the government has many other plans and very few young fit men are going to get exemption.'

Lily urged John not to seek funding elsewhere, but to complete Part I of his tripos in a single year. 'I am convinced,' she said, 'that national service for all is right and *every* career must be interrupted for the time being.'

John sent a postcard by return of post.

Thank you very much indeed for your understanding letter, Mummy dear. I am only writing a p.c. because I cannot as yet answer you fully. I want to see Daddy again first, and I also want another day or two to think my whole position out fully. Meanwhile please remember that whatever I ultimately decide to do in a day or so will be in answer to a call of duty and not in answer to personal whim or stubbornness. *Always* your loving son.

John

To his father he wrote a nine-page letter explaining the reasons for his decision to train for ordination, thus giving him exemption from military service. First, was his sense of obedience to God's call: 'I have had a definite and irresistible call from God to serve him in the church.' Second, there was service to his country: 'If medicos are exempt for their services in dealing with disease after the war,' he asked his father, 'how much more should ordinands for their services in dealing with diseases of the spirit? The country is best served if its citizens are obeying God. I respect you for your service; will you not respect me for mine?'

He concluded his long letter to his father:

> I want you to do what you think best from the point of view of the whole family and not of me. Have you definitely decided not to support me up here after my first year? I cannot believe that you have, since surely you see that I am doing my duty in the light of obedience to my call and service to my country?
>
> Even if we disagree, Daddy, remember that I for my part love you still and remain your deeply grateful son
>
> John

Lily now wrote to John every few days and dreaded what an envelope in his handwriting contained – fearing yet another letter which was deaf to all his parents' appeals. When one letter arrived in the post, she left it on the dining room table for two hours before she could pull herself together and open it.

In one letter she wrote, 'Dear Johnnie – I almost get cross sometimes – your view seems so soft and swollen headed sometimes . . . ' And some weeks later she added, 'Your decision seems so stuffy and crooked to me as tho' you had a complex of sorts. I am almost tempted to believe that Bash's influence is not all to the good . . . Please Johnnie, never again talk about not being able to come home unless you want to break our hearts altogether.'

Lily was dreadfully torn, wanting to be loyal to her husband while trying to understand her son. On a car journey back to Surrey from Deganwy in Wales, Lily and Arnold talked of little else but John, and several times took the wrong turning.

'I'm afraid, dear one,' Lily reported back to John, 'that the whole family thinks that you should do some form of definitely national service in the country's emergency. A capable, fit, and talented man like you should not continue your life as it is when many others are having to give up everything for the time being. I still hope that you may come round to this point of view – the war has touched you not at all as yet – it is so full of tragedy for so many people – there is much that you could do to help.'

On John's twentieth birthday, Lily sent him a war-time luxury: a cake made with five eggs – they kept their own hens at Woodlands Farm. John sat down and wrote to his father, thanking him for a cheque for £71 to meet college bills, opening with a few jocular pleasantries, day-to-day anecdotes, and reference to his seven to eight hours a day revision for exams, before getting down to more serious matters.

I was sorry to read the last sentence in your letter about 'a less pleasant subject'. I imagine that you were referring to the question of national service. May I put the whole business before you again as plainly as I can? I want to be frank and we haven't had an opportunity recently of talking about it all, so I'd like to bring you right up to date . . .

I don't want to appeal to you, Daddy, but you are such a shrewd judge of character and have such a deep knowledge of human nature, that surely you must see that I am not shirking national service? Far from it. The easier way for me would be to give in to your wish and do some sort of service, for I hate this family rupture. But Daddy I want you to realise that I *must* follow my call. Men down the ages have had to face similar problems, and those who have yielded to the will of the majority have often gone under and never come to the surface again . . .

Think not that I am going to live a normal, peaceful, comfortable, secluded life. I'm going to throw myself body and soul into the struggle for right. My desire is to see the world a better place, and I will not spare myself in this endeavour . . .

As for finance – you may not feel able to go on supporting me. But were you to be tolerant and magnanimous enough to do it, there will never lack gratitude in your
Ever loving son

John

Lily followed this up with a letter to Arnold arguing that, since the War Office had taken the line that John could best serve his country by continuing with his ordination training, and had given him exemption from military service, could he not be 'generous and tolerant, face facts' and pay his fees?

John had to wait nearly a month before hearing from his father. Arnold's reply came in the form of a priority telegram on 19 May 1941:

AM CONSENTING BUT WITH GREAT RELUCTANCE AND
UNHAPPINESS. STOTT

And so John would get his fees paid. But the rupture in relations between father and son was devastating. For two years, Arnold hardly spoke to John. In the holidays, when John made to embrace his father, Arnold always turned away from him. Bash became virtually a surrogate father to John.

But there's a further twist to the story. Some years later, having studied the Bible in more depth and been introduced to the idea of the 'just war', John resigned his membership of the Anglican Pacifist Fellowship. He no longer believed that the pacifist position was the only possible one for a Christian.

John's tutor at Trinity College was Patrick Duff who later became vice-master of the college. Apart from attending lectures, John was expected to write between two and four essays a week. On the whole he found the lecturers entertaining and the teachers good, though one was a poor speaker. 'His monotonous drone is soporific to the nth degree!' John told his parents.

Before he went up to Cambridge, Arnold Stott had a conversation with John.

'When you get to Cambridge,' he said, 'you will find an organisation called, er, the Cambridge Inter-Collegiate Christian Mission, or something like that. Don't join it. A lot of anaemic wets!'

'All right,' John replied. 'I won't, if you don't want me to.'

And he never did – but he went to most of their meetings through all his Cambridge years. Arnold had got the name wrong. The proper title was the Cambridge Inter-Collegiate Christian Union (always known by its initials, CICCU, pronounced 'kick-you'). Though he followed his father's wishes and never technically became a member of CICCU, John threw himself wholeheartedly into all its activities from the start. Personally, he found the Union's emphasis on the centrality of the cross and the doctrines of the atonement and justification by faith attractive – though by no means everyone agreed with him.

One evening he tried to explain the gospel to a fellow student.

'Salvation is Christ's free gift,' he said. 'We can neither buy it nor even contribute to its purchase. Christ has obtained it for us and now offers it to us gratis.'

'Horrible! Horrible! Horrible!' the man shouted.

John's contemporaries at Cambridge never forgot his self-discipline. He insisted on leaving meetings at half past nine in the evenings so that he could get up early the next day for his quiet time. He often walked out of a lively discussion at the stroke of 9.30. But he did continue to relax by bird-watching. John and his friend Oliver Barclay (who later became General Secretary of the Inter-Varsity Fellowship) rode their bikes on some Saturdays out into the fens and discussed theology while looking through their binoculars.

For two terms at Cambridge, John continued to practise his cello. But then he found that music had to give way to the pressures of study and Christian work. In his third term he gave his cello to Rugby school – but regretted this decision later. He bought a piano accordion, however, to accompany the singing at open air evangelistic services and visits to village churches in Cambridgeshire. With Oliver Barclay he sang in the choir of Trinity College chapel on Sunday evenings, before dining in hall and going on to the weekly CICCU evangelistic address at Holy Trinity, Charles Simeon's old church.

John sat the Preliminary Examination in Modern and Medieval Languages, Part I, in the summer of 1941, the end of his first year. Twenty-three 'Firsts' (first-class results) were awarded with his name among them. His tutor, Patrick Duff, wrote to him: 'Congratulations on your First, with almost exactly the same marks in every paper.' It was a remarkable achievement, especially considering the tensions with his father and mother over his pacifism.

In the summer vacation of 1941 (and again in 1942), John joined a team of helpers at a Children's Special Service Mission (CSSM, now Scripture Union) at Borth on the Welsh coast, a few miles north of Aberystwyth. Then he went on to Bash's summer camp, which now had a permanent holiday location at Claysmore School in the Dorset village of Iwerne Minster. John became Bash's right-hand man in the running of these camps – the word 'camp' being used long after these events were no longer held under canvas. Working from an office on the first floor at Claysmore with a view of the lily pond and croquet lawns, he soon gained a reputation for his efficiency, eye for detail, and almost workaholic perfectionism, combined with cheerful courtesy and mischievous sense of humour.

John worked hard throughout his second year at Cambridge – both at his studies and for CICCU and churches in the area. Others sometimes found his discipline tiresome and excessive. One student from a women's college, Myra Chave-Jones, was given the task of inviting John to lead one of their Bible studies. So she climbed the dark staircase to his rooms in Whewell's Court. About to knock on his big oak door, she spotted a neatly written notice:

Working 8 a.m. – 8 p.m. Please do not disturb unless absolutely necessary

What sort of a man is this? Myra thought as she crept down the stairs. *Perhaps leading a Bible study would be too much of a disturbance.* She may have been mistaken about this – but she never invited him.

Myra often saw him in the university library and realised the iron self-discipline which he exercised. 'He would enter silently, go to his accustomed corner, reach for the books in the same area, and settle down immediately with total concentration, apparently oblivious of whatever else was happening around him.' Many years later, when she moved to London after the war, Myra and John became friends and colleagues in founding 'Care and Counsel', a Christian counselling service.

John did, of course, still find time for bird-watching. In great excitement he discovered that, in May 1942, a pair of black redstarts was nesting either on the top of Trinity Chapel or on one of the St John's buildings next door. Black redstarts had never been seen in Britain before. Another pair was nesting on the Eden Lilley store. 'It makes an amazing noise,' John told his parents, 'like the rattling of stones together or the buzz of an electric machine when the current is suddenly turned on.' The black redstart became the symbol of the Cambridge Ornithological Society.

Next month, at the end of his second year and two months after his twenty-first birthday, the results for Part I of the Modern and Medieval Languages Tripos were published. John was again among the fourteen Firsts in French but, to his dismay, only achieved a 2.1 (upper second-class result) in German. His tutor, Patrick Duff, tried to console him. 'We are all quite sure that you are really a First Class man. But you do not always have enough self-confidence for examinations. You haven't been elected to a senior scholarship, but your entrance scholarship has been prolonged.'

The college did award him a senior scholarship a year later. Had the long hours as secretary to Bash's camps taken their toll? Or was it anxiety over the breakdown in relations with his father? Whatever the reason, he was now able to put French and German behind him and begin to read theology. But he never regretted his years studying foreign languages in depth. 'The greatest help,' he said many years later, 'in learning to use words with care and accuracy was writing essays in French and German. There is a precise word which fits every situation, and the sort of education I had has been a great help to me in my preaching and writing ministry.'

Arnold Stott, now promoted to the rank of Major General, continued to be opposed to his son's further residence in Cambridge. He was sceptical about the influence which teachers of theology would have upon John. He took the view that his son's outlook on life was unreasonably narrow and that studying theology would do nothing to broaden his thinking.

When the October term began in war-time conditions at Trinity (1942), John began his study of theology, not in a more normal tutorial group of four or five but one-to-one from John Burnaby. Burnaby was later to succeed Michael Ramsey as Regius Professor of Divinity at Cambridge. John arrived in his small dark study to find it filled with tobacco smoke from his pipe. His tutor lapsed into long silences either because he was deep in thought or didn't know what to say next. John didn't feel that it was his responsibility to initiate a conversation. And when the two men did speak they often disagreed.

'As it is recorded in Matthew 5,' said Burnaby, 'Jesus contradicted Moses about the law.'

'I disagree,' said John. 'The six antitheses ("you have heard that it was said . . . but I say . . . ") express Jesus' disagreement with the tradition which had grown up around the law and not with Scripture itself. I think that Jesus was contradicting the teaching of the scribes but not of Moses.'

Thirty-five years later, John would develop these ideas in his commentary on the Sermon on the Mount, *Christian Counter-Culture*.

In the summer term John enjoyed getting away from the smoke of Burnaby's study to work out of doors in the Trinity Fellows' Garden, though he was sometimes distracted by the singing of the blackcaps, garden warblers and a pair of lesser spotted woodpeckers feeding their young. He did most of his work in his own rooms or in the great reading room of the university library.

Most of his lecturers adopted a 'liberal' approach to the Bible and to theology. He often objected, not so much to the liberalism itself, but to the fact that his teachers tended (in his view) to rehash material from their own or other scholars' books. He complained that he heard little which was first-hand and preferred to go directly to original sources. He took the view that liberalism was becoming aridly negative and doing little to prepare students for Christian service.

It took two years to study Part I of the Theological Tripos. This meant that although John would graduate as BA after his first year of theology, he would remain at Trinity as a post-graduate student until summer 1944 and then move across Cambridge to Ridley Hall, the theological college he had chosen, with a view to ordination in December 1945.

On 22 June 1943, he did indeed graduate as BA with a First and was awarded a senior scholarship from Trinity College. After a long summer vacation, much of which he spent at Bash's Iwerne camp, he prepared for his final year at Trinity.

Relations with his father continued to be difficult. When John sent him a Wardonia razor for his birthday, his father replied that he already had two Wardonia razors but thought that perhaps a third might be a useful addition. More seriously he wrote in September, drawing his son's attention to the fact that it was the fourth anniversary of the outbreak of the war:

For the rest of my life it will be an abiding sorrow to me that you have chosen to stand aloof; if sufficient of your friends and countrymen had taken the same course, disaster too horrible to contemplate would have overtaken your country and the world. I believe you will later regret it, and, tho' memories are short, I believe it will diminish your power to be of help to others in the future.

The other thing that worries me is this camp business. I told you a few years ago that it was taking too much of your time but you denied it. It has been increasingly obvious ever since that I was right. I believe your close association with it has prevented your discovering other interests and hobbies; it has clearly associated you with only one aspect of life and I believe is mainly responsible for your narrow outlook and failure to face realities . . .

John replied and returned to Cambridge to begin his final year at Trinity as a post-graduate student. In November another letter arrived from his father. Arnold's tone was angry. He told John that it was an 'extraordinary anomaly' to remain at Cambridge at a time of war. He told him that the time had come for him to pay his own way. He could do this by selling his 'Birmingham Stock', a legacy from his grandmother. Coutts, the family bank, would make the arrangements. In the meantime he enclosed a cheque for £70 to pay off any sums outstanding up to the time John took his degree. If this amount was insufficient, John was to let his father know. If it was more than needed, he was to return the balance.

This was a blow for John. It would still be a full two years before he could be ordained and his grandmother's legacy wouldn't be enough to support him for that long. Alarmed, John went to see his tutor, Patrick Duff.

'I think we shall have to look for further grants and bursaries,' Duff told John. 'I will write to your mother.'

In his letter to Lily, Patrick Duff asked whether she thought the decision about selling the Birmingham Stock should be taken as a final decision or open to reconsideration. Lily sent the substance of this letter to Arnold, then based in York. Ten days later Arnold wrote another letter to John.

If in future you do not agree with, or wish to discuss, anything contained in a letter of mine, kindly communicate with me direct, and not indirectly through Mummy via your tutor or anybody else.

My last letter was not intended to close the door on discussion. I gave you my view and I have not changed it. My suggestion about your Birmingham Stock seemed to me a proper way of solving my difficulties. Altho' it has aroused such opposition, I have not yet heard any arguments against it.

Nevertheless, I confess that I had forgotten that Mr Duff wrote to me in March last and told me of your intentions, and I feel that he is right in feeling that, altho' no reply from me was required, my silence meant consent.

I have therefore decided that I shall have to continue to finance you, though my reluctance has in no way diminished.

I do not wish to see your accounts, but I shall expect you to let me know each term what sum you require from me to meet your obligations after exercising all reasonable economy.

John sent his father an affectionate reply with explanations, apology and gratitude. From this time, their exchange of letters became friendlier and the relationship when they met less strained.

The British government invited Arnold to make a memorable contribution to the country's war-time history. Back in May 1941, Rudolph Hess had flown to Britain, parachuting from his Messerschmitt over Renfrewshire and landing (though breaking his ankle) on a farm near Eaglesham, just south of Glasgow. Hess had grown distressed by the war and probably hoped to score a diplomatic victory by sealing a peace between the Third Reich and Britain.

Hess was quickly arrested. His strange behaviour and unilateral proposals quickly discredited him as a serious negotiator (especially after it became obvious he did not officially represent the German government). However, believing that Hess might have useful military intelligence, Churchill and the head of MI6 arranged to have him transferred to secure accommodation near Aldershot. The house was fitted out with microphones and sound recording equipment.

'I want Hess to be strictly isolated,' Winston Churchill told the security services, 'and every effort made to get any information out of him that might be useful.'

Hess became increasingly agitated as he grew convinced that he would be murdered. Mealtimes were difficult, since Hess suspected that his food might be poisoned, and the MI6 officers had to exchange their food with his to reassure him. Some of them began to think that Hess was insane.

The British Government asked Arnold Stott, as consulting physician to the army, to examine Hess in October 1943.

'I agree with the verdict of the examining psychiatrist,' Arnold reported back after a session with Hess. 'He is not insane, but certainly mentally ill and suffering from depression – probably due to the failure of his mission.'

4. DISCOVERING THE INNER LOGIC

The town of Cambridge played its part in the war-time story. The D-Day invasion of northern France was planned on the banks of the Cam. To John's astonishment, for four nights (28–31 March 1944) the army posted military guards at the gates of Trinity College. Officers from all three services arrived at the college to be coached for their part in Operation Overlord. College Master, George Trevelyan, gave over the Lodge for use as headquarters. Three months later, in June, the allies invaded France and in August Paris was liberated.

Sadly, one of those killed on the beaches of Normandy was Robbie Bickersteth, a friend of John's since his days at Oakley Hall. Before crossing the Channel he had married Penelope, and Robbie's death was an even greater tragedy because she was pregnant and later miscarried. Every year, on the anniversary of Robbie's death, John wrote to Penelope until she died in old age.

During his final year at Trinity, and now a post-graduate student, John attended few lectures in the university. He still took the view that his time was better spent reading original sources for himself, rather than listening to rehashes of this material by others. One day he bumped into one of the lecturers, Henry Hart, in King's Parade.

'Let me see,' said Hart, 'you attended one of my lectures once, didn't you?'

During the summer vacation in 1944, John made ready to enter Ridley Hall for his final year at Cambridge and in preparation for ordination.

A new student at Pembroke College spotted John outside his college in October 1944. He had met him once before but didn't expect John, who was on his bike, to recognise him. However, John stopped when he saw him and they chatted for a moment.

'Do you plan to go to the pre-terminal meetings of CICCU?' John asked.

'I don't know anything about them,' replied the fresher. John explained about CICCU.

'The first meeting will be this evening in Trinity OCR – the Old Combination Room above Great Court. Do you know where that is?'

The fresher shook his head. John glanced at his watch and leaned his bicycle against a wall.

'I'll take you there. It takes just seven and a half minutes.'

The two young men walked together along King's Parade to Trinity, across the Court, up the steps and to the OCR. John opened the door to show the new undergraduate the high-windowed empty room. Then they walked back and John retrieved his bike.

'See you tonight, then,' said John, and rode off to Ridley Hall.

Ridley Hall was established in 1881 with a trust deed which committed the college to an evangelical position. The first Principal was Professor Handley Moule. Although as a preacher and teacher Moule played an important part in making evangelicals more missionary-minded, critics however maintained that Ridley Hall men were pious but not learned. They may have been well taught, but Moule failed to tackle current critical issues. However, Moule became well known outside Cambridge as a respected evangelical leader, and was in demand as a preacher and speaker. He became a chaplain to Queen Victoria, then to Edward VII, and from 1901 was Bishop of Durham.

When John arrived at war-time Ridley, there were not many more than a dozen students at the college. The Vice-Principal was Professor C. F. D. ('Charlie') Moule, Handley's nephew. During 1944 he left to become Dean of Clare College, but John still attended his lectures. Charlie Moule (who died in October 2007 at the age of 98) combined brilliance as a New

Testament scholar with personal humility, friendliness and charm. Charlie's approach was more liberal than his uncle's. When John and his contemporaries noticed that Charlie was taking a line of which they thought the college's first Principal would have disapproved, they wagged their fingers at him.

'Charlie,' they asked, 'what would Uncle Handley have said?'

Donald English, who went on to become President of the Methodist Conference, knew John at this time. He recalled John's attitude to the liberal theology which most Cambridge theology lecturers adopted. 'The effect of both the university teaching and the situation at Ridley Hall was to send him even more deeply into detailed Bible study, both searching for and increasingly discovering the inner logic which it contained.'

While at Ridley, John often led Bible studies at four different colleges and loyally supported the weekly CICCU meetings in Holy Trinity church. Myra Chave-Jones remembered him as a steward looking 'handsome and impressively dignified in his sweeping graduate gown. It was always nice to be shown into a seat by him.'

As John's Cambridge years drew to a close, so the war finally ended. They celebrated Victory in Europe (VE) Day, 8 May 1945, with a great bonfire on Midsummer Common. Winston Churchill invited the Labour and the Liberal parties to continue in office until the defeat of Japan, which he didn't expect to occur for another eighteen months. When both parties refused, Churchill resigned and returned at the head of a caretaker administration.

With the national election campaign in full swing, John took Parts 1 and 2 combined of the Cambridge Ordination course exams. He was the only candidate to achieve starred distinctions in the two papers on doctrine.

Unusually, there was an interlude between polling day (5 July) and the declaration of the results (26 July), during which Churchill attended the Potsdam conference. Stalin seemed to have persuaded him for the moment that his intentions were benign. After a brief holiday, Churchill was back in Britain for the result of the general election, which proved to be a landslide Labour victory. The new generation which voted for the first time in 1945 had been shaped by the egalitarianism of the war years.

'It may well be a blessing in disguise,' his wife Clementine remarked.

'At the moment it seems quite effectively disguised,' Churchill replied. At 7 o'clock on the evening of 26 July, he drove to Buckingham Palace and resigned, declining the King's offer of the Order of the Garter.

With the bombing of Hiroshima and Nagasaki, Japan surrendered and the war ended earlier than expected. Arnold Stott, with characteristic reluctance, agreed to John staying on at Ridley for one further term, postponing his ordination until the end of the year. The condition of his agreement was that his son spent several hours a day reading a broad range of books in, as he put it, 'an attempt to widen your outlook and fill in some of the gaps in your education'. John readily agreed to this, hoping that his father would be happy with a diet of reading which included books on history, psychology and science.

But before his final term at Ridley, he acted as secretary to three camps at Iwerne Minster – his last. One man who was present at the final camp remembered an evening when several of them were gathered in the kitchen where they used to meet, with the grudging approval of Bash, to drink tea and gossip. John joined them in an unusually jovial and relaxed mood and started throwing eggs about.

'I'm not going to bed just because Nanny [Bash] tells me to!' he said, to the astonishment of his friends.

He clearly had been overtaken by an acute end-of-term feeling. More characteristically, however, he prepared a four-page memo for his successor as camp secretary. The document contained detailed advice about items such as school bursar, domestic staff, boilermen, travel vouchers, war-time petrol coupons, ration books, laundry, insurance, hire of chairs, cleaning the swimming pool, bank facilities, payment of bills, checking inventories, thank-you letters, analysis of expenditure, and so on.

Perhaps we may sympathise with his father who had more than once urged him to give up his camp duties and concentrate on his studies. Ironically, however, John had managed to achieve a double first-class honours degree, which Arnold had failed to do.

The Revd Harold Earnshaw-Smith, the Rector of All Souls Church, came to Cambridge in the autumn of 1945, to preach for the sixtieth anniversary of CICCU. John read the lesson and, at the end of the service, Earnshaw-Smith approached him.

'Has it been settled where you will serve your first curacy?' he asked.

'No, not yet,' John replied.

'Well, why don't you come to All Souls?'

In the course of making up his mind, John consulted his father.

'Human nature varies but little,' Arnold opined. 'So that I should think it matters little where you start. I think you will find you have a great deal to learn after all these years of sheltered academic life.'

It was provisionally agreed that John would join the All Souls staff in December with a salary of £230 a year.

'If I may say so,' John told Earnshaw-Smith, 'I am very much looking forward to coming to you. I know what a very great deal you have to teach me, and I do hope you will never hesitate to "reprove, rebuke, exhort". I am deeply anxious to learn.'

Before finally leaving Ridley Hall, John sent a note to about 150 friends and relatives telling them that he was to be ordained deacon in St Paul's Cathedral on 21 December 1945. Robbie Bickersteth's widow Penelope replied, 'How Robbie would have loved to be with you in body!' Gladys Beale, who had taught him music at Oakley Hall, wrote from Gloucestershire, promising him her prayers and adding, 'You have two great gifts, lack of which hampers many parsons, a clear speaking voice and being able to sing!' Florence Myers, who had cooked for the camps, told him to be sure to make arrangements for an honest midday meal, 'NOT bread and cheese!'

His sister Joanna, newly married, wrote from Manchester:

It's strange to think that the time has really come after all these years. As you know I haven't been able to understand your point of view all the time about it – but I can see quite clearly that it is what you want, and that it is what you have been working and aiming for, for years, and it *has* dawned on me that you are 'just the type of person needed'.

His aunt Ella sent him a cheque saying, 'I believe church vestments are very expensive,' while great aunt Emily told him, 'You *daily* have my prayers.'

In November, the London diocese required all its candidates for Order of Deacon to sit the ordination examination on the Christian faith, the Holy Scriptures, the Prayer Book and the Pastoral Office. Then, a week before Christmas, John joined the other candidates for a retreat in Hampstead, wearing a suit of plus-fours he had had made from Scottish tweed, bought on a visit to the Hebrides.

On 21 December 1945, John's family made their way to St Paul's to see him made deacon. Designed by the court architect Sir Christopher Wren, the cathedral was built between 1675 and 1710 after its predecessor had been destroyed in the Great Fire of London. Wren's masterpiece had been the venue for events of overwhelming importance: the funerals of Lord Nelson and the Duke of Wellington, Jubilee celebrations for Queen Victoria and then her memorial service, and peace services marking the end of the First and Second World Wars. The church had survived a bombing raid during the blitz in 1940.

Arnold and Lily, with Nanny Golden, together with many of John's friends, followed the signs down into the crypt. The new bishop of London, William Wand, arrived to conduct the service. John had been asked to read the Gospel, from Luke 12:31–40 (KJV).

'Let your loins be girded about,' John's voice echoed around the crypt, 'and your lights burning; and ye yourselves like unto men that wait for their lord, when he will return from the wedding; that when he cometh and knocketh, they may open unto him immediately . . . '

Bishop Wand laid hands on John and gave him a copy of the New Testament.

'Take thou authority,' the bishop said, 'to read the Gospel in the Church of God, and to preach the same . . . '

Outside, after the service, the bells, which had rung out to celebrate the liberation of Paris in 1944, pealed again for London's first peacetime Christmas for seven years.

'When you read the Gospel lesson,' Nanny Golden told John afterwards, 'I just felt I wanted all the world to hear you.'

A few days after Christmas, John learned that he had been awarded the

Pilkington Prize for his papers in his ordination exam. The prize amounted to the grand total of £1. 10s!

There was no curate's house attached to All Souls. However, John had a friend from his Rugby and Cambridge days, Marcus Dukes, who was the son of two doctors who lived at No. 1, Queen Anne Street, close to All Souls. Marcus's parents agreed to put John up for a week or two. In the event, he stayed with the Dukes, who were Quakers and not members of All Souls, for almost seven years.

5. CURATE IN A MIXED PARISH

Harold Earnshaw-Smith, the Rector of All Souls when John took up his duties at the end of December 1945, had been converted to Christ through the work of CICCU while studying classics at Christ's College, Cambridge. He had come to All Souls in 1936 after serving as vicar in two London churches and becoming more widely known as a preacher at the annual Keswick Convention meetings held for the 'deepening of the spiritual life'. Through the years of the London blitz, he and Church Army Sister Jordan worked night after night in air raid shelters deep underground. Hundreds of frightened London workers and residents spent their nights on the four platforms of Oxford Circus tube station, and Earnshaw-Smith held regular services for them.

When appointed to All Souls, he had told friends that the church 'stands in a wonderfully strategic position for the gospel'. With the BBC's Broadcasting House next door employing hundreds, Regent Street Polytechnic across the road, the Middlesex hospital and the great Oxford Street stores nearby, there were many opportunities to reach out to students, doctors, nurses and working people with both the message and the love of Christ. And there was a church primary school with six hundred children.

Earnshaw-Smith had quickly established links with the BBC and regularly presented a broadcast children's service. John found

Earnshaw-Smith an inspiring role model. For twenty minutes before a service began he would wander around the church going up to a pew and holding out his hands to welcome people.

'He put his surpliced arm round my shoulders,' recalled a medical student arriving in London for the first time, 'like the wing of a seagull. I felt very welcomed and touched.'

'I would willingly have blacked his boots,' John said of his new boss.

Earnshaw-Smith's administrative abilities, however, didn't equal his pastoral gifts. He had no secretary and possessed no congregational register. John was astonished to find him one day sitting on the floor of his tiny study sending out a circular, stuffing the envelopes and licking the stamps himself.

Since the bomb had badly damaged All Souls in December 1940, the congregation had made St Peter's, Vere Street, their home. The church, which was later to become a daughter church of All Souls, was where John ministered through all his years as curate.

One Sunday, John was on the receiving end of a little joke Earnshaw-Smith played on all his new curates at one time or another: he came up to him in the middle of the service and said, 'Let me see now, you're preaching this morning aren't you?'

Any image of All Souls as a fashionable church in a West End parish set in an upper class world is far from the truth. The parish stretches from Marylebone High Street to Tottenham Court Road and includes an area that is almost an overspill of Soho north of Oxford Street. In the 1940s and 50s there were many housing blocks with small flats and much over-crowding, Greek-Cypriot restaurants, Spaniards, Italians, some Indian and (later) Bangladeshi families. A stone's throw from the church, in Hanson Street, a Christian foundation ran Latimer House, a hostel for working boys. All Souls staff visited the hostel regularly, often leading evening prayers.

Mrs Denham, the All Souls verger's wife, supplied John with a list of mothers she thought the new curate should visit. As she went through the list with him, she made staccato comments about each one: 'old', 'deaf', 'widow', 'nice' and so on.

John set off for his first full day of visiting on 31 December 1945. The top name on Mrs Denham's list was a Mrs Todd. He found her house and rang the bell. After three rings no one appeared. It was a disappointing start.

Out in the street he watched a group of boys, some of whom he recognised, playing soccer.

Strange how cherubic boys in white surplices on Sunday can shout and punch like pagan toughs on Monday! he thought.

In Hanson Street, Chinese Mrs Yow was in. She looked very ill, with sunken pallid cheeks. Mr Yow was lying in bed, with a beaming smile, hugging baby Barry. They chatted for a while.

'May I say a prayer as we look forward to the New Year?' John asked.

A look of alarm flashed across Mrs Yow's face, but she agreed.

Next on the list was Mrs Hollidge, a deaf widow. John knew that she lived in a block with about twenty flats in it, but he had no idea which was Mrs Hollidge's. He wandered in and saw light under the door immediately to the left on the ground floor. The door was a little open. He knocked but no one came. He knocked again.

'Is anyone in?' he called.

He thought he heard movement but no one spoke. He peeped through the crack and saw an elderly woman who apparently hadn't heard his knocks and calls. Just then a man arrived at the block.

'Does Mrs Hollidge live here?' John asked.

The man nodded and John walked in. 'Within a few minutes,' he later recorded in his diary, 'my mouth was within two inches of her right ear, while strands of her grey hair found their way into my mouth.' Mrs Hollidge grasped his right hand in both of hers and stroked it.

'We cannot feel lonely if we know Jesus as our friend and Saviour,' he shouted.

Next stop was the home of Mrs Evans, an Irish lady with three children. Her daughters, Marie and Dorothy, who had acted in the school nativity play, were dressed as angels. John saw some spare angel costumes in the room. When he attempted to put a costume on himself, Marie and Dorothy screamed with delight. One by one they scrambled on to his knee for Ride-a-cock-horse and then on to his back for piggyback rides.

Then baby Desmond hit his head against a gas lamp and they all got scared until he recovered and stopped crying. When Mr Evans arrived home from work, John and the whole Evans family knelt for prayer.

This is lovely, John thought.

John preached his first sermon in the parish of All Souls at St Peter's, Vere Street, on the first Sunday in January 1946. He decided to use the framework of a sermon he had already preached near Cambridge six months earlier. He wrote the notes of his sermon on the tiny five-by-three-inch cards he was to use for most of his preaching life. His text was Romans 3:22–23, 'all have sinned and fall short of the glory of God,' and his theme, 'there is no difference'. His notes reminded him to emphasise: *Important face sin, as then appreciate remedy.*

A few weeks later, on a Sunday evening, he preached on 'Abiding in Christ' from John 15 – 'I am the vine,' says Jesus, 'you are the branches.'

Tony Waterson, a medical student at the London Hospital, was listening critically. Following the sermon, and as a response to it, Tony sent John a diagrammatic analysis of the sermon's structure and detailed explanation of the difference between sap in a plant and blood circulating in the body. The preacher found this useful.

'Now I've settled in a bit,' he said to Tony, 'is it too much to ask you to write a full critique each time I preach? You only need to tell me if you have a special word either of criticism or commendation. Could you be especially sensitive to two broad questions about each sermon: first, is it worth saying? and, second, is it well said? What I mean by the first is: *Is there a real message here, something vital, relevant, gripping?* By the second I mean: *Has the message gone across – or was it too heavy, too complicated, too boring?* I'd be so grateful if you could do this. It's really especially adverse criticism I want to hear – such as you might overhear while leaving church.'

And so Tony Waterson began the regular practice of sending John detailed written criticisms and comments on his sermons. Responding to one particular set of comments, John replied to Tony: 'My own greatest criticism of myself (which you've never mentioned!) ... is that I'm too heavy, and try to put over too much "theological" stuff for the background of the average listener. But I find it hard to control myself! I'm still rather puzzled by what you call my harsh or forced delivery. I think you mean intensity (do I frown a lot?!), but I'm not sure it really is something to eliminate, or something which really is myself and which it would be unnatural to cut out.'

Preaching regularly in a church in the West End of London was a demanding assignment – and there was plenty of competition. William Sangster attracted a congregation of 3,000, morning and evening, every Sunday at the Westminster Central Hall until the mid-1950s. Leslie Weatherhead was preaching at the City Temple at Holborn Viaduct and didn't retire until 1960. Martyn Lloyd-Jones practised his unique brand of expository preaching at Westminster Chapel until he retired in 1968. And Donald Soper preached at Kingsway Hall, the West London Methodist Mission, and standing on his famous soap box at Hyde Park Corner, until he retired in 1978.

Despite this readiness to invite feedback, John soon got a reputation for preaching sermons which were longer than the All Souls congregation was used to. One Sunday, Earnshaw-Smith preached at the neighbouring church of All Saints, Margaret Street. At the end of the service he said good-bye to the congregation at the church door, disrobed in the vestry, took leave of the vicar, and began his stroll home via St Peter's, Vere Street.

If there are any lingering members of my congregation, he thought, *I can greet them.*

Instead, to his surprise, he found that the service was still in progress, with John well settled into the pulpit and energetically expounding Pilate's question, 'What is truth?'

Earnshaw-Smith, who had already received some adverse comments on the length of the new curate's sermons, didn't let his curate forget this incident in a hurry.

On a March day in 1946, John visited the Latimer House boys' hostel to take prayers as usual. He walked into the table tennis room and got into conversation with a disabled teenager who was a newcomer.

'I've recently been discharged from the London Hospital,' the young man told him.

John invited him to meals at his flat at the top of 1 Queen Anne Street. He discovered that he was an orphan and that his disability was the result of polio. He had been brought up by a man he called 'grandpa' but when 'grandpa' had remarried he became severely depressed.

'Why should God send me all this suffering?' he asked.

When John explained the Christian gospel, it made little impression on the teenager. Sometimes he lived in a fantasy world imagining that he was a great actor.

'I have made up my mind to end it all,' he told John one day. 'Three weeks' time, on Good Friday, I'm going to take my own life.' He showed John an entry for Good Friday which read: *For better or for worse I drink this bitter cup if providence so wills.*

'Why have you chosen Good Friday?' John asked.

'Well,' the young man replied, 'it will give me time to get the poison – and it was the day of Jesus' death. Even though I have pretended not to, I really like Jesus very much.'

John pleaded with him, 'Life is precious and sacred. God will judge those who take it, even if it is their own. I will be a friend to you, as long as you live.'

The young man persisted: he intended to kill himself on Good Friday.

Before he left for a pre-Easter camp at Iwerne on 5 April, John asked the teenager to agree to two requests: 'First, I want you to promise that you will do nothing until I get back from my camp in Dorset. And second, I want you to read this Gospel of John.'

The teenager thought for a while, then took the Gospel and made his promise.

At the camp, John received two letters from the young man, full of bitterness against God. He returned to London before Easter and met him on the steps of St Peter's before he was due to lead a Good Friday service.

'Are you busy?' asked the teenager.

'Moderately at the moment, why?'

The young man came close to John, shaking with emotion. 'I've decided on this day which I'd fixed for ending my life to become a Christian instead!'

'Why have you made this decision?'

'It wasn't fair that they crucified Jesus like that.'

'Come back to Queen Anne Street after the service,' John said.

The young man came and they talked. John went through the 'ABC' with him – three basics steps that Bash, he and others used to explain how to become a Christian:

Admit (or *Acknowledge*) your need of Christ
Believe that Christ died for you
Come to him

John talked about the picture of Jesus, in Revelation 3:20, knocking at the door of the human heart, and his promise, 'Here I am! I stand at the door and knock. If anyone hears my voice and opens the door, I will come in and eat with him, and he with me.'

'Do you know Jesus has come in?' John asked the young man.

'I'm not sure,' he replied, 'but during the service in St Peter's I covered my eyes with my hands and felt as if someone had put his arm around me and said, "At last you have come to me".'

'Jesus does come in when we invite him,' John said. 'But there's also a cost. You have to repent – to say you are sorry – for your sins. Are you ready for that?'

'Yes, I'm ready,' the young man said.

'It will mean turning your back on any idea of taking your own life.'

The young man closed his eyes for a few moments. 'Yes, I accept that.'

'And it will mean telling others what you have done,' said John.

'Yes, I can take that, too.'

John was sure that he had become a Christian.

On Sunday 5 May 1946, John took the 11 o'clock service at Latimer House and then walked to St Peter's in Vere Street. People were leaving the morning service and when they had nearly all gone, a man in a frayed coat approached him.

'Can we have a chat?' he asked.

John agreed and it soon became clear that the man wanted money.

'I have a rule that I never offer anyone money,' John told him. 'But you can have an egg if you want.'

'I've nowhere to cook it. Couldn't you break your rule this once?'

'No, I can't. But if you come to my flat at 1 Queen Anne Street at one o'clock I'll see what I can do about some food.'

'I'll be there,' said the man and walked off.

John didn't expect to see him again. However, at one o'clock the bell rang and he appeared. The two men had a friendly lunch. The visitor's name was Harry Mossop. He spoke well and seemed to have been well educated.

'I was a commissioned officer in the Indian army,' he said, 'but drink got the better of me. And now I'm destitute.'

They talked, and eventually John explained the same ABC procedure that he had gone through with the disabled young man. 'Do you think you could take those steps?' John asked.

'I could probably make the effort,' said Harry.

'It's not so much about "making an effort" as inviting Jesus into your life,' said John. 'But you are right in one way. There's a cost to becoming a Christian. You wouldn't be able to touch drink again, or you would slip back.'

Harry rather liked the image of Jesus standing at the door of the human heart with a latch on the inside. 'I want time to think it over,' he said and got up to go.

'Will you come to the 6.30 service at St Peter's?'

'Yes.'

When John arrived for the service soon after six, Harry was sitting in the back pew. After the service, John approached him.

'Will you come back to my flat for some supper?'

Harry agreed and walked with John to Queen Anne Street. 'I've decided to do my utmost to go the way you've outlined,' he said as John got some food together.

'You really understand the steps I'm suggesting you take? Are you really facing the cost which would be involved?'

As they talked, John grew convinced that Harry meant business. The two men knelt down and prayed. 'Dear Lord, I'm asking you to come into my heart,' Harry said.

After a while he got up to go. 'I've never prayed aloud before. I'm grateful for the interest you've taken in me,' he said.

Harry did 'mean business' and the two men remained friends over a period of years.

6. UNDER CHARING CROSS ARCHES

Ever since he was a teenager at Rugby when he had founded his Association for the Benefit of the Community, John had felt a concern for those who were rejected by society. But what would it really be like to be one of London's underclass? John decided to try to get some idea. He stopped shaving for several days until he had a stubbly beard and put on some very old clothes. He still had his wartime identity card and, having put this in his shoe, set off to make the dramatic transition from Queen Anne Street to the Embankment area on the north bank of the River Thames.

He spent his first night under the arches of Charing Cross Bridge surrounded by tramps. He lay down in the company of men and women whose only covering, apart from their clothes, was newspapers. He didn't get much sleep. The pavement was hard. Men were coming and going, some very drunk and making a lot of noise. It was November 1946 and very cold.

As light dawned and the sun came up he was relieved that the new day was sunny and dry, though the air was crisp. He called at a number of the old ABC teashops where employees were kneeling outside scrubbing the steps. He had deliberately brought no money with him.

'Can ya gimme a job for a cup o'tea?' he asked in the best Cockney accent he could muster. 'Or even spare a breakfast?'

When nobody took pity on him, he began to feel rejected. He walked into the East End of London and, since he had had little sleep, lay down in the sunshine on one of the many bomb sites. Rosebay willow herb was growing in profusion, making a reasonably soft bed, and he fell asleep.

When evening came, he made his way to the Whitechapel Salvation Army hostel for the homeless and queued for a bed. When he got to the window where you booked, the officer in charge was brusque with the man in front of him. Momentarily, John forgot who he was meant to be that day.

'As a Salvation Army officer,' he burst out, 'you ought to try to win that man for Christ and not treat him like that!'

The officer looked at him sharply, wondering who he was, but said nothing.

He was allocated a bed in a dormitory with no cubicles or privacy. He slept only intermittently. Men were coming and going most of the night, some drunk and shouting, others mentally disturbed.

John left the hostel, walked down Commercial Road to Toynbee Hall, and once again attempting a Cockney accent, asked for breakfast. But this time it didn't work.

'OK,' the man on duty said. 'The game's up! You'd better tell us who you are.'

He didn't tell them he was a clergyman, but he got out his identity card and showed it to them.

Toynbee Hall was the charity which over the years attracted the support of Labour Prime Minister Clement Attlee, social reformer William Beveridge, and later disgraced politician Jack Profumo. Staff gave John breakfast and saw him on his way. He walked back to 1 Queen Anne Street to find his landlord Cuthbert Dukes (a distinguished pathologist), and his wife Ethel (one of the founders of the Marriage Guidance Council, now Relate) at home. As Quakers, with a strong social conscience, they were not at all fazed by their lodger's dishevelled appearance.

'Come into the drawing room,' said Cuthbert, 'and tell us all about your intriguing venture. Feel free to sit anywhere!'

John managed to stay awake while he gave them a graphic insight into a side of London life far removed from the western edge of All Souls parish.

In 1946 Arnold Stott was knighted for his distinguished services to the army. When the National Health Service came into operation, he was a whole-hearted supporter, insisting that medical care should be available to everyone, whether they could pay or not. He became well-known in medical circles for his chairmanship of the medical committee at the Westminster Hospital and his flashes of humour which enlivened the meetings. In 1948, he was appointed Extra Physician to the Royal Household and retired from the staff of the Westminster Hospital two years later.

Visiting the area around Harley Street presented John with different challenges from the tenement blocks to the east. Many people remembered the Stott family from their years as residents at numbers 58 and 65 Harley Street. It wasn't easy for John, when making a pastoral visit, and sitting in a West End drawing room, to suggest to a busy medical consultant that he should join him in prayer or a Bible reading. However, he tried to do this whenever possible and found it useful to make a habit of carrying his Bible so that residents knew, when he arrived, that he had (in his words) 'come on spiritual business'. This made it easier for him to take his Bible from under his arm and say, 'I wonder if you would allow me to read a few verses and pray with you before I leave?'

On Sunday mornings, it was John's job, as curate, to lead the children's church in St Peter's for half an hour before the main service at 11 a.m. These children were mainly from professional families in the West End area of the parish, and this sometimes provided an opening for him to visit homes where the parents had little or no connection with the church. Every year, in April, they visited the zoo in Regent's Park, and at Christmas there was a party. Many children grew up remembering John playing the tune 'The more we are together, the merrier we shall be' on his piano accordion.

But John wanted to do more to reach the unchurched boys of the parish. With the encouragement of the Rector, he established Covenanter groups for both boys and girls. Covenanters had been founded about fifteen years earlier as an interdenominational non-uniformed organisation for children and young people linked with a local church.

John's group met on Monday evenings and his helpers were mainly medical students from the Middlesex Hospital nearby. The boys were a rowdy lot, but they were able to develop an excellent soccer team which played in Regent's Park. John sometimes acted as referee and was proud of the group's reputation one year for having played twenty-four matches and won them all!

John was anxious to build links with boys living in the Langham Place area who typically left school at fourteen and got jobs as newspaper boys, market traders or bottom-of-the-rung jobs in the big Oxford Street stores. Many of them were from Greek or Turkish families. He also formed a junior group of Covenanters – 'Jucos' – mainly for boys in the All Souls Church School. These boys already knew him because he used to visit the school and act as coach for the soccer team.

John bought a Dutch ex-army jeep – his 'jalopy' – for £100 and used it to take Covenanter boys to the Glory Café, opposite the Middlesex Hospital, for egg and chips, where he developed a mischievous relationship with the Greek-Cypriot proprietor and his staff. The jalopy also came in useful for taking the boys to a Whitsun camp on a farm on the banks of the river Wey, and further afield in the summer to Cromer.

He and the boys crammed the old jalopy with tents, blankets, cooking pots and camping gear. These were poor London boys, very different from the middle-class types who had gone to the Iwerne camps under Bash's leadership. The Covenanter camps were rough and tumble, genuinely under canvas, and close to nature.

One boy, who first went to a camp at Cromer when he was thirteen, remembered John as his tent officer and padre. The boys from Langham Place included a boxer, Tony Mancini, and a barrow boy called Arthur. He remembered John waking the camp up in the morning by parading round with his accordion. 'He showed great interest in us. We could go to the Quiet Time tent. John had his own devotions beforehand, praying upright on his knees in order to keep himself awake. He shaved with a cut-throat razor without drawing much blood. Like many of his boys, I had my first taste of bird-watching, lying on my stomach in a field with John. He could remember us by name years later. Even when I returned from a long stay in Peru he greeted me by name at the door of All Souls!'

'It was a good camp,' John told the All Souls congregation. 'Despite friendly but determined opposition, the message brought to the boys at prayers each day bore fruit. Few of us have any idea of the struggle our boys have to undergo if they really give their allegiance to Jesus Christ. It takes a real man to stand up for decency and honesty, let alone for real Christianity, in the surroundings in which some of them live and work. Yet a few have boldly taken their stand. Will you pray for them? And when they come to church on Sunday nights – give them a welcoming smile?'

In July 1946, Harold Earnshaw-Smith had his first heart attack. He was only fifty-five. In the weeks when he was out of action, retired clergy helped by conducting some services – but much of the weight of running the parish rested on the young curate's shoulders.

A second curate, Gordon Mayo, didn't arrive until the end of 1948. When he delivered a sermon at St Peter's, Vere Street, Gordon shared his doubts over a particular theological issue.

'I'm out of my depths here,' he told the congregation, 'and haven't a clue how to make sense of this.'

Used to a more confident style of preaching from John, some members of the church warmed to this rare moment of diffidence from the pulpit. 'We found it a rather refreshing experience,' they confided in Gordon.

Following his first heart attack, Harold Earnshaw-Smith suffered from a series of recurring illnesses which kept him, for periods, away from his desk and the pulpit. Eventually, the All Souls Parochial Church Council agreed that John should have a secretary to ease his burden in running a busy parish.

'I hope you'll allow me to take off your shoulders just as much as possible,' John told Earnshaw-Smith. 'Of course, we'll need to work out the details, and I'd like guidance as to how much you'd like to be consulted and how far in day-to-day decisions you'd like me to carry on without worrying you. But it gives me great joy to think that I may have some share in helping to prolong your ministry here.'

But Earnshaw-Smith's ministry was not to be prolonged. In the second week of March 1950, he died in his sleep following an attack of cardiac asthma, aged fifty-nine.

'We are an orphaned church,' John told his congregation.

'I want you to act as priest-in-charge of All Souls and St Peter's,' the Bishop of Willesden told John, on behalf of the Bishop of London, 'until a new incumbent can be appointed.'

7. THE KING APPROVES

All Souls is a 'Crown living' church where the Rector is appointed by the monarch on the advice of the Prime Minister. Although he had abandoned his belief in God while at school, Clement Attlee took a keen interest in church appointments.

'It's difficult to have a relaxed conversation with him on any subject,' a friend said of Prime Minister Attlee, 'except bishops and cricket.'

Attlee was advised on church appointments by his Secretary for Appointments, Sir Anthony Bevir, who had worked at No. 10 since 1940 serving Chamberlain and Churchill before his current job.

'He's a walking *Crockford*!' Attlee said of Bevir (referring to the Anglican Clerical Directory).

Bevir arranged for a questionnaire from the Prime Minister's office to be sent to the All Souls churchwardens.

On 21 March the PCC (Parochial Church Council) met, chaired by Geoffrey Bles, the publisher whose authors included C. S. Lewis and J. B. Phillips. To the Prime Minister's question – 'What are the church's views now obtaining?' – Bles secured agreement that they would reply, 'Evangelical with conservative emphasis, combining a biblical preaching ministry with a dignified worship.'

As for the qualities they were looking for in their new Rector, the church council agreed that they were looking for a fine preacher; a capable man of affairs to deal with the restoration of All Souls; one who loved the poor and loved to work among them, in view of the many poor families in the parish; and, finally, they wanted a young man, who could win the affections and confidence of young people, and would take an interest in clubs for boys and girls.

A small delegation from the PCC went to 10 Downing Street with the churchwardens to make their views known to Anthony Bevir. 'We had to tell the Crown that we were only interested in one name,' recalled George Cansdale, a member of the delegation. 'We didn't ask for a married man.'

'John Stott is already widely known as a fine preacher,' the delegation told Bevir. 'He has proved himself as a remarkably efficient administrator throughout Earnshaw-Smith's recurring illnesses. He has always taken a special interest in the poorer members of the parish and, as a young man still only twenty-nine, he has worked energetically with the church's clubs for children and young people.'

On 30 March, the churchwardens met the Bishop of London.

'We wish to press for John Stott's appointment,' they told Bishop Wand.

Just over a month later, an embossed envelope arrived at No. 1 Queen Anne Street. John opened it and read:

10 Downing Street
Whitehall
3 May, 1950

Dear Sir,

Your name has been brought to the notice of the Prime Minister in connection with the vacancy of All Souls, Langham Place.

If you wish to be considered, with others, in connexion with this benefice, I should be glad if you would complete the enclosed form and return it to me.

Yours very truly,
Anthony Bevir

John returned the form and received another letter five weeks later.

10 Downing Street
Whitehall
8 June, 1950

Confidential

Dear Sir,

I am desired by the First Lord of the Treasury to say that he will be happy to submit your name to the Crown for appointment to the benefice of All Souls, Langham Place, Marylebone, with which St Peter, Vere Street, is shortly to be amalgamated. Mr Attlee makes this communication to you in the belief that, subject to the provisions of Parliamentary Enactment, you are prepared to give due obedience to the Bishop of the diocese in matters of discipline and ceremonial.

As His Majesty's approval must be obtained before any announcement can be made, I have to ask that you will treat this offer as confidential: and I shall be glad to hear at your earliest convenience whether it is agreeable to you.

Yours very truly,
Anthony Bevir

Things moved fast and four days later Bevir informed John that 'the King has been graciously pleased to approve your appointment'.

At the end of the month, John chaired his first PCC meeting as Rector-designate.

'The appointment strengthens our faith in regal infallibility,' Geoffrey Bles observed, 'and we trust that Mr Stott will remain with us for many years to come.'

The announcement in July that John Stott had become Rector of All Souls alarmed some members of the congregation. The young man was likeable enough but he seemed inexperienced, dogmatic and uncompromising in his views compared to the older Rector they had known and loved. 'I was amazed that this young upstart should take over from my father,' Elisabeth Earnshaw-Smith recalled later. 'He was so unlike the vicars I knew who were my father's friends.'

'I am more humbled than honoured by this appointment,' John told the All Souls congregation. 'I ask for your prayers. Do let us make the weekly church prayer meeting central to our life as a church.'

A few days after the announcement of his appointment, he mounted the pulpit stairs and preached his first sermon as Rector-designate. His text was Acts 2:42, 'They devoted themselves to the apostles' teaching and to the fellowship, to the breaking of bread and to prayer.'

'This is the model we must imitate,' he said, 'as we peer into the unknown. Study, fellowship, worship and prayer must mark a church which is to work together in evangelism. All Souls with St Peter's is a Parish Church. Our first duty is local, and yet our impact on the neighbourhood is small and the percentage of Christians in the population negligible. The multitudes are outside. Are we too respectable to go out and bring them in? Too afraid of public opinion to employ well tried methods? Too sensitive to convention to devise new means of reaching the unbeliever? The task is beyond the power of the clergy. A staff of 10 curates could not do it. There are only two alternatives. Either the task will not be done, or we must do it together, a task force of Ministers and people thoroughly trained and harnessed as a team for evangelism.'

Within weeks of John becoming Rector of All Souls, curate Gordon Mayo sailed for Africa, leaving the new man and the tireless Church Army Sister, Phoebe Jordan, to run the parish between them. John lost no time in arranging for Donald Eddison, who was already working in the diocese, to come and join him early the following year. They had been friends from Bash's camps and had both been at Trinity College, Cambridge. Donald also became Chaplain of the Regent Street Polytechnic, almost opposite the church.

In August, John set off on holiday with a couple of friends, one of whom was John Lefroy who was soon to join the All Souls staff. They squeezed into an Austin van, which John now owned, with three small tents. John's objective was to drive as fast and as far as he could to a distant corner of Britain. When they reached Stranraer, in Dumfries and Galloway, Scotland, John sat on the pier and finished writing the All Souls parish magazine. He wrote,

> I have not been able to get you all out of my thoughts. My mind has turned constantly to St Peter's. Here I am perched precariously at the end of Stranraer pier, looking out across the splendid harbour, encircled by graceful Herring Gulls and listening to the plaintive pipings of Oyster Catchers. A little Scottish lad of about 10, seeing me writing, has just sidled timorously up and said: 'Och, are ye a poet, mon?'

> But the question which rests most heavily on my heart at present is how to reach the hungry multitudes who are without Christ. We are not unmindful of the fact that many come to St Peter's who do not live in the parish. Nevertheless, God has entrusted to us the care of some 10,000 souls living within the parochial boundaries . . . We have an unmistakable, inescapable responsibility towards our neighbours who are strangers to Christ and his gospel of grace. This responsibility is clearly shared by the whole congregation. The task of evangelism cannot be delegated to the few. Worship and witness go hand in hand. We are all called to worship, and we are all called to witness in some way. I visualise (and hope before next month to be able to explain in detail) the training of a considerable number of church members for the task of bringing the gospel of our Saviour Jesus Christ to every house in the parish. We cannot play at this. It will mean real sacrifice in our busy lives to commit ourselves to thorough training once a fortnight for six months, and then to go out two by two to visit from house to house. The course of training will need to cover the theology of the gospel, the personal life of the Christian worker and the technique of evangelism. Can we hear this call of Christ to discharge our duty to the mass of non-churchgoers?

Establishing All Souls as a pioneering church in parochial evangelism, training church members for the task, was to be a major theme of John's in the next decade.

Meanwhile the three men pitched their tents close to sandy Ardwell Bay on the west coast of the Rhins of Galloway, the most south-westerly corner of Scotland. They slept in their tents near the shore, in a meadow belonging to a local farm. The farmer's wife cooked them an evening meal, and sometimes breakfast of porridge with thick fresh cream. They walked in the hills and along wide deserted beaches. They took a boat and rowed out into the bay to fish for pollock and watch the waders on the shoreline. In the early mornings they swam in the cold sea – usually naked, since people rarely used the path along the shore. One morning, however, they were not so lucky: a couple sauntered by while they were bathing and they had to stay submerged, slowly freezing to their very bones until the coast was clear.

On Tuesday 26 September 1950, John was formally instituted as Rector. The rebuilding of All Souls was still not complete so the service was held in St Peter's, with William Wand, Bishop of London, leading and preaching.

'Keep up your reading amid the pressures of a busy parish,' Bishop Wand instructed John. 'And make sure he has the time to do so,' he told the churchwardens.

Both Sir Arnold and Lady Stott were there, plus Bash (the Revd Eric Nash) under whose preaching John had become a Christian and who had hugely influenced his early years as a Christian and at the Iwerne camps. After the service, a reception was held at the Royal Institute of British Architects in Portland Place.

Bash found John's father standing smoking a cigarette and (as Bash later told John) 'looking very proud of you and yet out of his depth by turns'.

'Good evening, Sir Arnold,' said Bash, cheerfully.

Arnold slowly turned his head towards the speaker. There was a long pause.

'Who are you?' Arnold growled.

'I'm Nash, John's friend. We met in 1940. Do you recall me?'

There was another long pause. 'Yes, I do. What are you doing?'

'Oh, youth work,' Bash replied. 'You must be a proud man tonight, Sir Arnold. Wasn't it to be the Foreign Office for John, in those pre-war days?'

Arnold looked sour, almost startled, and puffed at his cigarette. 'I was never against this. I only wanted no hasty decisions.'

'You've hardly a grey hair,' said Bash. 'You wear very well!'

'I'm thin,' replied Arnold solemnly. 'You see?' he concluded and managed a smile.

Lily arrived, beaming all over her face. 'I must shake hands with dear Bash again!'

A thousand people made their way to All Souls Church for a service of rededication on Sunday morning, 29 April 1951. Many of them had memories of being unceremoniously forced out of the church by a German bomb eleven years earlier. Arthur Buxton, Rector when John had first set foot in the church as a toddler, read the first lesson, and William Wand, the Bishop of London, preached. John, Donald Eddison the curate and Sister Jordan had carefully planned and rehearsed the whole service – except for one thing. It hadn't occurred to them that the alms dish for receiving the offertory bags might be too small! John held it and watched in alarm as the sidesmen placed the bags on it, only to see them cascading off on to the marble steps. This was not a problem which gave the church treasurer a moment's anxiety, however!

Finally, the congregation streamed out into Langham Place, to the triumphant strains of Jeremiah Clarke's *Trumpet Voluntary*. All Souls Church was set to become a major presence in the centre of London with an influence which would spread to the ends of the earth.

St Peter's could seat at most some five or six hundred people and had been packed in the years after the war. You had to arrive early to be sure of a place. But the restored All Souls comfortably seated nine hundred, and one thousand quite happily when full.

In September, six months after the re-opening, the BBC broadcast an evening service from the new church for the first time. And later in the year a new deacon joined the staff.

Like his Rector, John Collins was still unmarried. The two men had overlapped briefly at Cambridge, where Collins had been President of the CICCU, and they had got to know each other at camp. Where should the new man live? Mrs Earnshaw-Smith and her family had vacated the

Rectory within a few weeks of her husband's death, but the house wasn't yet ready to be lived in. John looked forward to the day when he could move in and offer lodgings to some of his unmarried curates, and to two or three students or bachelor members of the church. In the meantime John Collins made his home in a decayed hotel in Manchester Square, full of alcoholics.

It wasn't long after becoming Rector of All Souls that things began to get on top of John. Feeling under great strain, he started having nightmares about finding himself halfway up the pulpit steps and suddenly remembering that he hadn't prepared his sermon. But then he attended what used to be called the Islington Clerical Conference. One of the speakers was the Revd Leslie Wilkinson, or 'Wilkie', Principal of Oak Hill Theological College. John later forgot what he said, except for one part of his talk.

'In my view,' said Wilkie, 'every clergyman ought to keep a quiet day once a month, in which to look ahead and seek to be drawn up into the mind and perspective of God regarding his ministry.'

John saw this as a heaven-sent message. 'Wilkie saved me,' he recalled later, 'though I don't think he ever knew it. I went home from the Islington Conference that January, and immediately marked one day a month in my engagement book with the mystic letter "Q" for QUIET. That monthly day became a life-line.'

A family home near Pinner on the western outskirts of London where Phyllis Parsons, a former member of the congregation, lived with her husband and two daughters, became John's retreat. Usually he arrived quite early in the morning, and Phyllis would put a room at his disposal, and leave him alone. She would bring him a cold lunch, but didn't disturb him, leaving him twelve hours in which to be quiet. He reserved for this monthly quiet day all the things that needed time – time to think, prepare, plan and pray, time to write his editorial in the All Souls magazine, a difficult letter that needed time to think through before answering. 'It immediately lifted the burden from me, and I've hardly ever had a "clerical nightmare" again.'

8. DESERTED FARMHOUSE IN WALES

At 8 o'clock on a Friday morning in August 1952, John left London along with John Collins in his old jalopy. They arrived at the village of Dale at 6 o'clock in the evening. Dale is on the coast of Pembrokeshire in South Wales, close to the mouth of the Milford Haven estuary, twelve miles from the railway station at Haverfordwest, and nearly the most westerly point in Wales. Since they were unable to find anywhere to pitch their tents, the Dale postmistress recommended a farmer up the hill who let them sleep in a Nissen hut which he'd erected as storage for his potato boxes. But the weather was so miserable that, as they went to bed, John Collins was more than ready to return to London next day.

However, they woke to a glorious Pembrokeshire morning with early sunshine sparkling on the sea. Walking the coastal path looking for a campsite, they eventually found a small sheltered valley which overlooked West Dale Bay. A little stream gurgled its way to the sea while overhead several pairs of buzzards circled. An uninhabited farmhouse with out-buildings was tucked in just below a large derelict aerodrome left over from wartime.

After trying unsuccessfully to locate the owner of the land with its ramshackle buildings to ask his permission to camp, they decided to pitch their tents anyway. A local family called Morgan, who farmed at Glen

View on the other side of the airfield at Marloes, cooked meals for the two Johns: eggs and bacon, salty butter from the farm and creamy milk. David Morgan killed two chickens in their honour.

They discovered that everyone in the area called the deserted farmhouse where they were camping either 'The Hooks' or 'The Hookses'. Clustered round the house, some across the stream, some nearer the cliff, the out-buildings had at one time served as cow shed, stable and barn. Beyond the buildings was the cliff edge and a magnificent seascape. When someone told them that the valley and its buildings belonged to the Dale Castle Estate, they made their way across the airfield, rang the castle bell, and were ushered into the presence of Colonel Hugh Lloyd-Philipps.

'We are London clergymen on holiday,' John explained. 'We are wondering if you would give us permission to carry on camping in the valley by The Hookses.'

At first reluctant, the colonel eventually agreed. They stayed for three weeks, and were visited by a succession of friends, until there was quite an encampment. They washed in the stream, bathed in the sea below the crumbling cliffs, ate breakfast and a picnic lunch, and were fed royally in the evenings by Mrs Morgan of Glen View. After their meals David Morgan entertained them from his repertoire of local songs and poems.

John found a little nook just below the cliff top where he sat in the hot sunshine of that idyllic 1952 summer preparing the eight addresses he was to give three months later at Cambridge in his first university mission. When he looked up from his Bible and notebook, he was surrounded by the bird life he loved: gannets fishing in West Dale Bay, diving like stones from the sky, and stiff-winged fulmars from St Anne's Head riding on currents of air. And about five miles off shore were the islands of Skomer, Skokholm and Grassholm, world-famous for their breeding colonies of sea birds.

The urgent need to combat the menace of German U-boats in the Second World War had put an end to The Hookses as a working farm. The level plateau on the top of the cliff had been taken over as an airfield, and from 1942 bombers and the famous De Havilland Mosquitos had taken off mainly on anti-submarine patrol, but also carrying out raids on enemy shipping off the French coast. Breezeblock huts housed 500 military personnel, and The Hookses farmhouse had been much sought after as accommodation for married couples.

John wondered whether the deserted farmhouse and its outbuildings might be for sale. He began to dream dreams of a Pembrokeshire haven for missionaries during breaks at home, a rural retreat for conferences and church 'away' weekends – a place where he could return to relax and sometimes write summer by summer. So before his holiday ended, he paid a second visit to the castle and was allowed to borrow the keys and look around the property.

He found that, although the house hadn't been occupied since the end of the war, it had been very sturdily built to withstand Atlantic storms, with walls some two-and-a-half feet thick. He returned the key to Colonel Lloyd-Philipps.

'If The Hookses ever comes on the market,' he said to the colonel, 'I would be interested to hear.'

On his return to London, John wrote to confirm this conversation.

That same month, the Rectory at No. 12 Weymouth Street was finally ready. Weymouth Street was only five minutes' walk from All Souls. No. 12 was a high narrow building wedged between a block of flats on the east and offices to the west. The house had thirteen rooms, and to get from the basement kitchen to the fourth-floor attic you had to climb ninety-three stairs.

What was a bachelor clergyman, who for five years had been living in a small flat, to do with such a house? The PCC readily agreed to John's suggestion that the building should be turned into a hostel, providing seven bed-sitting rooms for curates and others connected with All Souls, as well as living accommodation for the Rector, a housekeeper and a cook.

The basement housed the kitchen and a large communal dining-room. John took over the study just inside the front door, an elegant room with plenty of space for books, and one of the upstairs bedrooms. Harold Earnshaw-Smith's old study became the cook's bedroom. On the first floor the drawing room came to be constantly used for meetings of many kinds, while the church secretary later had her desk in one corner. The remaining rooms became bed-sits for a housekeeper, one or two single curates and a handful of post-graduates, often medical students at London hospitals, or ordinands. Some of them knew their temporary home as 'The Wreckage' while others dubbed it 'The Stottery'. Over the years these former residents came to form a far-flung community of academics, clergy, doctors and Christian workers scattered across the world. Two curates, Donald Eddison and John Collins, together with four students, were the first to move with John Stott into No. 12.

When accommodation for the boys' and girls' youth clubs grew inadequate, John stumbled across an empty building at 23 Duke Street, next to Selfridges, which had two halls available. He arranged to share the building with the church at St Paul's Robert Adam Street. Here the boys could play indoor soccer and let off steam, but it was too far to expect boys to come from Fitzrovia – the area bounded to the north by Euston Road, to the east by Gower Street, to the south by Oxford Street and to the west by Great Portland Street. So John continued to search for other premises, ideally big enough to accommodate sixty boys and girls, together with a room for the club for the elderly of the parish, known quaintly in those days as the Good Companions.

One day as he was walking down Cleveland Street, John passed a disused building with two halls, together with some rooms which were set back from the street, known as Holy Trinity Clubhouse, close to Great Portland Street Station. A church warden showed John round the derelict building and later negotiated a sale at a very reasonable price. After the sale, John organised a complete renovation of the premises to include two halls, one fitted for indoor soccer. There was also a flat for a warden – but as yet they had no warden.

Later, when John conducted a university mission in Canada, he made friends with a young man called Tom Robinson who was newly ordained and married. Tom accepted John's invitation to come to England and became the first warden of the newly named All Souls Clubhouse – a pioneering community centre which still flourishes today.

9. 'YOU'D BETTER COME AND BE MY SECRETARY'

In 1951, a young woman named Frances had taken a temporary job with the BBC, working in their offices at the Langham Hotel, opposite All Souls Church. One evening she was walking with another BBC secretary past the church steps. From the pavement they could see the warm glow of lights in the building, illuminating the painting of Christ crowned with thorns, hanging at the east end.

'Let's go in and have a look at that church,' said Frances to her colleague.

In the porch she saw a notice announcing Friday lunch-time concerts. Frances decided to go one Friday but was disappointed to find only a handful of people present, and no one made her feel welcome. She didn't go back.

Some months later she was walking in her lunch-hour past St Peter's Church in nearby Vere Street. The bells were ringing, the sun was shining, she was happy, and on the spur of the moment she went in. The church was full, and she was gripped by the sermon. John Stott was preaching, though she didn't know his name. She began attending the mid-week lunch-hour services in St Peter's regularly, drawn by the powerful preaching. It was some time before she discovered that St Peter's was linked to All Souls, and she began attending the church regularly on a Sunday morning.

On New Year's Eve in 1952, John preached on the story of Nicodemus, followed by his familiar appeal to 'open the door to Christ' based on Revelation 3:20. Frances listened and found the sermon compelling and personal. She secretly made her response to Christ, but was too shy to respond to the invitation to go forward to have a talk with the preacher. She spoke to no one, and instead walked quietly home on her own to her bedsit in the early hours of New Year's Day.

About nine months later, Frances felt that she ought somehow to make herself known and become more involved in the church's life. She picked up a congregational register form and found a little box you could tick if you wanted to help out in the church. She ticked the box, having no idea what this 'help' might involve, but thinking that perhaps someone would then make the next move.

When the Rector himself got in touch and arranged to talk with her, she told him that her name was Frances Whitehead. 'I think he soon realised that I must be a new Christian,' she recalled, 'and, because time was short, he invited me to come back again for a second talk. This time he took me through "the way of salvation".'

At John's suggestion, Frances joined an All Souls 'nursery class' to learn the basics of the Christian faith. Then she was given the practical job of addressing envelopes for the church magazine. Still later she led a nursery class herself and went through the ten-week annual training school.

By 1956 she was beginning to wonder if God was calling her to leave the BBC and go to Bible college, perhaps to train for missionary work, so she went to see John to ask his advice. After discussing various options, John came up with an idea of his own.

'You'd better come and be my secretary,' he said.

Frances didn't take the remark seriously. But about a week later her phone rang at the BBC. It was John.

'Have you thought any more about it?'

'More about what?'

'About coming to be my secretary.'

'No! I didn't think you were serious!'

Once more, Frances went to see John.

'I want formally to invite you to come and work as church secretary.'

Frances accepted the invitation with much trepidation, fearing that she would never cope with the demands of the job. Once ensconced at a desk in a corner of the Rectory drawing room, however, she began to help in the general administration of the church's busy and varied programme, while also trying to keep pace with the Rector's daily volume of dictation. Later she learnt to maintain the work of John's private office during his frequent absences, dealing with correspondence from all over the world, typing his books and articles, arranging meetings and interviews. For many years she handled most of the day-to-day routine work and finances of the various organisations John founded.

In whatever John undertook, she was secretary, administrator, bursar, and occasionally caterer and cook – closer to him than anyone else. 'When I first joined the staff, all was exceedingly formal. We stood somewhat in awe of John Stott who called everyone by their Christian name (I was "Frances" from the day I first met him), but no female church member was ever allowed to use his!' 'Frances' she has remained: but with affectionate additions: 'Frances the omnicompetent' at times, and to the early inhabitants of the Rectory, 'Frances – SOAK' (Source of All Knowledge).

At the end of August 1953, a letter arrived from a Haverfordwest Estate Agent saying that the owner was considering the sale of Hooks Farm House in Dale, and asking if John was still interested. He replied at once, enquiring about the price. He was told that the owner had refused an offer of £1,000 but that he might be prepared to accept £1,200.

John had the property surveyed, and was advised to offer no more than £500 for it since, though structurally sound, it was falling into increasing disrepair. This he did, only to be told that it had already changed hands for £850.

'Why wasn't I given the chance to raise my bid?' John asked.

'We assumed that a clergyman would be too impoverished to do so!' came the reply.

So The Hookses became the property of Peter Conder, Warden of Skokholm Island, who needed somewhere to live on the mainland during the winter. It looked as if ownership of The Hookses would remain a dream.

The Bishop of London, William Wand, encouraged John to make time for writing and invited him to be the author of his 'Lent Book'. John decided to use a series of talks he had given at St Peter's in the autumn of 1948 as the kernel of his book, and sent the bishop his manuscript in the summer of 1953. His aim was to introduce the New Testament, its authors and their writings to ordinary Christians. He recalled the words of the Queen Mother in 1951: 'I can truly say that the King and I long to see the Bible back where it ought to be as a guide and comfort in the homes and lives of our people.'

In summarising in separate chapters the messages of Jesus, Luke, Paul, Hebrews, James, John, Peter and the book of Revelation, John was anxious to draw out the distinctive contribution of each New Testament author. When he sent the manuscript to Wand, the bishop replied, making a number of friendly suggestions to do with technicalities of Greek translation and the chronology of the New Testament. He thought the book would be valuable in introducing people to Bible study.

Longmans published the book in January 1954 under the title *Men with a Message*. There is a striking passage in chapter one where John talks about the conditions of entry into the kingdom of God. Jesus told Nicodemus that 'no one can see the kingdom of God unless he is born again'. And new birth is 'a deep, inward, revolutionary change of heart effected by the Holy Spirit'. How can this change come about? There are three conditions: repentance, faith and self-surrender. 'This claim on our total allegiance,' wrote John in his first book, 'is one which we all need to face squarely today. Jesus never encouraged half-hearted discipleship. He asked for all or nothing . . . Such self-denial is true self-discovery.'

Meanwhile in Pembrokeshire, a few months after becoming the owner of The Hookses, but before he began to repair it, Peter Conder was appointed Director of the Royal Society for the Protection of Birds and moved to Bedfordshire. John heard this news soon after Longmans had paid him £750 for writing *Men with a Message*. So he offered Conder £800. Conder accepted, and a delighted John became the owner of the entire property.

A few months later Conder came to lunch at the Rectory in Weymouth Street.

'It hardly seems fair to have given you less than you paid for The Hookses,' John said and handed over a further £50.

During the autumn of 1953, Gwen Packer, a tall, elegant lady known to everyone as 'Packie' (or irreverently as 'the Mother Superior'), had moved into 12 Weymouth Street and was to become the longest-serving house-keeper. During the First World War the man whom she hoped to marry had been killed in action and she had declined all subsequent suitors. Packie took it for granted that this experience qualified her to give expert advice in all affairs of the heart. Many residents of the Rectory were to unburden themselves to her and seek her advice.

'Had I been younger,' she is reported as saying on at least one occasion, 'I would have set out to secure John Stott as the husband I never had!'

Residents of 12 Weymouth Street met at breakfast round the big table in the basement. One morning a Canadian resident taunted John. 'Why do you always read *The Times*?' he asked. 'You should read the *Guardian*. It's a much better paper – look, it's even got a picture of a black-headed gull flying past a lighthouse!'

John looked up from his *Times*, took the *Guardian* and glanced at the picture. 'Actually,' he said quietly, 'it's an immature Kittiwake.'

One visitor to No. 12 was surprised to find that John had fixed up a camp bed for himself in his study while a homeless man was sleeping in his bedroom.

'He does this quite often for needy folk,' the housekeeper told the visitor.

In 1953 a tall, slim Texan named Frank Boggs came to London to sing and direct the choirs at a series of evangelistic rallies in the Royal Albert Hall. John invited him for Saturday evening supper at the Rectory.

Wearing his trademark Stetson hat, Frank Boggs arrived and met John and his curates. They received him warmly and, after the meal, John was fascinated to hear Frank speak of a spiritual awakening during his college days at Baylor University, Waco, Texas.

'God has rocked our Baptist universities and churches,' Frank told John, 'calling many thousands into Christian service.'

To Frank's surprise, as he recounted these stories, John responded, 'Hallelujah!'

This didn't fit his image of an Anglican Rector.

Next morning he was delighted at the warmth of the welcome he received at an All Souls guest service. Later in the day he sat down and wrote a letter to his mother in Texas. 'John is an amazing blend of High Church/Low Church, of dignity and warmth, of amazing scholarship and the human touch,' he told her.

Another person who experienced an All Souls guest service was Chad Varah who visited in 1954, a year after founding the Samaritans, the world's first crisis hotline organisation. Varah's father, an Anglican vicar, was a strict High Churchman.

Varah listened as John gave a 'simple and masterly exposition' of the parable of the great supper in Luke 14:15–24. He was impressed at the way the preacher 'was able to get good-humouredly under their guard'.

'Christianity like a banquet?' teased John. 'I can see from your faces that you think of it as more like a funeral!'

Then Varah noted 'the skilful probing for each one's trouble – anxiety, fear, loneliness, guilt, dissatisfaction, doubt, lack of purpose – and the flicker of a response here and there as the diagnosis fitted. "Come, for all things are now ready." "Christ has done all – the banquet is spread – He Himself is the banquet – you are invited" and always the persistent re-iteration of "Come . . .".'

Chad Varah thought that John had 'a quietly persuasive style, with no mannerisms, tricks, or fireworks – earnest, urgent, without unction or sentimentality'.

Next day, John and Chad Varah met at the Rectory. John told Varah about his team of counsellors and how All Souls followed up new Christians. Forgetting to eat the sandwiches, which were all the lunch he had time for, John showed Varah the material used at All Souls to equip the church for the task of evangelism. 'Nothing is left to chance,' Varah noted. 'Here are copies of all the carefully-prepared leaflets, booklets, study courses, examination papers, letters of welcome, record cards, and other printed matter which steer the lay evangelist and his charges along a tried and tested course.'

As, during the 50s, All Souls grew more popular, John from time to time remonstrated with the congregation: 'No one should be attending All Souls if they are passing another evangelical church en route.'

One student, faced with this challenge, satisfied her conscience by making a considerable detour on her bicycle, Sunday by Sunday, from the flat she shared in north London, in order to comply with John's wishes.

'I can look the Rector in the face as one honestly entitled to be there!' she insisted.

10. SPECIAL RELATIONSHIP

By the early 1950s 'Billy Graham' was already a household name in America. He had visited England twice in 1946, including a six-month tour when he had spoken at many meetings. In July 1952 the World Evangelical Alliance formally invited Billy Graham to conduct a 'crusade' in Britain in two years' time and formed a special executive committee to make it happen. They went ahead and booked the Harringay Arena in North London.

As a member of the Council of the Evangelical Alliance, John had helped to set up the executive committee which took responsibility for the crusade. He could see that Billy was different. American evangelists had a reputation for making a great deal of money out of their crusades. John had noticed that when Billy came to England prior to his missions, he had anticipated the questions he would be asked by church leaders. On his financial policies, he told them that he received a fixed salary. He insisted that the accounts of the crusade should be published so that everything was above board.

John personally arranged for Billy and his team to stay at the Stratford Court Hotel near Oxford Circus, which made them temporary parishioners of All Souls. In his autobiography, Billy Graham described it as 'probably the smallest and cheapest hotel in London' – chosen to avoid any appearance of extravagance. Of course there were many cheaper hotels in the greater London area, but certainly, by the standards of most visiting Americans, it was modest.

John quickly became friend and informal pastor to the team. On Good Friday, about a month into the crusade, he presided at a service of Holy Communion for the team in St Peter's Vere Street – probably their first exposure to Anglicanism. Billy was just three years older than John, and a warm friendship quickly grew between them.

All Souls as a church was deeply involved in Harringay. John attended most nights, often taking friends for whom this was a unique opportunity to hear the gospel. People were interested to form their own opinion of the American preacher whose name appeared in every newspaper. For three months, buses made their way nearly every night from All Souls to Harringay, ferrying many hundreds to the meetings. About five hundred people who had responded to Billy's invitation during his appeals to 'get up out of their seats' were referred to the church for follow-up. Quite a few were drawn into membership at All Souls as a result.

On Saturday, 22 May 1954, 120,000 people filled Wembley Stadium for the final meeting. Archbishop Geoffrey Fisher, who had been cool and non-committal at the outset of the crusade, appeared with Billy on the platform. After offering a closing prayer, and apparently moved at the sight of so many making their way across the turf in response to the appeal, he turned to Billy's associate evangelist Grady Wilson sitting next to him on the platform.

'We'll never see such a sight again until we get to heaven,' Wilson reported him as saying.

Wilson put his arm found Fisher's shoulder and replied, 'That's right, Brother Archbishop, that's right!'

Within twenty-four hours of the close of the last meeting, Billy wrote to John, warmly thanking him for supporting the crusade. He had preached to the largest religious congregation, 120,000, ever seen until then in the British Isles. He had spoken both in Oxford and Cambridge to crowded congregations of students and dons. Winston Churchill had invited him to Downing Street, where they talked for forty minutes.

Why was it that, while many English churches were half empty, thousands came night after night to hear Billy Graham? John's answer was that he believed that 'Billy was the first transparently sincere preacher these people have ever heard'.

The Evangelical Alliance Council agreed that Billy should wait a year, and return then for a further week of meetings at London's Wembley Stadium in the early summer of 1955. When it came, the Wembley crusade, like the previous one, attracted huge numbers, undeterred for the most part by the unceasing rain which made the stadium a sea of umbrellas night after night. Twenty-three thousand people came forward as enquirers. John took the view that Wembley hardly fulfilled its promise when compared with Harringay. He thought the Wembley Stadium was so huge that it tended to be very impersonal. 'You can't see Billy across the turf at Wembley,' he concluded. 'I didn't like it so much.'

A few weeks after Billy Graham's Wembley crusade ended, Wilbur Smith, an American preacher (not be confused with the novelist of the same name), visited All Souls on the first Sunday in July 1955. 'The beautiful auditorium,' he told his friends back home in the States, 'was crowded with a very notable group of people. I believe apart from Westminster Abbey, and perhaps even including that, Mr. Stott regularly preaches to the largest congregation in any Anglican church in London. The church is filled morning and evening, even when it rains, and the evening audience is made up for the most part of young people, many of them students of the universities. The church carries on a tremendous programme throughout the week.

'Mr. Stott is an evangelical preacher from beginning to end. The service was Anglican, but not over-ritualistic, and the preaching was the preaching of an unadulterated gospel. He took for his text the healing of Naaman. A sermon on the subject *could* be quite ordinary – I mean nothing but a sequence of axioms, and a little uninteresting to folks who know the story by heart. But not the way he developed it . . .

'In a gracious but clear way, in the power of the Holy Spirit, he told that audience, many saturated with culture and learning, that there was only one cure for this disease of sin, and that was in Christ, the Lamb of God, and only one place where we could find that healing, and that was in the shed blood of Calvary. That morning my soul was bathed in the dew of heaven, and, may I add, that it has been a long, long time in my own beloved land that I have felt the whole service one of true *worship* offered to God as in that morning at All Souls Church.'

As the new owner of The Hookses, John was now faced with the task of putting it all in order. In December 1954, Atlantic gales lifted the roof of one of the outbuildings and carried it up on to the airfield. Fortunately Peter Conder had insured the property and this paid for the re-roofing. Just after Christmas, John drove down with his sister Joy to examine his purchase.

They found that the house was eligible for a post-war improvement grant, which helped towards connection to mains water, installation of a septic tank and enlargement of windows. While this work was being done, John had a Rayburn stove installed for cooking and hot water. These changes made the house habitable, and over the months and years ahead various working parties of friends joined John at The Hookses to help decorate it and make it comfortable. This idyllic spot on the south-west coast of Pembrokeshire was to play an important role in John's life.

On 4 April 1955, a few weeks before his thirty-fourth birthday, John wrote to twenty-two friends recalling that John Newton, among others, had in 1783 founded 'the Eclectic Society' with the object (as they had put it) of 'mutual intercourse and the investigation of spiritual truth'. He suggested reviving the society, and invited them to an initial meeting at the Crown Hotel, Amersham. The main purpose was fellowship, prayer and discussing matters of common interest and concern. The first meeting agreed that membership should be limited to Anglican evangelical clergy under the age of forty, and that they should meet twice a year.

The private nature of the meetings meant that members could be entirely free in debate, even questioning the received orthodoxies of the time without fear that an unguarded comment would be held against them. Peter Dawes, who went on to become Bishop of Derby, first met John at a meeting of the Eclectic Society. 'He chatted to me, was interested in what I was doing and gave me his whole attention. When I next met him he seemed to have remembered it all.' The society grew to over a thousand members by the mid 1960s.

In John, Anglican evangelicalism had found itself with a new leadership figure who belonged to a young generation.

In 1952, John led a CICCU mission at the University of Cambridge. Crowds at this, the first of many university missions he was to lead, were so great that stewards brought extra chairs into the side-aisles of Great St Mary's, the University church. Many years later, Owen Chadwick, the distinguished church historian, told John that 'the finest Christian preaching I ever heard in my life was the first sermon you gave in Great St Mary's to open the Cambridge mission'. On the final evening they had to turn latecomers away.

Three years later, John was back in Cambridge, not to lead a mission this time, but as senior assistant missioner to Billy Graham, who had accepted the CICCU's invitation, with John's warm encouragement.

When news leaked out that Billy was to lead this mission, a fierce debate began about religious fundamentalism. It began in the correspondence columns of *The Times* with a letter from Canon Luce, Headmaster of Durham School. Luce argued that the recent increase in fundamentalism among university students should cause concern to those who worked in religious education. 'No branch of education,' he argued, 'can make terms with an outlook which ignores the conclusions of modern scholarship in that particular department of knowledge . . . Is it not time that our religious leaders made it plain that while they respect, or even admire, Dr. Graham's sincerity and personal power, they cannot regard fundamentalism as likely to issue in anything but disillusionment and disaster for educated men and women in this twentieth-century world?'

A flurry of letters followed. Mervyn Stockwood, Vicar of Great St Mary's, pointed out that his permission for Dr Graham to use his church didn't imply any endorsement of his views. Michael Ramsey, then Bishop of Durham and later to become Archbishop of Canterbury, assured *Times* readers that many people would be grateful to Canon Luce for highlighting the problems created by the revival of fundamentalist evangelism. He recalled that a long line of great evangelists, including William Temple, had emphasised the need for decision and conversion hand in hand with an insistence upon the duty of thought and the rationality of the Christian revelation.

Bishop Barry, of Southwell, wrote on the other hand that, 'if I were vicar of St Mary's, Cambridge, I should have no hesitation in lending the church for Dr. Graham's mission'.

John waited for ten days and then wrote this letter to *The Times*:

August 25 1955

Sir, It is surprising that your correspondents on this subject have not paused to define the term 'fundamentalism'. They have assumed that your readers understood the term, that they understood it in the same sense, and that it accurately describes Dr. Graham. Actually, the term clearly has different meanings, and Dr. Graham has publicly denied on more than one occasion that he is a fundamentalist.

The word had a noble origin . . . [but more recently] has become associated with certain extremes and extravagances, so that now 'fundamentalism' is almost a synonym for obscurantism, and it is generally used as a term of opprobrium. It appears to describe the bigoted rejection of all biblical criticism, a mechanical view of inspiration and an excessively literalist interpretation of Scripture. It is doubtless in this sense that your correspondents have employed the term, and in this sense that Dr. Billy Graham and others associated with him have repudiated it.

Clearly a distinction must be drawn between fundamentalism and the traditional, conservative view of Scripture. It is neither true nor fair to dub every conservative evangelical a 'fundamentalist'. The conservative evangelical desires to lay a truly biblical emphasis on the necessity of divine revelation, to ascribe to the Scriptures no meaner an authority than did our Lord and his apostles, and to accept the biblical doctrine of Scripture as they accept the biblical doctrine of God and Christ and the Church. The real point at issue in this controversy, revealed by an episcopal disagreement in your columns, seems to be the place of the mind in the perception of divine truth.

All thoughtful Christians would agree with the Bishop of Durham, whose letter you published on August 20, that God's revelation is essentially reasonable, but would have to add that it is often in conflict with the unenlightened reason of sinful men. The Bible is itself aware of this conflict . . .

There is then in conversion not what the Bishop of Durham calls 'the stifling of the mind' but the humble (and intelligent) submission of the mind to a divine revelation. The proud human intellect still needs to be abased – in England as in Corinth – and the only way to enter the Kingdom of God is still to become like a little child.

Yours faithfully,

JOHN R. W. STOTT.

All Souls Church,
Langham Place,
W.1.

The Times debate ended with a leader which lent some support to Billy's coming mission by suggesting that the contemporary trend of biblical scholarship was opposed to the nineteenth-century theological liberalism espoused by some of the letter writers.

Billy Graham himself, far from accepting the label, told his wife how he suffered at the hands of fundamentalists who criticised his policies and sometimes his message. He wrote to Ruth: 'Some of the things they say are pure fabrications . . . If this extreme type of funda-mentalism was of God, it would have brought revival long ago. Instead, it has brought dissension, division, strife, and has produced dead and lifeless churches.'

Billy found the prospect of conducting a full-scale university mission at Cambridge increasingly daunting. 'I am deeply concerned and in much thought about the mission,' he told John. 'I have never felt more inadequate and totally unprepared. As I think over the possibility for messages, I realise how shallow and weak my presentations are. I shall be relying heavily on you and Maurice [Wood].'

When Billy arrived in Cambridge, John arranged for him to talk privately with C. S. Lewis, then a Fellow of Magdalene College. The three of them met in Lewis's rooms at Magdalene and spent an hour or so together.

'I was afraid I would be intimidated by Lewis,' Billy later admitted, 'but I was relieved to find that he immediately put me at ease. I found him to be not only intelligent and witty but also gentle and gracious. He seemed genuinely interested in our meetings.'

'You know,' Lewis said to Billy as they parted, 'you have many critics, but I have never met one of your critics who knows you personally.'

The Cambridge mission opened on Sunday evening, 6 November 1955, in Great St Mary's, the University church. Mervyn Stockwood, the vicar, insisted on being involved in the services and gave the blessing from the pulpit each night. On that first evening, undergraduates and their friends queued, sometimes for as much as forty-five minutes, to get into the church. By half-past eight some 1,200 people had squeezed into the church, filling the nave, the great galleries, and the tiny west gallery by the large organ. The organist played quietly as Billy made his appearance.

John, as assistant missioner, and Mervyn Stockwood walked beside Billy. Stockwood briefly introduced the mission and welcomed Billy to Great St Mary's. John led the congregation in a hymn, and then prayed for the mission. After a Bible reading they sang a second hymn, during which Billy, in his preaching gown and doctor's hood, climbed into the pulpit and surveyed his congregation.

'I thank you for your welcome,' Billy began. 'I approach this mission at Cambridge with a sense of weakness.' With a few jokes, he turned to his theme of the critical world situation, quoting authors, journalists, statesmen, churchmen, before his familiar phrase – 'the Bible says' – echoed around the church.

When he was emphasising human sinfulness, someone shouted from the gallery.

'What about the love of God, Billy?'

'I'm coming to that,' responded Billy and continued with his sermon for just over thirty-five minutes.

'And now I am going to invite any of you who wish, either here and now to receive Christ, or to set yourselves during the week to seek for him, to remain behind. After the end of the service I will return to explain simply the way to Christ.'

Stockwood gave his blessing and accompanied Billy and John into the vestry. For a while it seemed that very few were accepting Billy's invitation to remain. But when he returned and made his invitation, over a hundred people gathered below the pulpit.

In spite of good attendances and serious enquirers, Billy was uneasy. He had heard striking accounts of John's mission three years earlier. John was his closest adviser in Cambridge, and their friendship deepened. However, Billy was aware that John was better equipped for a mission to Cambridge than he was.

'I was really feeling boxed in and inadequate,' Billy explained later. 'I felt that John ought to be the preacher, and I should have been his assistant. John is one of my dearest friends, but he can also be a critic. And I felt in the first two or three nights I was preaching to please John rather than the Holy Spirit.'

Then, on the fourth night, Billy abandoned his prepared sermon and preached as he would to any other audience. To David Watson, it seemed on this night as if Billy 'accepted the apparent foolishness of the message of Christ crucified and preached it with simplicity and integrity. The power of God's Spirit was manifestly at work, changing the lives of many undergraduates.' By the end of the week about five hundred people had sought help or advice and made or renewed a commitment to Christ.

John wrote to Billy immediately after the mission. In his reply, written on the headed notepaper of Kensington Palace Hotel, London, Billy told John that he would frame John's letter and hang it in his study. 'It was about the finest letter I have ever received from any of my personal friends.' Billy told John that he thought the Cambridge Mission of November 1955 would live in his memory for ever as one of the highlights of his ministry. He had learned a great deal that he could use profitably in the States about how to conduct university missions – 'but, John, I learned more from you than all the rest'.

'We are both young,' Billy told John, 'with most of our ministry before us. It is my prayer that our friendship will grow and deepen . . . and be used of God as was the friendship of Wesley and Whitefield. There are few men that I have met and known for so short a time whom I have grown to love and appreciate as I have you, John. Thank you for all you meant to me at Cambridge.'

Responding to approaches from Canada and the United States to conduct a series of missions in Canadian and American universities, John sailed from Southampton on 4 November 1956 aboard the *SS United States*. His parents and Frances Whitehead stood at the dockside to wave goodbye.

He had written offering to conduct a service on board. The purser agreed and allowed him to use the ship's theatre. John stood in front of the stalls, while a small orchestra of piano, violin and xylophone led the singing. The purser read the lesson.

'There may be a variety of reasons why you are crossing the Atlantic,' John said, 'and perhaps it will be the opening of a new chapter in your life. But for many of us it will be an opportunity of taking stock. There will even be the possibility of knowing Christ as friend, trusting him as Saviour and, best of all, gaining him as treasure.' When he finished speaking, eight people asked for the booklet which he offered.

Mid-Atlantic brought heavy seas. He woke early on the Tuesday morning as his array of toilet accessories, including a glass of water, slid from the dressing table by his bed across on top of him. Later everything on his writing table slithered gracefully to the floor. In the morning, walking on the sun deck, the strong wind blew biting salt spray into his face. The tops of breaking waves were glacial green. John watched a puffin flying alongside, managing to keep pace with the ship. Fulmars wheeled effortlessly in the wind, skimming the crests of the waves, while silent kittiwakes swam in small flocks or flew away alone, 1,500 miles from the nearest land.

The ship arrived in New York on time. In Manhattan, John met members of the Billy Graham New York Crusade Committee, recorded a radio message, paid a flying visit to see the United Nations headquarters, watched the sunset from the Empire State Building, and then caught the night train to Canada.

About 500 students turned up on the first evening in the huge Convocation Hall for his mission at the University of Toronto. By Wednesday 900 had come to hear John speak on the subject, 'The Fact of

Sin'. *SIN BOOSTS ATTENDANCE AS FOUR RECEIVE CHRIST*, the headline in the student daily newspaper shouted on the Thursday morning. Each morning that week in Toronto, you could hear John's very English accent broadcasting talks live from the CBC studios. By the end of the mission, some two dozen students had become Christians.

'I made the cost of becoming a Christian high,' John told a local newspaper. 'I didn't want irresponsible enthusiasts to come and so I made the decision hard.'

John enjoyed a few days rest at the Niagara Falls. He walked down the track leading to the water's edge and reached the jetty from which the *Maid of the Mist* sailed in the summer. Counting thirteen different species of duck, he stayed at the foot of the falls until his hands were numb with cold and the light faded.

The last mission before the Christmas break was in Ann Arbor, where the 22,000 students of the University of Michigan formed nearly half the population. John arrived in a thick snowstorm and gave his main talks every evening in Rackham Hall, with plush cinema-type seats. He conducted many personal interviews.

'If I were sure that Christ was the Son of God,' one Armenian student told him, 'I would become a Christian and never, ever give it up!'

One married medical student, about to qualify as a doctor, as soon as he was convinced of the deity of Christ, knelt with John and became a Christian.

John sat in the barber's shop of the Students' Union, waiting to have his hair cut. A young mathematics lecturer came in and engaged him in conversation, describing some of the intellectual difficulties that he found in accepting Christian faith. John heard him out and then spoke of the 'change from self to unself' that would have to take place if ever he committed his life to Christ.

'You would have to make Christ the centre of your life, and move yourself over to the circumference,' John explained.

'Gee,' the dismayed lecturer replied. 'I guess I'm very reluctant for this decentralisation!'

John thought that 'decentralisation' was a magnificent modern word for conversion.

John flew to join Billy Graham in New York, from where they travelled together to Princeton for a conference on evangelism. They stayed at the Princeton Inn where John had a room next to Billy's. Their windows looked out over the closely cropped lawns of a golf course, past a little lake to the impressive tower of the graduate building beyond. For two nights John gained an insight into Billy's pressurised programme. Telegrams kept arriving all day. As John turned his light out, Billy was still talking on the phone, and he woke to hear him answering a long-distance call.

They took the train south for a twenty-four-hour journey to North Carolina, to spend Christmas with the Graham family. Billy drove John along the steep and winding road to their home in Montreat, a village on the side of a mountain. Billy and Ruth lived in a log-cabin style house, surrounded by woods, with a superb view across the valley to the mountains beyond.

John was the only guest, sharing the home with the Grahams, their dogs and three mountain sheep with black faces and legs. The youngest child, Franklin, was armed with daggers. A big Christmas tree lit up the sitting room, with presents piled underneath it.

'The adults must hang up stockings as well as the children,' Billy instructed.

On Christmas Eve they nailed seven stockings, each clearly labelled, in a row along the beam over the fireplace. When John undid his stocking on Christmas morning he found sea-sick pills, spare socks, and a Longines Swiss watch inscribed 'John Stott from Billy Graham', which he went on to wear for twenty-five years. But that wasn't all. There was a strange little plastic container.

'DEO', John read on the label. '*Deo*,' Latin for 'God'.

Then 'DORANT' – did this mean 'gift of God'? The Grahams had to explain to him what it was. Toiletries for men had barely begun to cross the Atlantic in the 1950s!

Billy took Christmas gifts round to the people in the neighbourhood, and each night led the family in a Bible reading and prayers. During John's stay, Cliff Barrows and Grady Wilson came to record the 'Hour of Decision' radio programme. Then they played golf with Billy while John admired yellow-bellied sap-suckers on the golf course.

John then travelled north to Winnipeg where he conducted a mission in the University of Manitoba in temperatures 25 degrees below zero with biting Arctic winds. He went to the Hudson's Bay Company Store and bought a fur hat with ear flaps.

A young science student came to see him. 'I have been in trouble with the police for car thefts and housebreaking in Calgary, my home town. Two of my friends are serving a prison sentence but I haven't been caught.'

John explained what it meant to be a Christian and what he must do. They prayed and the student committed his life to Christ.

'I shall go back to Calgary in the Easter holidays,' he said, 'to make a clean breast of the past – even if it means a sentence.'

John took this as a sign of a genuine conversion.

Following the final weekend of the mission, John caught a Canadian Pacific Railway train to Vancouver, a nearly 1,500-mile journey through the heart of the Rockies.

Arriving on the west coast, he flew across to Vancouver Island for two days' rest. In the evening he walked down to the sea alone, sat on some lonely rocks and watched the sun set over the Pacific ocean. Next morning he got up early, missed breakfast, and spent three hours watching birds near the harbour, before flying back to Vancouver Airport where about twenty students from the University of British Columbia came to meet him. They presented him with the yellow-and-blue-striped university scarf, and then lifted him into the air and carried him shoulder-high into the waiting hall.

John gave an interview to *The Ubyssey*, the student newspaper.

'Many people reject Christianity without ever giving it a fair hearing,' he said. 'They dismiss it as a religion of childhood and discard it with childhood's toys, without ever investigating it with the honest impartiality of an adult mind. Now we believe that the intellectual basis for Christianity is respectable. More than that, it's convincing. It can bear scrutiny. Our purpose therefore in this mission is to bring before the members of the university who care to come and listen, a reasoned statement of the Christian faith . . . I believe that Jesus Christ is the only person, and his cause the only cause, which is worthy of our thoughtful and total commitment.'

The university campus enjoyed a magnificent situation, with views across the water to snow-capped peaks. Students almost filled the auditorium every day to hear John speak, many of them eating sandwich lunches as he began his talks. He conducted personal interviews during the week, and some students decided to become Christians. Each day he broadcast morning talks on the radio from the CBC studios.

John flew to New York for more meetings with Billy Graham before travelling on to Harvard, the oldest university in the United States, and likely to prove stony ground. 'Trying to find a Christian at Harvard,' a student worker had said in the 1940s, 'is like Diogenes going around with a lantern looking for an honest man!'

John stayed in 'The Preacher's Room' in Lowell House. The organisers of his visit approached Dr Pusey, the university President, about the possibility of arranging a faculty reception for John to meet Harvard staff.

'Even if the Apostle Paul himself were to visit Harvard,' Pusey replied, 'the faculty wouldn't turn out to meet him!'

About 200 students attended John's talks. The deans and professors who chaired his meetings told him that this was 'very good for Harvard'.

A fourth-year biochemist from a wealthy background grasped John's hand during a tea party on the final Sunday. He had been wrestling with the problem of his allegiance to Christ. 'God wins,' he conceded. 'But it will cause an earthquake at home!'

This was the first for John of many trips across the pond. The Inter-Varsity Christian Fellowship (IVCF) had assigned Keith Hunt to look after him, as he did on many subsequent American visits as their friendship grew. Gladys Hunt, joint historian with her husband Keith of the IVCF in America, reflected later on the effect on John of this pioneering visit to the States. She thought it must have been a terrifying experience for him. 'Yet his reception and the embrace of the enthusiastic and uninhibited Americans gave him a platform that he extended around the world. I think of how uptight emotionally he was in those early days – and how he now gives *latino embrazos* so freely. Part of that is the mellowing of aging . . . but we think that this trip was a launching point for him personally.'

11. MODELLING JESUS

Slowly and with the help of John's friends, The Hookses began to take shape. They replaced the floor of the barn loft which was riddled with wood worm, and divided it into sleeping quarters for groups of young people who came down from All Souls. Some members of the church gave or bequeathed modest sums of money to help restore or convert the outbuildings.

Late December, before or after Christmas, was a favourite time for John to snatch a few days at The Hookses. Catching the midnight newspaper train from Paddington on one occasion, he was in his sleeping compartment with double bunk, one bed above the other. In Cardiff, a rather drunk Welshman stumbled in to share the compartment with him. John discovered that his fellow passenger was an official in one of the mining unions, and a communist. Learning that John was a clergyman, he was shocked.

'It's time you became productive, man — you are a parasite on the body politic!'

One of the first books John wrote at The Hookses was *Basic Christianity*. He drew on addresses he had given to students at university missions in different parts of the world during the 1950s.

John writes about the character of Jesus. With Christ, he says, there was no discrepancy between his words and his deeds. His character was unique. When he asked a hostile audience, 'Can any of you prove me guilty of sin?' no one answered. They were all sinners. He was without sin. He lived a life of perfect obedience to his Father's will. All other men and women were in the darkness of sin and ignorance. He was the light of the world. All other men and women had a spiritual hunger. He was the bread of life.

What, John asks, did his disciples think of Jesus? We can rely on their evidence. They lived in close contact with him for three years. They ate and slept with him, experiencing the cramped conditions of a small boat. They shared a common purse. They got on one another's nerves. They quarrelled. But they never found in Jesus the sins they saw in each other. Familiarity normally breeds contempt, but not with Jesus and his disciples.

What did Jesus' enemies concede? They had no bias – at least in his favour. The Gospels tell us that they 'watched' him and 'tried to entrap him in his talk'. When he was on trial, they had to bring false witnesses against him: but even they didn't agree with one another. Pilate, after attempting to save him, said he was 'innocent of this man's blood'. Herod could find no fault in him. Judas the traitor, later filled with remorse, returned the thirty pieces of silver with the words 'I have sinned . . . for I have betrayed innocent blood'. A thief on the cross said, 'But this man has done nothing wrong.' A man in charge of a hundred Roman soldiers said, 'Surely this was a righteous man.'

The picture of Jesus which emerges is of a man with a balanced personality. He's not like a crank. He believes ardently in what he teaches but he doesn't sound like a crazy fanatic. What he says is unpopular but he's not an eccentric.

There's as much evidence for his humanity as for his divinity. He gets tired, needs to sleep and eat and drink like other people. He experiences human emotions of love, anger, joy and sorrow.

He made friends with ordinary fisherman and publicans, put his hands on lepers and allowed prostitutes to touch him. He gave himself in healing, helping, teaching and preaching. In the end they flogged him, spat in his face, pushed a crown made of thorns on his head, nailed his hands and feet to a cross – and as they drove those nails into him he prayed for them:

'Father, forgive them, for they do not know what they are doing.' He succeeded where we fail. He had complete self-mastery. He never retaliated.

This disregard for self in the service of God and your neighbour is what the Bible calls love. There's no self-interest in love. The essence of love is self-sacrifice. We do sometimes see nobility in the actions of men and women – and we should thank God for it. But the life of Jesus was filled with it moment by moment. Love was with him a 'never-fading incandescent glow'. Jesus was sinless because he was selfless. Such selflessness is love. And God is love.

Basic Christianity became one of the most successful Christian books of the twentieth century. In all corners of the globe readers became Christians. One Australian described how he was given *Basic Christianity*, found it inescapably persuasive, and read the last few chapters many times until he had exhausted all the possibilities of dodging the issue.

Many readers wrote to John and told him, 'My life has changed completely. God has given me purpose, direction and joy. Thank you for writing a book which changed my life.'

During the spring and early summer of 1958, it had become clear that Sir Arnold Stott was failing. He spent each day in his favourite chair at Bullens Hill Farm, near Guildford, where they had moved in 1956. He seldom if ever went out, and didn't find retirement easy. Before leaving to conduct meetings in Australia, John discussed with his mother and sisters what he should do, were his father to deteriorate or even die, while he was away. Lily agreed that he should fulfil his responsibilities, and only then fly home.

Father and son were now reconciled after the tensions of the Cambridge years, although they kept off the subject of religion in conversation. Sir Arnold did come every year to the annual doctors' service which John had initiated. John felt that his father was very ignorant of the Christianity he had rejected, and was pleased to find him slowly reading through his copy of *Basic Christianity*. He was about halfway through it when John left for Australia in June.

'I will read the rest while you are away,' Arnold told his son.

John's plane arrived in Perth twelve hours late, but in time for him to go straight from the airport to the first of his meetings. From Perth he travelled to Adelaide where, after two hours' sleep, he preached at the morning service at the cathedral and in the evening at Holy Trinity Church, where the guest service was modelled on All Souls. The church was crowded beyond capacity, with people sitting on chairs wherever they could be squeezed into the chancel.

After a visit to Melbourne, he flew on to Sydney, speaking three times on the following Sunday and at several public meetings. His mission was held in the Wallace Theatre at Sydney University. The lunchtime meetings were packed, with over 700 students sitting at desks, in the aisles, on the floor, crowding in the doorways and standing at the back. John was relieved that his British sense of humour wasn't lost on Australians. He conducted many personal interviews during the afternoons, with Christian and non-Christian students.

An African ordinand named Gresford Chitemo was studying theology at Moore Theological College, Sydney. He and a fellow student were repairing a motorcycle just near the college grounds when a taxi arrived. John Stott got out.

As Gresford looked at him, it seemed to him that there was radiance in his face.

'Look at a man of God!' he said to his friend.

'Everybody you see, Gresford, you say is a man of God!'

Next day the two men went to Sydney University to hear John preach. They sat together in the hall and John began to deliver his talk.

'How did you know that he was a man of God?' Gresford's friend asked.

They felt as if something was touching their hearts.

On the Tuesday morning of the mission, a telegram arrived for John, while he was preparing a sermon. His father had died. He was seventy-two. The memory of that morning never left John. Although he had been half expecting the news, he felt shocked and helpless to be so many thousands of miles away. He found it difficult to collect his thoughts sufficiently to deliver the next mission address an hour or two later.

That evening he telephoned Lily. They agreed that the funeral would take place the following week, but that the memorial service in the Chapel of Westminster Hospital would await John's return. For the moment, John had to put aside his grief and, with a heavy heart, preach that day as usual in the crowded Wallace Theatre. He described it later as 'the most difficult address I have ever given in my life'.

John's final meeting in Sydney was due to be held in the university's Great Hall. Unfortunately, at the end of a two-month preaching tour, his voice was giving trouble. He consulted an ear, nose and throat specialist.

'It's not the parson's occupational diseases,' the expert told him. 'It's a bug which is doing the rounds in Sydney at the moment.'

John was afraid he wouldn't be able to get through the evening's event and considered telephoning the mission committee to say he couldn't preach. Friends, however, persuaded him not to do this.

Half an hour before the meeting began, John waited in a side room with some supporting students. He turned to the mission committee chairman.

'Would you please read the "thorn in the flesh" verses from 2 Corinthians?' he whispered.

As the chairman began to read the verses, John – his throat raw and sore – listened. The conversation between Paul and the Lord came alive in a new way.

'I beg you to take it away from me,' said Paul.

'My grace is sufficient for you,' replied the Lord, 'for my power is made perfect in weakness.'

After he finished reading, the chairman prayed for John, who then walked to the platform and sat down. He saw that a thousand students had crammed the hall to hear him. When it was his turn to speak, he had to talk softly without forcing his voice. He croaked his words in a monotone, unable to modulate his voice or convey his personality. But all the time he was praying.

'Fulfil your promise to perfect your power through my weakness!'

It seemed to him that, despite his disability or perhaps because of it, there was stillness in the meeting and a sense of God's presence. At the end of his address he gave straightforward instruction on how to come to Christ, and then issued his invitation to do just that.

There was an immediate response. After a week in which many students had quietly thought about the cost of Christian discipleship, those who decided to commit their lives to Christ did so with a steely resolve in the absence of superficial emotion. Since that evening, John has returned to Australia seven or eight times. On each occasion someone approached him with similar words.

'Do you remember that final service of the 1958 mission in the University Great Hall when you lost your voice? I came to Christ that night.'

Throughout his time in Melbourne for a university mission, he stayed with Jack and Georgie Langford and family, arriving some days before the meetings began. The family lived in a modern house with a rounded front and a big tree by the back door whose overhanging branches drooped themselves over the roof. The Langfords had two teenage daughters, Myra and Jaqueline, and an eleven-year-old called Robyn.

They held a musical evening in the Langford house, with Myra playing the piano, Jacqueline the flute and Robyn the cello.

'Would you like to play my cello?' Robyn asked John.

Although he hadn't played a cello for nearly twenty years, John accepted the invitation and found that he could still produce the right notes.

'I was the youngest member of the family,' Robyn remembered later, 'very bouncy, too talkative and, as you can imagine, was "put on my best behaviour" for this important English clergyman whom I was not to bother. The impact of our visitor was enormous on us as a family. John's humility was stunning and unforgettable to me as a child. He joined us in the washing up, came on picnics, and taught us songs and prayers to sing as a family as we drove out to the bush. I was never treated as a nuisance. He listened to my interminable riddles and played my cello. He modelled Jesus to us.'

On his first Sunday in Melbourne, John was an Anglican in the morning (preaching in the cathedral), a Methodist in the afternoon (speaking at a broadcast service for the Central Methodist Mission) and a Presbyterian in the evening (preaching to a congregation of 1,000 in the leading Presbyterian church in the heart of the city).

Despite the joy and relaxation of staying with the Langfords, he could hardly face the Melbourne University mission which lay ahead. The Sydney mission had been physically and spiritually demanding, ending in the inspiring event in the Great Hall when, although he had lost his voice, there had been a good response. After this high, he felt a sense of anti-climax. Feeling drained and depressed, he desperately wanted to get home to be with his mother and sisters who were mourning the loss of Sir Arnold.

But he knew that somehow he must proceed with the Melbourne mission. This would be impossible unless he were lifted out of his depression, given a fresh vision and an anointing from God. So on the Saturday evening, he locked himself in his bedroom in the Langfords' house.

'I will not come out until I have been recommissioned and re-equipped,' he told himself.

He read the Bible. He prayed. Hour followed hour. Then he came to Psalm 145:18: 'The Lord is near to all who call on him, to all who call on him in truth.' He tried to lay hold of this promise.

'Lord,' he prayed, 'I am calling upon you now, and doing so in sincerity and truth. I have fulfilled the conditions. Will you fulfil the promise?'

As he prayed, he seemed to experience the presence of God and was able to go ahead with the mission.

Compared to Sydney, the Melbourne mission got off to a slower start. About 800 students turned up for lunch-hour meetings in the Wilson Hall, a modern building with glass sidewalls and plush seats. A dramatic mural behind the platform depicted humanity's search for truth through the mists of ignorance and doubt. But there seemed to be little visible response to the talks John gave. However, gradually the atmosphere thawed and John found himself constantly in demand for interviews and advice.

On the last Sunday night, the venue for the final meeting of the mission was Melbourne Cathedral. As the university was non-residential, John worried that students wouldn't come into town from their homes and digs in the suburbs. His fears were groundless.

As he entered the cathedral with choir and clergy, he saw a huge crowd of about 1,800 people – half from the town and half from the university. When he finished his address and made his appeal between three and four hundred people stayed on for a continuation service. John spoke on personal commitment to Christ. Many people came forward after he said the final prayer. With his team, he was kept busy answering questions until nearly ten o'clock.

After five days of meetings in New Zealand, John boarded a plane for the long flight home. They touched down for a break at Waikiki, Honolulu, in Hawaii. Warm Pacific breezes blew and, after buying himself a pair of bathing trunks, he made his way to the beach to find silvery sand under an overcast sky. He tested the water and found it unbelievably warm. He watched American and Chinese children surfing. Since they made it look easy, he plucked up courage and decided to hire a surfboard for an hour.

His board was big and heavy. He watched those around him kneeling and standing on theirs, gracefully balanced. But his attempts to surf were a failure. It was hard enough to keep on his board lying, let alone kneeling and standing. And in his excitement at trying to surf, he had overlooked the fact that even a cloudy sky at this latitude can allow the rays of the sun through. On the plane to Los Angeles that night he became sick and the next morning his whole back was a huge blister. He did soon recover but returned to London wiser for his Hawaiian experience.

12. APPROACHING RENEWAL

In June 1959 Buckingham Palace staff, having satisfied themselves that he possessed the qualities they were looking for, appointed John a chaplain to Her Majesty the Queen. The duties involved preaching annually in the Chapel of St James's Palace, occasionally at Windsor Castle and once at Sandringham. It entitled him to wear a scarlet cassock, a badge on his scarf and (should he so wish) special buttons on an evening waistcoat! The All Souls congregation was delighted at the news. Churchwarden George Cansdale gave All Souls workers and helpers the opportunity to contribute half-a-crown each, enabling them to present John with a cheque for £31. 10s. to pay for the cassock.

September 1960 found John at The Hookses. He wrote to John Lefroy about a problem with which he often wrestled. He confided to his friend that he had a continuous nagging fear that 'our conservative position is untenable'. He wondered whether he should dismiss his doubts as temptations without examining them. He didn't imagine that anyone would ever get a complete answer to every problem, but he thought that by study and prayer he might grasp more firmly the general and positive principles on which the conservative view of the Bible rested.

He was quite happy to be 'a despised evangelical' so long as he could resolve his own doubts. He told John Lefroy that he had been greatly helped by reading carefully Norval Geldenhuys's *Supreme Authority*. Geldenhuys had undertaken a detailed study of the New Testament and early Christian writings. He had concluded that these writings revealed, first, the historical fact of the supreme authority of the Lord; second, that the Lord's apostles had been given unique authority to lay in a once-and-for-all way the foundations of the church; and third, that the early church had acknowledged these two facts and accepted the apostolic writings as authoritative. The result of this was the coming into being (through the guidance and overruling of God) of a canonical New Testament clothed with the authority of the Lord and his apostles.

John was also encouraged by the fact that, although he was surrounded by liberal critics, he saw himself as standing in a noble tradition which went back not only to the reformers but also to the Puritans, the eighteenth-century evangelicals, Charles Simeon in the nineteenth century, and able scholars like Jim Packer in the twentieth.

John didn't believe that all liberals approached the Scriptures with strongly rationalistic presuppositions. Some were genuinely wrestling with difficulties, as William Temple did when he delayed his ordination until he was satisfied that he could assent to a belief in the virgin birth. John could understand where that sort of liberal was coming from.

The type of liberalism he rejected was that which would be captured some years later by David Edwards when, in his debate with John, he constantly used the phrase 'the climate of educated opinion'. For John, that was never satisfactory as a source of authority for the Christian. Although his understanding of the authority of Scripture hasn't changed fundamentally over the years, it has been enriched as he has taken hermeneutics – the methodology of interpreting and understanding the Bible – much more seriously. 'We need to say humbly and penitently,' he told me, 'that we evangelical people have not always taken seriously the hermeneutical task. I think I've seen more clearly that there is no point in having a supreme authority if you can't interpret it accurately. So authority and interpretation inevitably go together. In this respect I would be willing to say that those of us who are conservative evangelical people do not believe that every word of the Bible is literally true.'

He gave the example of the Book of Job: 'It is impossible to take a sentence out of the Book of Job and say, "This is the Word of God," because we know that much teaching in Job has been included in it in order to be contradicted and not in order to be confirmed. Twice in Job 42 God says to Job, "You have not spoken of me what is right." That is a very clear statement that there are some things in the Book of Job, and no doubt in other places, which need to be understood in their context.'

With these and similar thoughts, he survived the doubts which troubled him about the conservative approach to Scripture. And as the years went on, he refined and clarified his thinking.

In the Spring of 1962, John embarked on a second visit to Africa. He conducted his first mission at the University College of Sierra Leone in Freetown on the west coast. After his final address, a group of students returned with John to his rooms to continue talking. Shortly before midnight, when the others had gone, there was a knock at his door.

John opened it and in walked Ishmael, a Muslim student from the Gambia. He questioned John closely and intelligently about the Christian faith, about the reason for the cross and the person of Jesus Christ – 'his big brown eyes searching mine,' John wrote in his diary, 'and his whole soul seeming to hunger for God'.

'Is it possible to know God, to "see" him?' Ishmael asked.

Ishmael reminded John of Nicodemus who came to Jesus by night. He gave him a copy of John's Gospel.

'I promise I will read it,' Ishmael assured him.

After conducting missions in Nigeria and Kenya, and a holiday in the Rift Valley, John's final engagement of the African tour was a week's mission at the University College of Rhodesia and Nyasaland in Salisbury.

One of the African students invited seven of his friends to meet John for questions and discussion in a small common room.

'I just love these Africans,' John enthused. 'They're so much more warm and open and sincere than the rather cold and supercilious Europeans. We had a really valuable time, clearing up a number of their problems. We talked freely about Jesus Christ as the great breaker down of the barriers of race and rank, and I have every hope that they will join the Christian fellowship. It would certainly be a marvellous thing if the Christians at the University College of Rhodesia and Nyasaland were to demonstrate within the tensions of the university that a truly multi-racial fellowship is possible through Christ.'

Although there was no legal apartheid in Rhodesia, John noticed hotels and restaurants – and even churches – for 'whites only'. In the university, designated as multi-racial, there was little social integration, so that even at his meetings the hall tended to divide into racial groups. He was pleased to see three or four small African boys in the Salisbury Cathedral choir.

Three times in the 1960s, John visited Keswick Convention to give the Bible Readings. The convention owes its name to the small town of Keswick in the Lake District, where it has been held annually since 1875. In the 1960s the Convention was attracting seven thousand people annually to two vast tents under the banner, *ALL ONE IN CHRIST JESUS*.

Rowland Appleton, a member of the Keswick Council, welcomed John on the steps of the hotel and showed him to his room. John went across to the chest-of-drawers under the window, removed the top drawer, turned it over, and reinserted it upside down. Satisfied that this would make a good surface on which he could work, he spent much of his time in Keswick in his room, writing on this improvised desk.

The chambermaid in the hotel didn't judge the preachers by the quality of their sermons.

'Who is the best preacher at the convention?' someone asked her.

'No contest,' she replied. 'John Stott.'

'Why?'

'Because he keeps his room the tidiest!'

Others though judged him on the quality of his addresses, and the Keswick tape library meant that his talks were heard across the world, sometimes by missionaries in isolated places. But addressing the convention some years later, John began with some surprising but memorable words.

'I am,' he said, 'always a sinner and often a failure.'

This was not so much said as a device to endear himself to his audience, but because he knew it to be as true of himself as of others.

One well-known Christian minister once asked John a question in those halcyon years when All Souls was packed with young professional people and students.

'John, what do you think of as you walk to the pulpit and climb its steps just before you preach, knowing that a thousand people will be hanging on your words?'

'As I make that journey to the pulpit,' John replied, 'I just say over and over again, "I believe in the Holy Spirit".'

But there were some whose experience of the Holy Spirit was, outwardly at least, more dramatic than John's. John had had some experience of what became known as the Charismatic Movement in the late 1950s through his visits to California.

Later, an American pastor visited John at the Rectory in Weymouth Street and sat opposite him in an armchair. They discussed the phenomenon of speaking in tongues.

'Have you ever heard anybody speak in tongues?' the pastor asked John.

'No, I haven't.'

'Would you like to?'

To John's astonishment, and before he had chance to say 'yes' or 'no', the American broke into unintelligible speech, with his eyes open looking at John.

This experience shocked John. It made him feel that if this was something you could turn on and off like a tap, it really wasn't a gift of the Spirit, in the way that was claimed.

Then in September 1962 Michael Harper, one of John's curates, had his experience of 'renewal'. Since towards the end of the 1950s, he had been chaplain to the Oxford Street stores. A Londoner who had been converted to Christ in his first year at Cambridge, Michael's experience of renewal hadn't happened at a pentecostal meeting, but through reading the Bible.

'It was earth-shaking,' Michael recorded, 'baptised in the Spirit, everything leapt off the page.' The phrase 'baptised in the Spirit' became a familiar and controversial one in the Charismatic Movement.

At this time, staff of All Souls were re-examining the call to holiness and life in the Spirit. After curate John Lefroy's prolonged illness a few years earlier they had spent long hours praying that he would be healed. This and other factors had encouraged All Souls staff into a deeper and more systematic study of the doctrine of God's Spirit. At a staff away-day John invited Michael Harper to tell the whole story of what he felt had happened to him. When Michael finished his account, John Lefroy spoke.

'Michael, I believe you've been baptised in the Spirit.'

Worried about possible division in the church, John spoke to Michael.

'You are perfectly free to speak of your experience in terms of personal testimony,' he told him. 'However, it would be best if you did not preach on the subject.'

Michael agreed. 'Look, I will never preach on this. I'm not in the business of splitting All Souls.'

John was interested, intrigued, even gripped by Michael's experience. But he felt uncomfortable when Michael spoke in tongues.

The issue began to divide All Souls staff. Some claimed that speaking in tongues was a special gift of God. Others were dubious about its theological or biblical basis. Some people wrote to John saying, 'You've really got to get rid of this Harper man.' But John never hinted that Michael should go.

Rumour had it that Martyn Lloyd-Jones had decided that what some people were experiencing in this new pentecostalism could indeed be called 'the baptism of the Holy Spirit'.

Roopsingh Carr, then working in London and a member of All Souls, asked John a question.

'Is there such an experience as the baptism of the Holy Spirit?'

'I don't know, Roopy,' was John's reply before he had chance to study and reflect in depth on the issues raised by the new movement.

And so he took time during a visit to The Hookses to think through the question. Now it was time to share his conclusions. At the long-established Islington Conference, when Michael Harper was on the point of leaving the staff anyway, John declared his mind publicly on these pentecostal teachings and experiences. In 1964, when the theme of the Conference was, 'The Holy Spirit in the Life of the Church', John was billed to speak on the subject, 'The Individual Christian and the Fullness of the Holy Spirit'.

The subject attracted the largest attendance anyone could remember, about a thousand clergy and lay people. People were looking for guidance in trying to understand the much-talked-about Charismatic Movement, with its emphasis on a special experience of the Holy Spirit, speaking in tongues and healing. John's reputation as a Bible teacher, with first-hand experience of the new movement among his own colleagues at All Souls, ensured a large audience.

John denied that, either at Islington or in the ensuing booklet which contained the substance of his talk, he was throwing down a gauntlet or issuing a confrontational challenge to charismatics.

'I personally searched the Scriptures,' he said, 'deliberately in order to discover the truth about the subject. I opened my mind afresh to all that was being said, written and claimed, and spent two years reading, thinking, praying and discussing. It was as a result of this prolonged period of study that I came to my conclusions. My motive was practical and personal rather than academic or controversial. We are brethren. We love one another. We are concerned to know God's will in order to embrace it ourselves and commend it to others, not in order to score cheap points off one another in theological debate.'

Charismatics believed that Christians needed this second experience of God's blessing, whether or not you called it 'baptism' or 'fullness'. Non-charismatics could draw only one conclusion from their arguments: that there were first-class Christians who had received this charismatic blessing and second-class Christians who hadn't. This wasn't a recipe for harmony in local churches and fellowships.

At the packed Islington Conference, John politely but firmly denied that there was such a thing as a post-conversion Spirit-baptism. Scripture taught, he said, that the fullness of the Holy Spirit was a distinctive blessing of the new age, the Christian era, and that this was a universal blessing to be enjoyed by all Christians. It was intended as a continuous blessing. He dealt carefully with what were frequently cited as contrary instances (notably in Acts 8 and 19). The baptism of the Spirit, he insisted, necessarily accompanies conversion. It's a once-for-all experience.

'As an initiatory event,' John told the conference, 'the baptism is not repeatable and cannot be lost. But the filling can be repeated and in any case needs to be maintained. If it is not maintained, it is lost. If it is lost, it can be recovered. The Holy Spirit is grieved by sin and ceases to fill the sinner. Repentance is then the only road to recovery. Even in cases where there is no suggestion that the fullness has been forfeited through sin, we still read of people being filled again, as a fresh crisis or challenge demands a fresh empowering by the Spirit.

'We must assert that neither the baptism nor the fullness of the Spirit need be accompanied by spectacular signs. The initial baptism of the Spirit may be quiet and unsensational while the continuing fullness of the Spirit manifests itself in moral qualities rather than in miraculous phenomena.'

In its original or later form, *The Baptism and Fullness of the Holy Spirit*, John's booklet has never been out of print.

Not everybody heard about John's views or agreed with them, and from this time All Souls had to compete with church congregations which took on a more charismatic flavour. After leaving All Souls, Michael Harper established, with others, the Fountain Trust, and became for some years a leader in the Charismatic Movement of renewal. In 1984 he became Canon of Chichester Cathedral, and in the early 1990s was received into the Orthodox Church.

In December 1964 John made the first of six visits to the triennial Urbana Missionary Convention at the University of Illinois. He was driven there in a seven-seater Cadillac limousine from Chicago, where he had preached a sermon which was broadcast on TV and radio.

Some of the 6,000 student delegates had travelled for days to get to the University of Illinois. One father, on hearing that his son planned to attend, was devastating in his reaction.

'Go ahead,' he said, 'but if you decide to become a missionary don't bother to return home.'

John's task was to give a daily forty-minute Bible exposition and then to join a panel of speakers before lunch. In the afternoon there was an hour's forum when the delegates fired questions at the morning speakers.

Arthur Glasser, US home director for the Overseas Missionary Fellowship, sat next to a minister at one of John Stott's Bible Readings on 2 Corinthians.

'God helping me,' the minister said, turning to Arthur at the end of John's talk, 'I'm never going to enter the pulpit unprepared again and, God helping me, I am going to do biblical exposition. I want to let people hear the Word of God like Stott did this morning. I never realised how fascinating and instructive that kind of preaching is.'

One Yale student whose first exposure to John was at an Urbana conference was Mark Labberton. In later years he would get to know John intimately. He found that, since John was known as the primary Bible teacher at Urbana, his question-and-answer sessions were especially well attended. Mark remembered being more intrigued to know who John actually was as a person than by the content of his Bible teaching.

As Mark listened to John handling these sessions with consummate skill, he wondered: 'How did this person get formed? Who is this person who is communicating this gospel he believes so strongly?' Over the years he came to the conclusion that the explanation for John's success as a preacher was not so much his sense of the nature of the gospel or his approach to exposition (although these things were important), but that it was his persona which was so powerful. 'My assessment of him as a preacher has grown as my experience of him as a person has grown. The thing that distinguishes him among many people is that I have found him the more impressive the more I have known him, rather than the other way round. Some people are disappointing on closer inspection. Not so with John. He has sought faithfully to live the story of the one he proclaims. This has been true in places where the culture is very different from the one where he has lived most of his life.'

The final evening meeting at Urbana on 31 December 1964 was open to the general public. Billy Graham was the main speaker and between fifteen and sixteen thousand people attended. The organisers asked John to preside at the concluding communion service. 'I introduced them to a little liturgy,' he recorded. As the service finished at midnight, all rose to sing, 'We rest on Thee, our shield and our defender' as 1965 dawned.

John, at forty-four, was just the age when he might be considered for an English bishopric. With a Cambridge double First, as a Chaplain to the Queen, a linguist, a naturalist with a love of the countryside, yet committed to urban ministry, and a rich experience of the world beyond these shores, he had much to offer.

Michael Saward, when working as his Radio and Television Officer, had a conversation with Michael Ramsey, then Archbishop of Canterbury.

'None of the evangelical bishops will stand up and be counted,' Ramsey grumbled.

'Perhaps that is because only a few of them are recognised as being evangelicals by my generation,' Saward replied.

Later in the same day John Stott's name came up in conversation.

'I do find that man so intransigent,' Ramsey growled.

'Archbishop,' Saward replied, 'you complained about lack of backbone in evangelicals this morning. You really can't have it both ways!'

When John heard this, he believed that Ramsey may have had in mind his role in the committee appointed by the archbishops on the reservation of the sacraments. 'I was certainly intransigent about that,' he said.

Adrian Hastings took the view that it was probably for the best that John didn't become an English bishop. 'A modern Anglican bishop,' he wrote, 'has to relate sympathetically to all wings of the Church of England, and in strict evangelical eyes an evangelical who accepts a bishopric, like Edward Woods or even Donald Coggan, is almost bound to be judged sooner or later as something of a sell-out. British evangelical history in fact is replete with lost leaders – men who, as they grew older, have found it impossible or at least undesirable to stick quite closely enough to the movement's doctrines and norms.'

Clark Bedford and his wife, Sandra, arrived at All Souls from New York in Autumn 1965. Clark had been appointed organist and choir-master at the church and, Clark remembered, they were 'thrilled to be in London working with this famous preacher and writer'. They found that John was 'very gracious and kind and his speech and manners were "frightfully" British'.

'We were not a little awe-stricken,' Clark told me, 'but we settled in and found him to be a delightful person. Time passed, and soon we were at the staff Christmas party. Of course we had the traditional English plum pudding with *brandy butter*! The Rector obviously loved it. We had come from a large and famous Baptist Church in New York, so this was interesting. After the meal the Christmas crackers were passed out – another new experience for us. They were red paper cylinders filled with little doodahs and at one point we linked arm to arm holding one end of the cracker and a neighbour holding the other end. At the given signal everyone yanked hard, there was a big pop and the items rolled out of the cylinder. There were silly little toys, noise makers and strange, funny paper hats. I was a little embarrassed and hesitated putting mine on. But lo! Across the room, the Reverend John Stott had the hat on his head and a noise maker in his mouth. I couldn't believe it! So much for English dignity! We enjoyed it immensely.'

After Sir Arnold's death in 1958, Lily was often seen at All Souls and acting as hostess for John at the Annual Garden Party which he gave each summer in the grounds of the London Zoo, and later at Bedford College, Regent's Park, for the volunteer workers of the church. To John's delight, she visited The Hookses from time to time, coming to love the place as much as he did. Frances Whitehead remembered Lily as 'knowing her own mind, kind and gracious – though people were somewhat in awe of her'.

While John was conducting a student mission in Asia in Autumn 1963, Lily, aged eighty-three, suffered a stroke. Joy cabled, but her brother didn't receive the message until six days later, and was then unable to get in touch with her as storms had caused a breakdown of telephone communication between England and Hong Kong. Lily improved somewhat but remained something of an invalid, cared for at Bullens Hill Farm by Joy. John visited as often as he could and found her cheerful and comfortable. She could speak, but got some words muddled, even calling John 'George' for some reason. She died in January 1966. It was some comfort to John in his grief that her final days had been peaceful.

13. DRAMA AT THE CENTRAL HALL

In the late 1920s, Martyn Lloyd-Jones had abandoned a career in medicine to become a minister in a small Presbyterian church in Wales. Two years before John arrived at All Souls as curate, Lloyd-Jones had become sole pastor at Westminster Chapel in London, and preached there almost every Sunday night until 1968 when ill-health forced him to retire.

Lloyd-Jones had no formal theological training, but read widely, especially on the Puritans, and kept himself up to date on current affairs. His preaching was what is known as expository, drawing out the meanings of every phrase in passages of Scripture in his sermons and attempting to apply them to his congregation. For this he had a large and loyal following.

He had turned his mind to the issue of what unity evangelicals should prize. In June 1965 he addressed the Westminster Fellowship, an inter-denominational ministers' fraternal that met in his chapel from the end of the war.

'Theologically orthodox Anglicans,' he argued, 'and others with similarly orthodox beliefs should consider leaving their denominations. Instead of trying to "infiltrate" the various bodies to which they belong, evangelicals should stand together.' By 'orthodox' he meant those Christians who held strictly to the Protestant faith as believed at the time of the sixteenth-century Reformation and especially as held by Calvin.

In the summer of 1966, when Lloyd-Jones was sixty-seven and Stott was forty-five, John gave three Bible readings at a meeting for doctors in Oxford. At the end of one of them, Lloyd-Jones took John to one side and surprised him.

'I would like you to be my successor at Westminster Chapel,' he said.

Totally taken aback, John replied, 'While I am greatly honoured, I have no sense of calling to leave All Souls, or indeed the Church of England.'

The Evangelical Alliance (a body formed in 1846 to ensure that evangelicalism remained a vital presence in Britain following the rise of the High Church Oxford Movement) invited Dr Lloyd-Jones to give the keynote address on the theme of church unity in the Methodist Central Hall, Westminster. In particular, the organisers asked him to speak in response to a report which stated that the time was not ripe for evangelicals to seek to form a united church. It would be the second National Assembly of Evangelicals and, in view of the importance of its subject, the first really major gathering of British evangelicals since 1846 to be organised by the Alliance. The date was set for 18 October 1966.

The Alliance had a new General Secretary, author and Baptist Minister Morgan Derham. Lloyd-Jones met the Alliance Council beforehand to share with them what he planned to say. Although the strength of the case he intended to put rather took the Council by surprise, no one raised any formal objection to the outline of the talk which he summarised. However, Morgan Derham decided that Lloyd-Jones intended to make the assembly meeting the decisive event in his crusade for evangelical separation from mainline denominations. So he rang John, who had been asked to take the chair at the assembly.

'I believe,' Morgan Derham told John, 'that Dr Lloyd-Jones may well exceed his brief, which is simply to explain his case, but not to make an appeal for action. Frankly, if he does this he will be violating his rights as a guest at an Evangelical Alliance event. And if he does so, I feel that you, as chairman, would be well within your rights to challenge him.'

John was grateful for this advance warning.

When the great day arrived, many hundreds of evangelicals made their way to the Methodist Central Hall. The impressive building had, since its opening in 1912, played host to events of national and international importance. The suffragettes, campaigning for the vote for women, met there in 1914. Mahatma Gandhi addressed the Temperance Movement in 1931. During the Second World War the basement area became the largest air raid shelter in England, housing hundreds of people every night. Here, General de Gaulle announced the foundation of the Free French Movement to the world in 1940. William Sangster had attracted a congregation of 3,000, morning and evening, every Sunday until the mid-1950s.

On the evening of 18 October 1966 the hall quickly filled. In the vestry, the atmosphere among the platform party was warm and friendly as they prayed together.

'I suggest now,' said John as chairman, 'that we make our way to the platform.'

'Where would you like me to sit?' Martyn Lloyd-Jones asked.

'Sit at my side,' John replied.

'Which side?' Lloyd-Jones asked with a twinkle in his eye. 'You have *two* sides, John!'

There were merry, if slightly forced, chuckles.

John had been allocated ten minutes for his chairman's remarks. As agreed beforehand, he referred to his own conscientious, continuing membership of the Church of England: 'Its formularies are biblical and evangelical. Evangelicals are therefore the Anglican loyalists, and non-evangelicals the deviationists.'

John made four brief points on church unity. 'First, spiritual unity should be expressed visibly. Second, the visibility of this Christian unity must include the mutual recognition of the ministries and sacraments – there must be full communion. Third, this visible unity of the Church must be founded on the Biblical faith. Fourth, this visible unity of the Church must also allow room for divergence of belief and practice in matters of secondary importance.'

John concluded his remarks by referring to Lloyd-Jones as 'in every particular my elder and better. I hold him in great esteem and affection in Christ.'

As General Secretary of the Alliance, Morgan Derham then spoke in appreciation of the main speaker of the evening. One who was present thought that he 'eulogised the doctor with faint praise'.

At last, it was time for Lloyd-Jones to get to his feet. 'It would be churlish of me not to thank Mr Morgan Derham for the remarks he has made,' he began, 'but I wish he had not done so. He has robbed me of my valuable time!'

As the doctor got into his talk, he warmed to his theme. 'Ecumenical people put fellowship before doctrine,' he said. 'We, as evangelicals, put doctrine before fellowship . . . I make this appeal to you evangelical people this evening, what reasons have we for not coming together? Some will say we will miss evangelistic opportunities if we leave our denominations, but I say "Where is the Holy Spirit?" . . . You cannot justify your decision to remain in your denomination by saying that you maintain your independence. You cannot disassociate yourself from the church to which you belong. This is a very contradictory position, and one that the man in the street must find very hard to understand. Don't we feel the call to come together, not occasionally, but always?'

The atmosphere as he spoke was electric. In the audience were many Anglican clergy – John felt especially responsible for them. 'From the platform,' he later recalled, 'I could see younger men with flushed faces, sitting on the edge of their seat, hanging on every word, and probably ready to go home and write their letter of resignation from the Alliance that very night. I hoped at least to restrain some hotheads from doing this.' Members of the audience who valued their existing denominational allegiances were horrified by what the doctor was saying.

Douglas Johnson, of the Inter-Varsity Fellowship, thought that John looked 'flushed, rattled and annoyed'. And indeed John thought that using the opening address to make an appeal for action was an improper use of the assembly.

When Lloyd-Jones eventually finished, John rose to thank the speaker and announce the closing hymn. However, he had something more to say.

'I hope that no one will make a precipitate decision after this moving address,' he began. You could have heard a pin drop as he abandoned a chairman's neutrality. 'We are here to debate this subject and I believe history is against Dr Jones in that others have tried to do this very thing. I believe that Scripture is against him in that the remnant was within the Church and not outside it.'

The assembly delegates sang their closing hymn and a buzz of conversation began. 'Thank you for your timely intervention,' John Laird, General Secretary of the Scripture Union, and not an Anglican, said to John. Others were also supportive – but not all.

In his home in Oxford that evening, Jim Packer's phone rang. 'Jim – is John Stott mad?' the caller asked. But the following day, someone who had been at the meeting observed to Jim, 'Martyn Lloyd-Jones has gone off his rocker!'

The Church of England Newspaper described Lloyd-Jones's proposition as 'barmy . . . nothing short of hare-brained'. Others wondered whether the doctor had the organisational skills to get his idea off the ground.

A week or two later John Stott took the initiative and called on Lloyd-Jones to apologise – not for what he had said (which he continued to believe) but for misusing the chair and almost turning the meeting into a debate.

'I scarcely restrained myself from answering you and developing the debate,' Lloyd-Jones replied.

The incident generated so much controversy within evangelicalism that the Evangelical Alliance National Assembly had to be cancelled the following year as a direct consequence. And from 1967, the Westminster Fellowship ceased to offer a welcome to Anglicans.

When John became President of the Evangelical Alliance he told a 'President's Night' event that 'some evangelicals, like myself, believe it is the will of God to remain in a church that is sometimes called a "mixed denomination". At least until it becomes apostate and ceases to be a church, we believe it is our duty to remain in it and bear witness to the truth as we have been given to understand it. Some of us who do this, however, are thought not to care about the truth. I want to say to you with all the strength of conviction that I possess that we care intensely about the truth, because we believe that God has revealed it fully and finally in Jesus Christ.'

14. COMING OUT OF THE GHETTO

By the mid-1960s, John and his colleagues on the Church of England Evangelical Council (CEEC) decided that the evangelical movement had grown to the stage when it was time to say something publicly that would represent a milestone in its development. So the Council agreed to be among the sponsors of a major Congress. From August 1964, John acted as chairman and Raymond Turvey, Vicar of St George's, Leeds, as secretary to a National Evangelical Anglican Congress (NEAC) planning committee. They booked Keele University for April 1967, and agreed that the Congress would be preceded by a preliminary study course in the parishes followed by further courses well into 1968. There should be full participation by delegates rather than simply teaching from the platform, and the Congress would end by issuing a statement.

By 1966 a major programme of parish study groups was in full swing, followed by *Guidelines*, a book of essays by the Congress speakers sent to all delegates. Delegates were asked to represent the views of the parish study groups from which they came.

On 4 April 1967 some thousand delegates together with thirty observers converged on Keele University campus. Keele was one of the new universities, set amid farm and woodland, with lakes, lawns and rhododendrons.

The evangelical Anglicans who arrived by no means formed a uniform movement. 'There were,' as a young John Gladwin put it, 'the Puritans and Anabaptists who sat uncomfortably in a comprehensive church. There were the pietists who thought the Church of England the best boat to fish from. There were the young charismatics seeking renewal and revival. There were the radicals who wanted to embrace most things modern. In the midst were a group of leaders, young and old, lay and ordained, who held this disparate and sometimes disorderly movement together – in the best tradition of Cranmer, Hooker, Baxter and Simeon.'

John travelled to Keele at the start of that week in April to find Raymond Turvey and his team sorting out rooms, checking lists, going over the needs of the Congress with university staff.

Archbishop Michael Ramsey opened the Congress by speaking on the theme, 'Jesus is Lord'.

'My subject tonight,' he began, 'is the person of Jesus Christ, and I want to do no more than consider with you the meaning of the Easter faith "Jesus is Lord". Jesus lived nearly 2,000 years ago. Christians claim that he is alive now and that he matters immensely for the human race, but those who are not Christians say that this claim is absurd and may be ignored. I ask tonight: why do we believe the claim to be true, and how does it matter for the world?'

Archbishop Ramsey spoke about the historicity of Christ's resurrection, and the centrality of his cross. He appealed for openness across the range of Christian traditions.

Jim Packer used his talk to make an appeal for Christian obedience to revealed truth. Jim had come to Keele with limited expectations, but found his hopes rising as the Congress tackled its task. After walking from one room to another between meetings, he spoke to John. 'It is clear to me that this is an epoch-making conference in which the Holy Spirit is notably at work.'

On the Wednesday morning, John expanded on his own contribution to *Guidelines*, 'Jesus Christ, our Teacher and Lord'. He drew on feedback he had received in letters from delegates and in previous discussions. He especially addressed those delegates who would be wrestling with the concept of authority.

'If Jesus Christ were to appear in person on earth today,' he said, 'and if He were to speak to the Church in such a way that His person and His message were clear and incontrovertible, it is charitable to suppose that the great majority of churchmen would heed His message, believe it and obey it . . . If we could be certain that what the Scripture says Christ says, that the message of the Bible is the Word of Christ, then surely we would (or at least should) be ready to receive it and conform our lives to it.

'The truth of God is neither what you or I think, nor what the Church teaches, but what the Spirit says to the Church through the Word. And since churches and individuals err when they are "not governed with the Spirit and the Word of God", the greatest need of the Church in this as in every age is humbly to submit to the authority of the Word and prayer-fully to seek the illumination of the Spirit.

'I am conscious that some of you may think this places unacceptable constraints on academic freedom, or to verge simply upon a blind obscur-antism. But is not this submission of our minds to the mind of Christ an intellectual imprisonment? No more so than the submission of our wills to the will of Christ is moral bondage. Certainly it is a surrender of liberty, for no Christian can be a "free thinker". Yet it is this kind of surrender which is true freedom – freedom from our own miserable subjectivity, and freedom from bondage to the current whims and fancies of the world. Is it stunting to spiritual growth? No, it is essential to it, for Christian growth is nothing if it is not growth into Christ as Lord and Head.'

The practical upshot of this, John argued, is that pastors are to preach the Word of Christ, and Christians are to live by it – any attempt to reunite churches must be based on it. 'Only when we submit in this way to Jesus Christ as our Teacher and our Lord, is the reunion and the renewal of the church a realistic possibility.'

Then the delegates got to work in earnest, studying a series of themes in the life of the church in their groups. They began their work on the Wednesday afternoon, revising a draft statement which had been prepared beforehand, and continued with brief pauses until after nine in the evening. The chairs and secretaries of the groups then met to draft their reports, and it was six o'clock the following morning before the last section was complete. The revised statement was in the hands of delegates before lunch on Thursday. What the *Church Times* described as 'this superhuman programme' rolled on relentlessly as the revisions and redrafting continued, 'beaten into shape by a thousand people in three gruelling days'.

It was rumoured that Philip Crowe, who was at the heart of the drafting process, only managed four hours of sleep during the entire Congress. For his part, John survived the first night's drafting, but fell asleep during the second. He and Michael Green were the final editors of the draft statement which was submitted to the Congress. They had the task of judging, from the drafts submitted and the resolutions passed by the sub-groups, what was the mind of the Congress.

In his introduction to the published Congress statement, John commended it as expressing 'the convictions of a large but average evangelical constituency' rather than the work of experts. John believed that some evangelicals had been guilty for generations past of neglect of scholarship, a lack of social vision, and insularity within the church: 'a church within a church'.

'The mood of the Congress,' he said, 'was one of penitence for past failures and of serious resolve for the future. This has meant for many of us not a change of fundamental position, but of stance and even of direction.'

An important area in which Keele marked a change of direction for evangelical Anglicans, and where John himself had most to learn, was the relationship between the church and the world. Here the Congress broke new ground for most delegates.

A key figure, who helped the Congress to think clearly in this area, was a member of John's congregation at All Souls: Norman Anderson, Professor of Oriental Laws in the University of London. 'Evangelicals can congratulate themselves,' the *Church Times* reported, 'on the presence in their midst of a spokesman who must be among the most academically distinguished in the whole Assembly. Yet he is modest, friendly and informal in manner, with none of that unnerving earnestness sometimes found in Protestantism.'

Norman Anderson admitted that he himself had come late to this recognition of the need for Christian involvement in society. With a few exceptions, he and his friends had largely accepted the inequalities of life as part of the order of things. The urge to evangelise, and to 'witness for Christ', had not been accompanied by an equal determination to achieve radical social reform.

Sir Kenneth Grubb, Chairman of the House of Laity and an observer at Keele, believed that the Congress achieved three remarkable things. 'It has given evangelicals a justified sense of their standing; it has emphasised their loyalty to the church; it has demonstrated that they have much to contribute, not only to individual faith, but also to the great spiritual challenges of contemporary society.'

Father Bernard Leeming, the Roman Catholic observer, commented that 'evangelicals and Roman Catholics do indeed hold many fundamental doctrines in common'.

John thought that Keele marked 'our evangelical coming of age, for there we publicly repented of our immature isolationism and resolved to take a more responsible part in the life of both the visible church and the secular world . . . the evangelical constituency made a public penitent renunciation of pietism'.

Reporting on Keele, the *Guardian* newspaper spoke of 'the impressive and seemingly relentless growth in the last twenty years of the evangelical movement within the Church of England', and quoted in their headline the phrase 'coming out of their ghettos' which John had used in the press conference.

The Keele Congress in April 1967 institutionalised a process whereby evangelical laity and clergy in the Church of England began to take seriously their intellectual challenges and brought this process to the notice of the church at large. They made public commitments from which there could be no going back. The Congress set an ambitious agenda for evangelical parishes, supplemented by a range of conferences across the country. The church at large was reminded of the evangelical presence in a new way. Evangelicals could no longer be ignored.

'You can always hear John Stott at All Souls, even if he's not there,' they used to say back in London, alluding to the way his curates soon began to sound like him in mannerisms and intonation. But not long after Keele, a curate arrived who broke this mould.

Ted Schroder had grown up in New Zealand and was converted, as a schoolboy, through a local parish mission. At the University of Canterbury, New Zealand, while reading English and History, he joined the Christian fellowship and soon became its president. He came to England to do a second degree, and visited John at 12 Weymouth Street. They met again at Keele, which Ted had attended as a theological student.

Ted was surprised to receive a letter from John inviting him to consider joining the All Souls staff on ordination. John liked and admired Ted because he was a 'man's man', with a strong mind, absolute honesty and a hearty sense of humour.

Looking back on his time at All Souls and the training John gave him, Ted gave me his perspective on those years: 'John had a way of organising so that you had a rounded comprehensive understanding of ministry. This set me up for life. John gave me two notebooks and I had to write down every person I visited in the parish and notes about the visit. Every fortnight he would go through the book with me and talk it over. It forced me to pay attention to what I was doing and made me realise how important visiting was. This stood me in good stead later when I had curates myself. I tried to instil the same discipline in them. He showed me how he organised his card catalogue and filing system and that gave me an insight into how to organise my own study methods.'

John assigned Ted to the Club House which he had established for the youth as well as the elderly poor. This brought him in touch with the people on the east side of the parish which was so different from the west side, home to doctors and foreign embassies. Then John put Ted in charge of the team who visited the home-bound. 'Many of them were poverty-stricken: they didn't have running water in their flats and made do with a tap in the hallway outside. Their only form of heating was a gas or a coal fire. At Christmas I took them Christmas lunch. John had a real heart for that work which wasn't seen by a lot of people. He was very compassionate towards the poor and elderly, and knew every one of them by name. When I reported back he would know all about the person I was talking about. As a curate, you thought you were going to this very fancy West End church and were going to be in the limelight. But John soon taught you that the people who mattered were those at the bottom who could easily be forgotten.'

John never excluded the mentally ill or severely eccentric characters in the congregation. He believed in the transforming power of the gospel. He took an interest in the relationship between theology, psychology and mental illness. There was also tension between the mainline evangelical approach and more charismatic approaches which emphasised exorcism and healing. John tended to see emotional problems as what they were rather than as demonic. There was, Ted told me, 'a nuancing and a sensitivity in his approach. He reacted against excessive claims of healing in the renewal movement.'

John's prayer life and the humility of it were an inspiration to Ted. They often knelt together in prayer in John's study on Saturday evenings.

Not everything, however, was rosy in their relationship. Ted thought that John had a tendency to keep people at arm's length. He wanted to be in control of his own space and relationships. This came out in his preaching. There was a certain detachment about it. Although John always used to say that the preacher has to obey the instruction 'feed my sheep not feed my giraffes,' he came across to some as being 'six feet above contradiction'. Ted saw it as an aspect of his upper-class British reserve. Although John would tell his curates to 'get inside the doubts of the doubters', he found it hard at this time of his life to do this personally. 'You never got the impression he had any doubts,' Ted remembered.

Ted grew concerned that John's diary was too crowded and that he was trying to do too much. 'He wouldn't even come out of his study to eat. He would put "do not disturb" on his study door. I would have to go in and drag him down to eat. I violated his privacy because I felt somebody had to do it. He was intimidating to a lot of people and nobody would ever confront him. When he did come down for a meal, and we were all round the table, everybody would fall silent. They were frightened of doing or saying the wrong thing. It was unnatural. I couldn't abide this. It wasn't realistic. I didn't see it as a virtue. I got a name for hauling him down. I could see he was human elsewhere with his family and with other folk in the parish and I wanted him to be human in the Rectory. I remonstrated with him about his schedule: "If you try to do too much you are going to make mistakes and harm your health."'

John was taking health drinks to keep going, rising early and going to bed late. 'Do less speaking and more writing,' Ted suggested. 'You are going to reach more people through your writing. You are accepting too many speaking engagements all over the world. You've got to slow down.'

'I was down in south London doing a visit,' Ted told me, 'and I had an appointment with him at three o'clock. Coming back I got caught up in traffic and couldn't make the appointment. I got to a phone box and rang to say I wasn't going to make it. John was very cross. He said he had this half-hour allotted to me and had carved it out of his busy schedule. He could have used it for something else. This was a sign of his over-scheduling. He couldn't accept that other people had agendas which could also be interrupted through no fault of their own. He apologised later on for reacting as he had.'

These were the days of student revolutions, the Vietnam War, the Beatles, and young people experimenting with drugs. Ted was working as chaplain at the Polytechnic of Central London where Maoists and other left-wing zealots had no time for Christianity or indeed any religion. Ted wanted the preaching at All Souls to address this culture. With a huge gap to be bridged, he didn't believe you could continue in traditional ways.

One day he and John were processing out of All Souls at the end of a service at which John had preached.

'So what?' Ted said to John. 'You preached a good exposition of the passage. But I want more application to the modern world.'

John recognised this fault in himself, even if for his part he didn't think that Ted was much good at Bible exposition. Walking back to the Rectory a few weeks later, John and Ted discussed a Schroder sermon.

'If only you and I could combine our approaches,' John said, 'it would be very powerful. My desire is to be loyal to Scripture. Yours is to be relevant to the modern world. Both of them are important.'

The two men came to see that they needed to combine their strengths. Ted had worked as a journalist for a daily newspaper in New Zealand and had been forced to learn what interested people. Despite John's reluctance to use personal illustrations in his sermons and his limited skill in application at this time, Ted paid tribute to John's gifts as a communicator. 'He could lift words off a page. He could speak engagingly and with clarity.'

Ted was one of those who encouraged John to visit the theatre and cinema which, like many evangelicals of his generation, he had renounced soon after his conversion as worldly. Ted suggested that it would be a way of entering the mind-set of contemporary society.

When the Warsaw Pact troops drove their tanks into Czechoslovakia in the Prague Spring of 1968, John happily allowed All Souls to be used as a refuge for students and others who had been stranded outside their country. All Souls began to be known for being hospitable to hippies and to Christian students who were very unconventional.

One Monday morning, when the All Souls staff team gathered for their weekly meeting, John was in the chair as usual. Some staff members were discussing an issue which didn't particularly interest John. He switched off until rudely interrupted in his reveries.

'John!' Ted cried, 'you're not listening!'

John blushed. For, as he later admitted, Ted 'was quite right, and it is intolerably rude not to listen when somebody is speaking'.

Other tensions were surfacing in team relationships. John had become too immersed in the evermore diverse demands on his time from beyond the parish. Staff thought that John was away from All Souls too much.

But despite the tensions, people noticed that John took notice of Ted. Visitors who had been away from the parish were amazed on their return to find that John had grown sideburns and begun to wear a flowery tie!

John was moving towards the 'double listening' (to the Scriptures and to the contemporary world) which was to become so central to his thinking.

Left: *Joanna and Joy were intrigued to have a baby brother* (page 21).

Below: *Oakley Hall School 1929-1935. When John arrived at the school in September 1929, the Stotts' chauffeur parked the big Chrysler in the shadow of an ivy-covered building of Cotswold stone* (page 25).

Right: *He was enjoying games* (page 25).

Below: *Soon after John's eighteenth birthday in 1939, the producer of the school play chose him for the title role in Shakespeare's Richard II* (page 36).

Bottom left: *Lily was concerned both about John's adamant determination to be ordained and his doubts about whether he could in conscience fight for his country* (page 40).

Bottom right: *Ironically John had managed to achieve a double first-class honours degree, which Arnold had failed to do* (page 59).

The blast had so damaged All Souls' famous steeple that thirty feet of it had to be taken down and rebuilt (page 44).

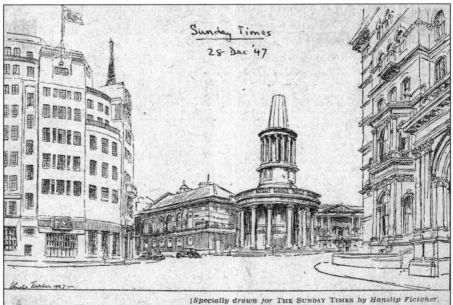

Sunday Times
28 Dec '47

[*Specially drawn for* THE SUNDAY TIMES *by Hanslip Fletcher*

Trafalgar Square with its Christmas tree has been London's Yuletide centrepiece, but here is a place that provided much of the country's holiday entertainment—the B.B.C. building on the left, with All Souls', Langham Place, in the centre.

Left: *John became Bash's right-hand man in the running of these camps* (page 50).

Below: *One Sunday, John was on the receiving end of a little joke Earnshaw-Smith (below left) played on all his new curates at one time or another: he came up to him in the middle of the service and said, 'Let me see now, you're preaching this morning aren't you?'* (page 64).

Above: *John sometimes acted as referee and was proud of the group's reputation one year for having played twenty-four matches and won them all!* (page 75).

Above: *When the Rector himself got in touch and arranged to talk with her, she told him that her name was Frances Whitehead* (page 91).

Right: *With the Queen Mother at a nurses' Carols by Candlelight, All Souls, December 1955. He recalled the words of the Queen Mother in 1951:* 'I can truly say that the King and I long to see the Bible back where it ought to be as a guide and comfort in the homes and lives of our people' (page 93).

Above: *In John, Anglican evangelicalism had found itself with a new leadership figure who belonged to a young generation* (page 101).

Middle left: *Billy Graham preaching at All Souls in the 1950s.* 'We are both young,' *Billy told John,* 'with most of our ministry before us. It is my prayer that our friendship will grow and deepen and be used of God as was the friendship of Wesley and Whitefield' (page 105).

Bottom left: *During the spring and early summer of 1958, it had become clear that Sir Arnold Stott was failing. Before leaving to conduct meetings in Australia, John discussed with his mother and sisters what he should do, were his father to deteriorate or even die while he was away. Lily agreed that he should fulfil his responsibilities, and only then fly home* (page 113).

Above left: 'I just love these Africans,' *John enthused* (page 121).

Above right: *Keswick Convention 1972* (page 122).

Above: 'Where would you like me to sit?' *Martyn Lloyd-Jones asked.* 'Sit at my side,' *John replied.* 'Which side?' *Lloyd-Jones asked with a twinkle in his eye.* 'You have two sides, John!' (page 132). (Photo: Pat Thomas)

Right: *Urbana Convention 1973.
Since John was known as the
primary Bible teacher at Urbana,
his question-and-answer sessions
were especially well attended*
(page 127).

Middle right: *In April 1972, a trial
excavation revealed that John Nash
had joined up the columns inside the
church by huge thick inverted arches,
underneath which formed a frame
to hold up the building* (page 156).

Middle left: *Talking to Princess
Alexandra at a London Lecture*

Bottom: *John made one of three
visits to Bathurst Inlet on the
northern shore of Canada's North
West Territory, just inside the
Arctic Circle* (page 174).

Above: *Mark Labberton succeeded Tom Cooper as study assistant in 1980. John liked American study assistants because he knew they were pushy enough to get things done* (page 193-4). *(Mark wears the 'Who is John Stott anyway?' T-shirt and Tom 'I'm a fan of John Stott'.)*

Below: *With study assistant Toby Howarth*

Above: *Sixty-fifth birthday with Noël Tredinnick (far left of picture) and Richard Bewes (second from the right).*

Below: *On 19 April 1991 the All Souls orchestra performed at the enthronement of George Carey as the 103rd Archbishop of Canterbury. Five days later Dr Carey hosted a reception at Lambeth Palace to mark John's seventieth birthday* (pages 234-5). (Photo: Richard Bewes)

Above left: *The degree was conferred on him at a ceremony at Lambeth Palace on 18 July 1983. Lambeth made it clear to John that the degree had been earned on account of his many writings and was not 'honorary'* (page 212).

Above right: *Steve and Dot Beck. 'This is Steve,' Dot said to John. John eyed Steve up and down, and evidently approved of Dot's choice of boyfriend* (page 213).

Above: *Leading a 'Christian in the Modern World' course at the London Institute 1985* (page 214).

Above left: *Addressing Lausanne II, July 1989.* 'What does the Manila Manifesto add to the Covenant or the process of Lausanne?' *an interviewer asked John.* 'It clarifies it,' *John replied* (page 231).

Above right: *As he looked at the bird through his camera viewfinder, the owl's head and body filled the picture.* 'She stared,' *he recorded in his journal,* 'even glared at me with her penetrating yellow eyes' (page 244). (Photo: John Stott)

Right: *New arrivals at The Hookses were often surprised to see the internationally-known preacher and writer wearing grimy clothes and grinning with satisfaction* (page 248). (Photo: David Cranston)

Above: 'It is impossible,' *John told a friend*, 'to express my sense of gratitude to God for his providential gift of The Hookses. The intoxicating Pembrokeshire air, the beauty of seascape and landscape, the stillness and seclusion, and the rich variety of bird life, together make a uniquely satisfying combination of blessings' (page 247).

Below: *In January and February 1999, John Yates accompanied John to China, Thailand, Taiwan and Hong Kong* (page 251).

Above: 'Birdwatching is an excellent recreation, for it takes you out into the wilderness with all the sights, sounds and smells of nature, and it is relaxing and absorbing to the mind. I don't think birdwatchers get nervous breakdowns!' (page 251).

Below: *With study assistant Corey Widmer, India 2002* (page 258).

Above: *To John's surprise, when the interpreter translated several of his phrases, the audience erupted into laughter. The English original words were not intended to be funny* (pages 261-2).

Below: *Billy Graham said,* 'I can't think of anyone who has been more effective in introducing so many people to a biblical world view' (page 264).

Above: 'When I enter the pulpit with the Bible in my hands and in my heart,' *John said*, 'my blood begins to flow and my eyes to sparkle for the sheer glory of having God's Word to expound' (page 267).

Below: *From my desk in the Langham Den where I wrote some of this book, I enjoyed a glorious view across the little stream next to which John had pitched his tent fifty-six years earlier, over a grassy slope to the sea with waves breaking on the shore in West Dale Bay* (page 274-8). (Photo: Roger Steer)

15. NEW MAN AT ALL SOULS

John now embarked on one of the greatest achievements of his life: his contributions to and editorship of the series he founded under the title *The Bible Speaks Today* (BST). This was originally conceived as a ten-year project, but in the event it took over thirty years to complete the New Testament. The series of expositions (John preferred this word to 'commentaries') was an important strand in the development in his thinking as influenced by Ted Schroder – the 'double listening' theme. John had three guiding principles in the long years that he worked on the series: first, be loyal to the text, second, be relevant to the modern world and third, be readable.

His first volume was published in 1968 under the title *The Message of Galatians*. Reviewing it, Michael Green made a witty comment which drew attention to a key characteristic of John's preaching and writing style. 'St Paul,' Michael wrote, 'might be pleasantly surprised to see how neatly he had subdivided his material when writing this Epistle.' It was a fault that John came to recognise in himself: members of his reading group remember him saying, 'We need to repent of our evangelical tidy mindedness.'

Finding other contributors to the series was a major task. John wrote a detailed memo to accompany his invitation to possible authors in which he made clear that he was looking first for accurate biblical exposition.

NEW MAN AT ALL SOULS

'My endeavour,' he said, quoting his hero Simeon, 'is to bring out of Scripture what is there, and not to thrust in what I think might be there.'

'The series,' John told potential authors of the commentaries, 'is deliberately entitled "The Bible Speaks Today". It is *today's message* we want our readers to hear and heed ... The application will sometimes be to the burning theological and moral issues of the day, and sometimes to our personal and social responsibilities as Christians ... For these reasons I am choosing as contributors an international team of men [sic] with "pastoral" and "preaching" rather than purely "academic" gifts.' He was looking for writers who could produce a readable style, 'a text which flows'.

Not everyone he asked to contribute accepted his invitation. And not all contributions were suitable when finally submitted. He rejected one writer's manuscript altogether and it never saw the light of day. He had to send several others back to the authors three or four times. But Michael Wilcock, who wrote the commentary on Revelation, remembered that John comments were 'almost always *suggestions* – "don't you think it might be better if ... ?"'

John based his commentary in the series on 2 Timothy, *Guard the Gospel*, on addresses he had given at Urbana 1967–8, and at Keswick the following year. In the same way his Keswick 1972 Bible readings from Matthew 5–7 helped to lay the foundation for his third book in the series, entitled *Christian Counter-Culture: the Message of the Sermon on the Mount*.

In May (1987) a letter arrived from America. It was signed by Ruth Graham Dienert.

Dear Dr Stott,

Perhaps you will remember me as a second grader the Christmas you spent with my parents, Ruth and Billy Graham. I remember you as a kind, warm stranger with a lovely accent! I even remember your thoughtful gift to me that Christmas – a funny little wooden goat, when you punched a button underneath him, he would collapse! As a matter of fact, I think it is still with me – tucked away with other childhood treasures!!

However, I have grown up and have children of my own!

And the reason for this letter is to tell you how much I have been blessed by *Christian Counter-Culture*. I used it for the basis of my study of the Sermon on the Mount this spring as I taught the women of my church and community.

Editors and staff at IVP in America all agreed that John was the most meticulous writer they had worked with. 'Almost all speakers accepted their tape transcriptions from the triennial missionary convention [Urbana] as ready for publication. Not John: he knew the differences between print and spoken communication.'

The *Church of England Newspaper* acclaimed John's study of the Sermon on the Mount as 'Paperback of the Year'. Richard Holloway, Bishop of Edinburgh, reviewing it for the *Church Times*, was in two minds. He described how on a train journey, 'there I was at the beginning of Lent on a high-speed retreat conducted by John Stott as I shot from Scotland to London, and he fairly rubbed my nose in my own moral and spiritual feebleness . . . Unlike a lot of contemporary writers on the Bible, John Stott's intention is to let the Bible speak to us, to confront us with the Sermon on the Mount in a fresh and personal way, without shirking critical issues. In this he has succeeded admirably . . . Reading the book was a salutary shock to me, because, like many people who like to be thought of as progressive and up-to-date, I'm a bit soft-centred when it comes to dealing with personal morality, though less so in the area of institutional morality. I need to be re-acquainted with the absolute standard of the holiness of Christ, in private as well as in public behaviour . . . ' Richard Holloway admitted, however, that he was 'somewhat repelled by the confident and often harsh tone of Dr Stott's frequent admonitions'.

Sir Timothy Hoare came from a family whose name remains a household word in banking circles. A member of the church at St Helen's Bishopsgate, Tim (as he was known to his friends) spent some days with John and a few friends at The Hookses in the spring of 1968.

'As soon as I arrived,' Tim recalled, 'before I had unpacked, I was led off to the cliffs to admire a raven's nest on the cliffs, with chicks on show. After lunch John would have his HHH (horizontal half-hour). Apart from local walks, we had a drive to St Anne's Head to see the fulmars. Another day we went to St David's where we visited the factory which had made the carpet for All Souls. I noted how slow our drive was through the town as John was always waving or stopping to chat to people.'

In the evening John gave the group a Bible study on what we may learn from birds (many years later he turned his love of this theme into his book *The Birds Our Teachers*). They discussed evolution and the date of Adam, the present state of Red Indians in Arizona and the Vietnam War. Tim noted that John would round the discussions off with a brilliant summary, leaving the rest speechless as he retired punctually to bed.

During Tim's stay, John spent time every morning writing in 'The Hermitage'. Nearby, Tim remembered, 'was the tool shed with meticulously ordered and labelled tools. There was a dovecote where he bred white fan-tailed pigeons. There were also beehives and goldfish in a pond.'

The Hermitage had been created in 1960 to provide separate self-contained accommodation for John. On a triangular patch of land, with walls on two sides and the third open to the sea, they built an enclosing wall, largely of glass, and added a roof. This served as John's study until 1990. Then, with an unexpected windfall for John from the sale of a magnificent Victorian bookcase which had belonged to Sir Arnold, they built a sitting room-cum-office with kitchenette and shower room, and a separate bedroom, creating an independent flat.

Beyond the Hermitage is the coastal path, the cliff – and then the ocean as far as the eye can see. Here, at his desk, binoculars beside him, John wrote his many books in longhand with standard abbreviations, for Frances Whitehead to read with practised ease, typing each manuscript either in London or in her adjoining office at The Hookses.

Back at All Souls, there were still some optimistic women who thought that eligible bachelor John, still in his forties, might succumb to their charms.

'One of these,' organist Clark Bedford remembered, 'attacked John after the evening service with her umbrella. She was upset about his lack of willingness openly to confess his love for her. So as he stood greeting all the parishioners one by one, she bolted in and began to hit him on the shins with her umbrella. Whack! Whack! Whack! The people standing in line to greet the Rector were shocked. The victim tried to remain calm, jumped around a little, and then a couple of people pulled the woman away. But after this and other annoying and sometimes hilarious (at least to some of us) experiences, he was always kind to the individual making the fracas.'

Another quite different memory left a deep and lasting impression on Clark. The incident happened on a Sunday evening after John had preached three times and had taken tea with some elderly parishioners. A long line of people stood waiting to shake hands with him.

After some time John saw a blind young man on the other side of the porch walking quietly to the exit. John left the line of people and walked over to talk with him. 'It would have been the easiest thing to have ignored him,' Clark told me. 'It had been a long day. I'm sure he was tired. But he cared about that man with the cane and took the effort to make him feel special that evening. What an example for me! Would I have done that? I'm not sure. But from time to time in the various situations of my life, I find myself asking, "What would John do? How would he handle this? What would he say?" I worked with him for six years, and I continually found him to be an example of what a consistent Christian should be. In addition, he was a delightful human being.'

As the 1960s drew to a close, John began to think and pray about the future direction of All Souls and the course his own life should take. On Saturday 20 September 1969 the PCC met in Buckinghamshire for a day conference, with a memorandum from the Rector as their main agenda item. John's memo set out his vision for restructuring the staff, the key proposal being the appointment of a 'vicar' as chief pastor of the congregation, with both administrative and pastoral leadership. The PCC and standing committee continued to refine the proposals over coming weeks.

But who should be the vicar? Over breakfast at the coffee shop of the Strand Palace hotel, John discussed this with his friend Dick Lucas, Rector of St Helen's, Bishopsgate, from 1961 to 1998.

'The man you want is Michael Baughen,' said Dick.

'I'd never thought of flying so high,' replied John, 'and getting somebody who is already a well-known evangelical leader.'

In 1964 Michael Baughen had moved north to be Vicar of Holy Trinity, Platt, just south of the heart of Manchester, where he had successfully completed a big building project. John invited him to call to see him when he was next in London. When Michael was in the capital conducting rehearsals for the launch of the songbook *Youth Praise 2*, he called early at 12 Weymouth Street and joined John in his study. After brief courtesies of welcome, John looked straight at Michael.

'I want you to take over from me at All Souls!' he said.

John's words came without any warning. Michael couldn't believe his ears or conceive that such a thing was realistic. After the session with John, which lasted longer than Michael had expected, Frances Whitehead offered to drive him through London to Kensington for the rehearsal. En route, Frances enthused, encouraged, and did everything in her considerable powers to persuade him to accept.

A few weeks later John travelled to Crewe with Ted Schroder for a further meeting with Michael. They met in the station buffet and worked hard in trying to persuade him to come, but received an ambivalent response.

'The signal,' Michael said to John, 'is at yellow. Proceed only to the next signal!'

Michael doubted that John would be willing to share the leadership. However, after Michael came to London for the launch of *Youth Praise 2* at the Royal Albert Hall, John sent him a telegram:

LET THE SIGNALS TURN TO GREEN!

But there were still many questions in Michael's mind. Could it work? Would it fail? When All Souls PCC approached the Bishop of London, Robert Stopford, the bishop agreed with Michael that the plan wouldn't work if John retained leadership of the church, with people appealing to him to overrule Michael if they disagreed with his leadership. So Stopford worked out a scheme to hand over all leadership of the church to Michael, with John just retaining the power to sign any legal papers as Rector.

After a lot of heart-searching, Michael and his wife decided they were prepared to put the signals to two yellows and agreed to proceed. With his churchwardens, John visited the Crown Appointments Secretary at 10 Downing Street.

'Since the Crown must retain its sovereign rights,' Sir John Hewitt told John, 'no promise can be made that Michael Baughen would be appointed Rector should the time come for you to resign. However perhaps I may say that, unless there are cogent reasons, I shall not feel obliged to look elsewhere.'

In May 1970 John wrote to everyone on the All Souls congregational register explaining the reasons for restructuring the church's leadership. 'I am very happy to announce,' he wrote, 'that the Rev. Michael Baughen has accepted this new post. Indeed we are extremely fortunate that he is coming to be vicar, for God has greatly gifted him and blessed his ministry. His wife Myrtle is fully committed as his partner (she is a teacher with a special interest in immigrant children), and they have three children – Rachel (11), Philip (7) and Andrew (6).'

John explained to his congregation that, although he would now have more time to read, think, write and travel, he looked forward to being part of the life of the parish and the staff team during some months of each year. John and Michael agreed that John wouldn't attend PCC meetings, and John was quite clear that authority in the church would rest with Michael.

'I am convinced,' Michael told me, 'that the unusual arrangement would not have worked without John's humility, his utter refusal to listen to any complaints and his total support of me.'

The Baughens would live in the Rectory, and John would eventually occupy a new flat to be built over the garage at the back. On an informal visit before the family moved in, Michael walked into the kitchen at Weymouth Street and met the cook. 'You're Margaret and I'm Michael,' he said. And he addressed Anne, the cleaner, in the same way.

The family moved into the Rectory at the end of November 1970, ready for Michael's formal licensing as vicar on 19 December. Big changes in the worship were to come. Noël Tredinnick replaced Clark Bedford who moved to Cardiff and took a position with the Welsh Opera. New music, including *Youth Praise* and *Psalm Praise*, came into use and the orchestra arrived on the scene. All Souls would never be quite the same again.

16. WHERE THE BATTLE FOR HOLINESS IS WON

On Christmas Day 1970, John joined Joy and Lily's unmarried sister 'Auntie Babe' at the Bullens farm near Guildford, and on the following afternoon Joy drove him to the airport. A foreign visit would allow Michael Baughen to establish his position at All Souls. John flew to the Urbana Conference in Illinois (his third visit), giving Bible readings on John 13–17, Jesus' Upper Room discourse, to students from all across America and some from Canada. From Urbana, John's next stop was Trinity Evangelical Divinity School, Deerfield, which conferred an honorary DD on him.

From Deerfield John flew to California, using his three hours between planes at Los Angeles to glimpse Hollywood, before settling down for the long flight to Sydney where he was booked to speak at three conferences.

At Sydney, he went from the airport to spend the night as the guest of Archbishop Marcus Loane and his wife Patricia at Bishopscourt. The following morning they drove west into the Blue Mountains where the Loanes had rented a house for the week. When they arrived, Marcus turned to Patricia.

'Darling, I hope you've got the keys.'

'No, darling,' she replied, 'I gave them to you during breakfast!'

They were eighty miles from Sydney, at a locked house, with the keys still on the breakfast table at Bishopscourt.

'Well, there's nothing else for it,' Marcus said to his wife. 'I'll drive straight back to Sydney, while you and John have a picnic lunch.'

'Hold on a minute,' said John. 'Don't you realise you're in the presence of an experienced British burglar? Allow me to break in!'

The Loanes were not at all keen on this idea. Archbishops didn't normally engage in forcible entry. However, John had spotted a bedroom window with a crack across its top left corner. With evident reluctance, Marcus allowed him to break the corner glass and remove it. The damage done, the Archbishop then reached through to open the window and clambered into the house.

Marcus Loane tended to be conservative in his ideas and outlook. At breakfast back at Bishopscourt, John teased him: 'You should allow yourself to be dragged into the seventies!'

'Into the sixties, you mean!' observed the Loanes' daughter, who had come to breakfast barefoot that morning, to her father's disapproval.

'And another thing,' said John, 'why do you insist on sticking to the Authorised Version of the Bible and the 1662 Book of Common Prayer?'

'Well,' replied Marcus, 'your sideburns are a throwback to the nineteenth century!'

After addressing a conference in Canberra, and enjoying a brief bird-watching break, John embarked on a round of speaking engagements in Sydney and Adelaide and an afternoon watching the test match in the Adelaide Oval. Here John's attention was occasionally distracted by 'dapper little Australian "willie wagtails" which were disporting themselves on the field, without showing any respect for the test cricket, and by the silver gulls, one of which was knocked unconscious by a fast ball and had to be carried off the field (where it was revived by a vet)!'

John spoke at more meetings in Hong Kong, Singapore and South India before returning to London after an absence of two months.

Soon after the publication of the 1971 revised edition of *Basic Christianity*, John received this letter from Bexhill-on-Sea:

22.5.71

Dear John,

Thank you for writing *Basic Christianity*. It led me to make a new commitment of my life to Christ. I am old now – nearly 78 – but not too old to make a new beginning.

I rejoice in all the grand work you are doing.

Yours sincerely,

LESLIE WEATHERHEAD

Leslie Weatherhead was a prolific writer and President of the Methodist Conference in 1953. His most influential years were as minister of the (Congregational) City Temple church in London when he was a national figure.

Books changed lives. But throughout his travels in the 50s and 60s, John had become increasingly aware of the serious shortage of good Christian books in the developing world. After a visit to South Africa, he wrote, 'I remember a youth worker in Soweto whose eyes, when I presented him with a book, filled with tears. He said it was the first Christian book he ever possessed apart from the Bible.'

Since 1964, John had been involved – through the Evangelical Fellowship in the Anglican Communion (EFAC) – in providing academic support for church leaders from the developing world to come to England for study. By the early 1970s his own publications were earning substantial royalty income which he said he didn't need for himself. He visited a solicitor and told him that he was eager to find a way to use this income to provide books for pastors, teachers, students and seminary libraries in the developing world. So in April 1971, John and a small group of his friends founded the Evangelical Literature Trust (ELT).

Over the years, and later as part of the work of Langham Partnership International, the trust made grants to pastors, professors, theological students, post-graduate scholars and writers, college and seminary libraries, and even to small publishing houses, enabling them to launch Christian literature in translation in local languages. John had grown convinced that the college or seminary is the key institution in the church, since, as he put it, 'all the church's future clergy pass through the seminaries, and it is there that they are either made or marred, either equipped for ministry or ruined through loss of faith and vision'.

From January 1974, a programme enabled future scholars to obtain their doctorates at first in the West, in order to fulfil their role as leaders in national colleges and universities. By 1977 the trust, with help from its sister organisation the Langham Foundation in America (later to be renamed John Stott Ministries) had agreed to take over major responsibility for their funding and they became known as 'Langham Scholars' on both sides of the Atlantic. Virtually every Langham scholar has returned to work in his or her home country on graduation. Later, as the programme developed, some scholars attended academic institutions in the developing world.

By 1992 John had assigned from 95 to 98 per cent of his royalty income to the Evangelical Literature Trust, which now, as Langham Literature, funds the various literature projects of the Langham Partnership International in the developing world. He hasn't kept exact figures of his royalty earnings from his many books, but it is estimated that they totalled well over half a million pounds by 1996 and are very substantially more today.

Since the Baughen family arrived in the Weymouth Street Rectory, John had been working during the day in its big basement room while commuting nightly to north London to stay with friends. However, work had been going on to convert an old single-room flat above the Rectory garage into self-contained accommodation for him. This had access only from Bridford Mews, and was in a poor state.

Early in 1972, his new home was finally ready, with an upstairs living room and study cantilevered over the Mews to give extra space, and including a kitchenette under the eaves. A twisting staircase led down to a bedroom and bathroom, with access through to the ground floor of the Rectory and Frances Whitehead's office. John gave one wall of his room to books, with rows of card index drawers on the floor beneath. On the other walls he hung prints of All Souls and of Trinity College, Cambridge, and on the stairs a large engraving of Charles Simeon with his famous umbrella, striding out in knee breeches, gaiters and stock, his gown flowing out behind him. By the dining table he gave pride of place to a view of The Hookses, painted by Geoffrey Rawlins, a former curate.

Since before Michael Baughen's arrival, John had been secretly discussing with an inner circle the possibilities for the future of All Souls Church itself, involving building work on an infinitely bigger scale than at the Rectory. The options for major improvements that might be open to them even included starting afresh on a new site in the area. They tried to keep the discussions confidential since it had been quite enough for the congregation to hear that they were losing John as their chief pastor, without rumours that they might also lose their church.

John made a rare faux pas, however, during his lecture tour of Australia. Speaking to the local press at the Archbishop's house in Perth, he was lulled into a false sense of security by the remoteness of the setting. An innocent-looking young woman journalist drew him into answering questions about relating ancient buildings to the modern world.

'I wish someone would bomb the church so that we could rebuild it to meet contemporary needs,' he said.

When he prepared to fly on from Perth, John was amazed on arrival at the airport to find the tarmac crowded with journalists eager to hear more about his drastic plans. Back in England, members of All Souls who read the *Daily Telegraph* choked over their cornflakes when they came across a story under the headline, 'Rector says "bomb the church".' According to the *Telegraph*, 'Mr Stott said: "There would be a terrible public outcry if the building went, but the church cannot be hamstrung for every old building. I would like to sell the English cathedrals to the National Trust, or keep the structures and radically change the insides. The Church should not be the custodian of antiquities.'

Every cloud has a silver lining and, after the rumpus following John's gaffe died down, everyone at All Souls was now free to discuss openly the future of the church.

At Michael Baughen's first annual church meeting in March 1971, a lady walked on to the platform and hit him over the head with an umbrella.

'Over my dead body will you do anything to this church!' she said.

However, after many months of consideration, the options were whittled down to one: raise the floor of the church and create a hall beneath it. In April 1972 architect Robert Potter watched as a trial excavation revealed that John Nash had joined up the columns inside the church by huge thick inverted arches underneath which formed a frame to hold up the building. Nash had then filled the foundation area with earth because of the high water table in London at the time. The engineering challenge for the new building was huge!

Over the next few years, while the church again made its home at St Peter's, Vere Street, some 6,000 tons of earth were removed, the inverted arches exposed as a feature of the refurbished church, and the floor raised to provide space for all the new facilities.

In 1972, John gave the Presidential address at the annual conference of the Inter-Varsity Fellowship at Swanwick on the place of the mind in the Christian life. 'Nobody wants a cold, joyless, intellectual Christianity,' he said. 'But does that mean we should avoid "intellectualism" at all costs? Is it experience, rather than doctrine, that really matters? Many students close their minds with their textbooks, satisfied that the intellect should play little, if any, part in the Christian life. How far are they right? For the Christian, enlightened by the Spirit, just what is the place of the mind?'

He made no secret of the fact that partly in his sights were 'Pentecostal Christians, many of whom make experience the major criterion of truth'. His argument was that the great doctrines of creation, revelation, redemption and judgment all imply that we have an inescapable duty both to think and act upon what we think and know. We are created to think. The fact that humanity's mind is fallen is no excuse to retreat from thought into emotion, for the emotional side of our nature is equally fallen. In spite of the fallenness of our minds, commands to think, to use the mind, are still addressed to us as human beings. God invited rebellious Israel, '"Come now, let us reason together," says the Lord' (Isaiah 1:18).

John insisted that the fact that God is a self-revealing God and has revealed himself to humanity indicates the importance of our minds. Redemption carries with it the renewal of the divine image in us, which was distorted by the fall. This includes the mind. Paul described converts from paganism as having 'put on the new self, which is being renewed in knowledge in the image of its Creator' (Colossians 3:10) and as being 'made new in the attitude of your minds' (Ephesians 4:23).

What is faith? John asked. It is neither credulity nor optimism but reasoning trust. Faith and thought go together, and believing is impossible without thinking.

He argued that the battle for holiness is nearly always won in the mind. It is by the renewal of our mind that our character and behaviour are transformed (Romans 12:2). 'Whatever is true, whatever is noble, whatever is right, whatever is pure, whatever is lovely, whatever is admirable – if anything is excellent or praiseworthy – think about such things' (Philippians 4:8). We certainly shouldn't think of the mind as being against the things of the Spirit: 'Those who live according to the sinful nature have their minds set on what that nature desires; but those who live in accordance with the Spirit have their minds set on what the Spirit desires. The mind of sinful man is death, but the mind controlled by the Spirit is life and peace' (Romans 8:5–6).

In order to combat the risk of the use of the mind resulting in a barren intellectualism, he concluded his talk with a powerful section showing how knowledge should lead to worship, faith, holiness and love. The text of the lecture was published by IVP as an influential booklet, *Your Mind Matters*.

In Autumn 1972, John spent a term as a guest member of the Faculty at Trinity Evangelical Divinity School in Deerfield, Illinois. His friend David Wells, a member of the Faculty, welcomed him at the airport, drove him to the college and took him to his apartment in a small block for married students on the edge of the twenty-five acre campus, between playing fields and the lake.

His duties were to give a course of lectures and seminars in biblical preaching, and two or three other courses in books of the New Testament. He gave a series of lectures on the Sermon on the Mount to a packed hall, with latecomers standing at the back. He also began to invite some of his students, a dozen at a time, to coffee and cookies in his apartment.

The students soon reciprocated and invited him back to meals in their own rooms.

During the term he visited the ten colleges of a recently formed coalition, the Christian College Consortium, from Westmont in California to Gordon in Massachusetts. Several times he delivered his lecture 'Your Mind Matters', followed by classes, question-and-answer sessions, or meetings with faculty or students. He also managed to take Mondays off for bird-watching.

Life on campus, interspersed with travels on behalf of the Consortium, and long weekends away for IVCF or the Fellowship of Witness, continued at a demanding pace. John began to suffer from blinding headaches – so much so that there was even talk of a brain tumour. Eventually doctors traced the cause to the dry heat of the apartment, and with improved ventilation the scare was over.

John returned to his normal robust state of health, ready to face the next major challenge of his life.

17. GIANT AT LAUSANNE

The Lausanne Congress grew out of an initiative by Billy Graham way back in 1958 when he had called together a small group including John, which met in Montreux to discuss world evangelisation. From this had come the world Congress in Berlin which John had attended in 1966. Berlin led to regional congresses financed by the Billy Graham Evangelistic Association.

By January 1970, Billy had seen the need for a second world Congress to discuss and carry forward all the implications of Christ's great commission to his disciples. The planning was entrusted to an international committee drawn from sixteen nations, under the executive chairmanship of Australian Jack Dain, Anglican Bishop of Sydney, with Billy as honorary chairman.

With the official title, 'The International Congress on World Evangelisation', the Congress opened on 16 July 1974 with some 2,500 members from 150 countries and 1,300 other participants – observers, consultants or guests, and several hundred journalists. They met in Lausanne, Switzerland, on the northern shore of Lake Geneva where the Palais de Beaulieu conference centre had an auditorium with 4,000 seats, facilities for simultaneous translation, and space for workshops and seminars. *Time* magazine described it as 'possibly the widest ranging meeting of Christians ever held'.

Half the speakers and participants were from the developing world. The aim was nothing less than to develop strategies for the evangelisation of the world. The Congress slogan emblazoned above the platform read, in the six official languages, 'Let the earth hear his voice'.

Reporting for the British magazine *Crusade*, John Capon wrote that 'the order of service is very reminiscent of a Billy Graham crusade with Tedd Smith and Don Hustad providing the familiar piano and organ accompaniment, and the energetic, ever-smiling Cliff Barrows as master of ceremonies introducing a rather traditional range of musical talent'.

The planning committee asked John to give the opening keynote address on 'the nature of biblical evangelism' and to provide a biblical definition of the five words: 'mission', 'evangelism', 'dialogue', 'salvation', and 'conversion'.

John's head was projected on to a vast screen behind him and his words simultaneously translated into five other languages. One delegate remembered how 'peering over his fashionable half-moon glasses [John] consistently managed to make both the profound simple and the simple profound'. He began his talk by calling for 'a note of evangelical repentance' and a willingness to listen to some of the critics of evangelicalism.

'I believe some ecumenical thinking is mistaken,' he said. 'But then, frankly, I believe some of our evangelical formulations are mistaken also. We have some important lessons to learn from our ecumenical critics. Some of their rejection of our position is not a disapproval of biblical truth, but rather our evangelical caricatures of it.'

The balance between evangelism and social action was an issue which might have polarised the Congress into two distinct factions. Some older Western delegates retained a deep suspicion that where Christian social (let alone political) action prevailed, meaningful evangelism was inevitably threatened. It wasn't easy for them to listen to radical voices from developing world speakers highly critical of a Western evangelicalism.

Against this background, here was John from the developed world pleading for a recognition that Christ's commission to 'go and make disciples' doesn't stand alone, and that as Christians we are called to serve. In the servant role, he told the Congress, we find the right synthesis of evangelism and social action. The Great Commission (go and make disciples) neither explains, nor exhausts, let alone supersedes the Great Commandment (love your neighbour). 'If we truly love our neighbour we shall without doubt tell him the Good News of Jesus. But equally if we truly love our neighbour we shall not stop there . . . Love . . . expresses itself in service wherever it sees need.'

One enduring fruit of the Congress was the Covenant to which it gave its name. When the main addresses and papers had become available, some months before the Congress began, the organisers had asked John to produce from them a draft which might be submitted to the Congress. He worked through all these papers in order to try to extract from them their major thrust. And then, during the Congress itself, he worked on the draft further in the light of the speeches that were actually given.

The Congress organisers established a small drafting committee with John as chairman, Hudson Armerding (President of Wheaton College) and Samuel Escobar from Peru, assisted by Leighton Ford and Jim Douglas. Day by day during the Congress the committee continued to refine the draft Covenant, balancing as best they could the conflicting viewpoints and emphases as they emerged.

The committee submitted its third complete draft to the whole assembly, and invited comments. Sustained by two 'ministering angels' who kept him supplied with Swiss chocolate and grapes, John worked through two whole nights to revise the draft in the light of 3,000 replies.

Given the unwieldy nature of such a large gathering, the drafting of the Covenant required all John's skills. Gordon Landreth, secretary of the British Evangelical Alliance and one of the delegates, said that 'what amazed us at the time was the way this document had managed to encompass so many diverse concerns and to tread a middle course through so many theological and ecclesiastical minefields. John's skills were undoubtedly reflected in this. We in the British party at Lausanne also felt he was a good counter to American simplistic and brash formulations of theology and strategy.'

Leighton Ford described the final form of the Lausanne Covenant as 'one of this century's exemplary statements on Christian beliefs, concerns and commitment'. Several of the paragraphs represented long hours of intense agonising over precise words and meanings which have continued to attract attention over the ensuing years.

The last full day of the Congress included a prolonged session in which the Lausanne Covenant was presented to the participants. As chairman of the drafting committee, John introduced and explained the Covenant. John Capon saw this performance as clearly establishing him as the key figure in contemporary world evangelicalism. 'He displayed complete mastery of the complex document in his hand (not surprisingly in view of the fact that he was up all night revising it) and expounded it in a way which brought to life the passion beneath the cold print.'

The Lausanne Covenant is still widely regarded as one of the most significant documents in modern church history. It is a covenant with God himself, as well as a covenant with other Christians, and is available now in The Didasko Files series under the title *For the Lord we Love*, which includes a commentary and study questions written by John.

Tom Houston, who was later to become International Director of the Lausanne Movement, described John at Lausanne as 'the giant in the land'. A delegate from the developing world was sure that 'all of us who attended this conference realised that he carried the entire spiritual burden of the conference on his shoulders'.

At the closing Communion Service Bishop Jack Dain and Billy Graham, the two Chairmen, personally signed the Covenant, while 2,000 of the 2,400 participants signed cards to indicate their personal commitment to it. For some of the 400 who declined to sign it at the time, their misgivings would centre on paragraph 9, which included perhaps the most anxiously-debated clause in the Covenant: 'Those of us who live in affluent circumstances accept our duty to develop a simple lifestyle in order to contribute more generously to both relief and evangelism.' The names of the signatories were sealed away and never made public.

However, it is no secret that Billy Graham's wife, Ruth, was one of those who chose not to sign, primarily because John insisted on inserting the statement about a simple lifestyle. While Ruth admired John, she found his espousal of a simple lifestyle too confining.

'If it said "simpler",' she explained to John, 'I would sign it. But what is "simple"? You live in two rooms. I have a bigger home. You have no children. I have five. You say your life is simple and mine isn't.'

John refused to delete the offending sentence. He had no doubt that it was wrong to eat too much, and to waste food, especially when so many were starving. As for possessions, one way to decide whether we *need* something was to consider whether we *use* it, for we evidently don't need what we don't use. It would, he thought, be a start if all of us went through our belongings annually, in order to give away what we did not use.

Lausanne signalled a public shift in mainline evangelical understanding of the relationship between evangelism and social concern. In the commentary on the Covenant which John later wrote during one month at The Hookses, he pointed out that in the past evangelical Christians had an outstanding record of social action. In the twentieth century, however, partly because of a reaction against the 'social gospel', evangelicals had tended to divorce evangelism from social concern, and to concentrate almost exclusively on the former. And so the Covenant expressed the Congress's sorrow for past neglect of Christian social responsibility and naive polarisation, in having sometimes regarded evangelism and social concern as mutually exclusive.

Since Christian duty arose from Christian doctrine, the Covenant outlined the four main doctrines out of which Christian social duty springs: the doctrines of God, humanity, salvation and the kingdom. God is not just interested in the church but in the world. He created all men and women, and all will have to give an account to him on the day of judgment. Therefore 'we who claim to be God's people should share the breadth of God's concerns'.

Because of John's personal insistence at Lausanne that social action was a part of evangelism, he almost certainly lost influence among some sections of evangelicalism in North America, and gained in respect and stature in the developing world. But many young Americans were also transformed in their thinking. Billy Graham's son Franklin was twenty-two, and attended Lausanne to assist with the travel arrangements. Until then he had shown little sign of embracing whole-heartedly his parents' faith and Christian commitment. But mingling at Lausanne with developing-world Christians, and recognising the physical hardships many of them suffered, touched his heart. A few weeks later in a Jerusalem hotel room, he threw a packet of cigarettes into a rubbish bin and knelt by his bed.

'Dear Father,' he prayed, 'I want you to be Lord of my life. I am willing to give up any area that is not pleasing to you.'

Franklin's father thought that 'Lausanne might one day be seen to stand with the three or four decisive moments when church history has changed direction'.

The Congress rejected the concept of creating a massive new structure for world evangelicalism. Instead it set up a Continuation Committee of which John was to be a member until 1981.

The first meeting of the Lausanne Continuation Committee was in Mexico City in January 1975. John flew in from India. Billy Graham opened the proceedings after dinner on the first evening, tracing progress historically from Montreux in 1960 through the Berlin Congress of 1966 to Lausanne in 1974. Then he came to the work of the Continuation Committee and described two concepts of Lausanne's work which had emerged from the many letters he'd received from participants – 'narrow' and 'broad'.

'The narrow view,' said Billy, 'is that our paramount task is evangelism. Now, there is no possibility of evangelicals uniting on any other subject. To attempt to do everything would be a great tragedy. We must leave other things to other bodies like the World Evangelical Fellowship and instead ourselves be characterised by a "this one thing I do" commitment. The broader concept is that we should get involved in everything God wants done.'

Having described these two approaches, Billy made it clear that he favoured the first. 'If we accept the second,' he said, 'we shall get off the mandate given us at Lausanne. So we mustn't get bogged down in other peripheral matters.'

Billy's words troubled John. He knew that many younger developing world leaders in the Lausanne Movement shared his convictions about evangelism as more than proclamation, yet were unwilling to oppose Billy.

John stayed up for several hours that first night at Mexico City preparing a rebuttal.

The following morning he was due to give a Bible exposition and turned once again to Jesus' prayer for his church in John 17, a prayer for its mission, truth, holiness and unity. 'Do Christ's followers have any liberty to cherish a narrower concern than this?' he asked.

In the open session that followed, the first speaker firmly endorsed the 'narrower' view of the Continuation Committee's role as Billy had described it the evening before. When he sat down, John caught the eye of chairman, Jack Dain. He didn't enjoy publicly disagreeing with Billy Graham.

'I want to argue,' he said, 'for the broader view. First, in Scripture Christ calls us to be salt as well as light. Second, history tells us that the church has a constant tendency to unbalanced preoccupations. Third, the Lausanne Covenant itself deals with a whole number of topics besides evangelism understood in its traditional sense. Bear in mind the expectation of evangelicals throughout the world. Many of them are concerned not just for the renewal of the church but for the reform of their national life by the Christian penetration of non-Christian society. If we go back now, and concentrate exclusively on evangelism, it will not be an implementation of the Covenant but a betrayal of it.'

John sat down and, as he put it later, 'the fat was in the fire'. Some delegates were shocked that he had publicly disagreed with Billy Graham. Some were in tears. Standing in a lift, Ramez Atallah of the Bible Society of Egypt heard two of Billy's assistants accuse John of challenging Billy Graham for the worldwide evangelical leadership.

The debate raged for the rest of the morning. Two or three members attempted to draft some broad guidelines. John felt their form of words to be unacceptable.

'I feel so deeply concerned that we are about to betray Lausanne's vision, covenant and spirit,' he said, addressing the committee again, 'that I am afraid I will have to resign if the committee members decide to go the way they are indicating.'

To John's surprise, Jack Dain from the chair immediately supported him.

'I'm afraid that I too would resign,' said Jack, 'since I couldn't possibly return to Australia with the narrower concept. Australian participants are already implementing the broader vision.'

This may have been a mistake. The American committee members interpreted it as a threat, an illicit form of blackmail – the behaviour of obstinate children who wouldn't cooperate if they didn't get their own way. As proponents of divergent understandings of, and approaches to, evangelism, John Stott and Peter Wagner were put in a room on their own. 'Don't come out until you have a definition of evangelism you can agree on,' they were told.

Eventually they agreed a form of words which began with the general wider mission of the church, and went on to affirm the primacy of evangelism within it. But more troubles followed for John.

The Americans suggested that Billy Graham should be, in name at least, the 'Supreme President' of the Lausanne organisation. John was afraid that the developing world delegates would be too polite and too loyal to Billy to voice their real feelings (even though Billy wasn't present). So he rose again to speak.

'I hope none of you is in any doubt,' John said, 'about my personal affection and admiration for Billy Graham. I have little doubt that he will go down in history as one of the greatest Christian leaders of this century. However I want to urge you that he should be one of several equal co-presidents. He himself has consistently said that he doesn't wish any overall leadership position in the post-Lausanne organisation. To be "Supreme President" would perpetuate the kind of paternalism he wants to avoid, and would be misunderstood in the developing world.'

Several delegates supported this proposal and the committee found itself again divided. John decided that he must tell Billy to his face what he had said in the committee. And so he went by appointment to Billy's room at 8.15 the following morning. He explained why he thought the idea of his honorary leadership was not on.

'I fully agree with you, John!' said Billy. 'In fact I'm glad you have come to see me because I couldn't sleep much last night. I spent a lot of time in prayer. I shouldn't have given in to the American group's pressure without more thought. I feel the Lord was telling me in the night that I should be neither head of the organisation nor even a "minister-at-large". Indeed, if I had accepted the leadership the previous evening I would have resigned it this morning!'

By this time, Billy and John were late for the committee meeting. When they arrived the atmosphere was tense. After reading two passages of Scripture to the committee, Billy frankly admitted his mistake in yielding to pressure, and declared his unwillingness to accept a leadership role beyond being honorary chairman of the Consultative Council (with which everybody was in agreement). He spoke warmly of John, and his personal friendship and loyalty.

The wounds began to heal. John was put on the drafting committee to prepare a statement summarising progress, and this was accepted with a few minor amendments.

Reflecting on his stay in Mexico City for the first meeting of the Continuation Committee, John felt that the Americans had tended to hold the floor too much, while developing world representatives were too reticent. And three days had been too short to get to know one another and develop mutual respect and understanding. But he was critical of his own performance: 'I think I was too quick on the draw. Although I do not regret anything I said, or even the way I said it, for I think I kept my cool and remained courteous, yet I was too quick to cast myself in the role of defending Lausanne and its covenant and of acting as protagonist for the Third World. I much regret this now, and wish I could learn to listen longer before speaking!'

The Lausanne Continuation Committee met again in September 1976 in Atlanta where four working groups were established, all of which are still active. John was appointed chairman of one, the Lausanne Theology and Education Group, later renamed the Theology Working Group, which organised a series of consultations which took John to Pasadena in 1977, to Bermuda in 1978, and to Colorado Springs in 1979.

18. UNCLE JOHN

In 1974 Jim Packer addressed the Senior Evangelical Anglican Conference (SEAC) on developments in the seven years since the Keele Congress. Towards the end of his talk, he turned to the relationship between traditional evangelicals and charismatics.

'I want to plead,' Jim urged, 'for every effort to be made to establish better relations between evangelicals and the charismatics within their ranks. No one should hesitate to say that God is in this thing.'

Replying to what Jim had said at the SEAC conference, John made his own position clear.

'Now I could not personally declare "God is in this thing" without qualification, for I would want to qualify this statement in a number of ways. Nevertheless, I confess that I have tended to be too negative towards this movement, and too reluctant to recognise and welcome whatever within it has seemed to be a work of God.

'I would also like to make a public apology to Michael Harper that I have allowed our friendship to become tarnished over the years, and that I have been slow to meet him and to talk with him.'

Since the Islington Conference in 1964, and the publication of John's booklet, *The Baptism and Fullness of the Holy Spirit*, John had received letters from many parts of the world which said something like: 'We hear that you have changed your mind, that you now have been baptised with the Spirit, that you speak in tongues, that you have asked IVP to withdraw the book, and they have refused to do so.' And so, in 1975, in a revised edition of the booklet he wrote: 'This is not so. The revised edition gives me the chance to correct this false rumour.' However, he did practically rewrite the book, since he felt that he had been less than generous in his evaluation of the movement. He wanted to put on record that he had no doubt that God had blessed the Charismatic Movement to both individuals and local churches.

Charismatics who disagreed with the line John took in his booklet saw it as a controversial statement, designed to be a check on elements and manifestations of the Charismatic Movement of renewal. But John maintained that his concern had simply been to discover and interpret what Scripture said. He had no polemical intent or desire to hurt or embarrass anybody. 'My objective in this is that all of us may grasp more clearly both the greatness of our inheritance in Christ, in order to enter into it more fully, and also the greatness of our responsibility to manifest all the fruit of the Spirit in our lives and to exercise those gifts of the Spirit which in his gracious sovereignty he has bestowed upon us.'

By 1975 Michael Baughen was firmly in the saddle at All Souls and could reasonably expect to be Rector, not only in practice but in law and name as well. Therefore in May, John sent in his resignation to the Prime Minister's Appointments Secretary who at once consulted the churchwardens about the future. Less than a month later John told the congregation at All Souls that the Queen had approved the appointment of Michael Baughen to succeed him as Rector, and that Michael had accepted the appointment.

Michael and the PCC invited John to remain in the fellowship of All Souls with the title 'Rector Emeritus'. In lieu of a personal gift, John asked that any who wished should make a contribution to the refurbished All Souls now under construction. The PCC invited donors to send a personal greeting for inclusion in a presentation album to be given to John as he moved to becoming Rector Emeritus. In the event, gifts were sufficient to provide a new pulpit in anodised aluminium and a matching communion table.

From all over the world grateful friends and admirers sent John messages. From New Zealand a seven-year-old wrote, 'Thank you for baptising me, Uncle John'. Another mentioned *Basic Christianity* 'which led to my conversion'. One card told how the writer 'was converted following your Keswick relay talks four years ago'. Another wrote simply, 'Thank you for showing me the way to Christ'.

John's sister Joy sent a card with 'most loving wishes for your next emeritic, exergetic, energetic and happy 25 years'. Colin Peterson wrote from 10 Downing Street on behalf of the Prime Minister 'to express his gratitude to you for your exceptional service to this Crown living over many years, first as a curate and then as its distinguished Rector'.

In the flat at the back of the Rectory, Frances Whitehead plucked up courage. For over twenty years she had called John either 'Rector' or 'Mr Stott' but never John.

'I refuse to call you Rector Emeritus,' she said.

And so, at last, it became John. A new era was certainly beginning.

In November 1975 John attended the World Council of Churches' fifth assembly as an adviser, as he had done seven years earlier at Uppsala. Each adviser was allocated to a work group of a dozen or so delegates and expected to contribute at the invitation of the chairman. John arrived late at his workgroup after the introductions had taken place and, since most members were not wearing their name tags, he had no idea who they were. The chairman spoke with a slight German accent and was obviously a theologian. After ten minutes John found himself arguing with him vigorously, especially on the relation between evangelism and social action and on the impossibility of talking about 'evangelising structures'.

At the end of the session, a member of the work group turned to John.

'Do you know who the chairman of our group is?' he asked.

'No,' John replied, 'I've no idea.'

'Well,' John was informed, 'it's Professor Jürgen Moltmann of Tübingen!'

Moltmann was one of the best-known living German theologians. When John returned for the next session, he approached the chairman diplomatically.

'If I had known who our distinguished chairman was,' he said to Moltmann, 'I would have kept my mouth shut!'

Moltmann's reply is not on record.

Later Desmond Tutu, newly elected as Johannesburg's first black Dean, began to speak. Amongst other things he said that the Apostle Paul 'was confused' and 'a prisoner of his own culture' who 'sometimes didn't know what he was talking about'.

John's newly found diplomacy deserted him. 'If I had to choose between the blessed apostle Paul and the Dean of Johannesburg,' he said, 'I would have no difficulty in deciding who to follow!'

Desmond Tutu didn't seem to mind John's outburst, and the two men became good friends. John was an ardent supporter of Tutu's struggle against apartheid.

As well as his contribution to the work group, John was allowed ten minutes to speak to the full assembly. In his address, John didn't beat about the bush. He said that he believed the WCC needed to recover the doctrine of humanity's lostness (over against the popular universalism of the day), confidence in the truth, relevance and power of the biblical gospel (without which evangelism is impossible), the uniqueness of Jesus Christ (over against all syncretism), the urgency of evangelism (alongside the urgent demands of social justice), and a personal experience of Jesus Christ (without which we cannot introduce others to him).

When John returned to his seat after speaking from the platform, Dr Krister Stendahl, Swedish theologian from Harvard, leaned over to offer his reaction.

'I didn't agree with one word you said!' he announced.

Canon David Paton, however, like John a Chaplain to the Queen, seemed to appreciate John's 'balanced approach in difficult circumstances'. But in his diary John recorded that 'at least one African brother came running up to me afterwards, almost livid with rage that I had dared to criticise the WCC in the way that I had done'.

The relief and development charity Tearfund, the vision of George Hoffman, sprang from very small beginnings at the Evangelical Alliance during World Refugee Year in 1959–60. John was an early supporter, and in 1975 he wrote an influential booklet to accompany the soundstrip, *Walk in His Shoes*. Tearfund believes the booklet provided for many staff and supporters a life-changing moment of understanding.

The booklet reflects the Lausanne approach. John challenged all those who were alert to Jesus' commission to evangelise but had somehow never heard his call to care for the poor, the sick, the hungry and deprived. He referred to the sermon which Peter preached to the household of Cornelius when he summed up Jesus' ministry with the words, 'he went about doing good' (Acts 10:38). This is a beautiful description reminding us that Jesus never did any harm to anybody but in every circumstance did positive good.

John referred to the balance of Jesus' public ministry in which his emphasis was on the announcement of the reign of God, and on his summons to people to repent and to believe the good news. But Jesus was concerned also for our minds, that we should understand the characteristics of God's rule, the principles of its growth and the conditions of entering it. It was fully in accord with this teaching that Jesus engaged in practical service too. He healed the sick, fed the hungry and comforted the sad. And he performed the lowly service of the slave when he took water and a towel and washed the apostles' feet.

We mustn't, John argued, imagine that to share the gospel with our neighbour exhausts our responsibility to him, and that if we have done this we have done enough. If we are even to begin to follow the real Jesus, and to walk in his shoes, we must seize every opportunity to 'do good' – and this 'doing good' must be an expression of our love. Our good works will show the genuineness of our love, and our love will show the genuineness of our faith.

John went on to serve as President of Tearfund from 1983 to 1997.

In 1976 John employed the first of a long line of study assistants. Roy McCloughry was newly married, had finished a Master's degree, and was looking for something useful to occupy him perhaps before embarking on a PhD. When he approached John and asked if he could do with a part-time assistant, John jumped at the idea, and the Langham Trust agreed to provide the money.

John made it clear that he was looking for 'a general assistant', someone who was willing to help in any way according to need, and this remained the study assistant's role. It might involve anything from preparing (and washing-up) for the monthly prayer breakfast in the basement of 12 Weymouth Street, to reading whatever John was writing at the time, so as to offer a second opinion and a younger person's perspective. John asked his assistants to get hold of books from libraries, track down references, compile an index or bibliography, read manuscripts and correct proofs. They were expected to help John entertain people, do shopping, drive him to engagements, accompany him on overseas trips, dispatch gift books to developing-world correspondents, photocopy articles, send letters, faxes, and later emails on his behalf.

On Roy's first morning, John gave him a job.

'The Archbishop of Burma has written to me,' he said. 'He had a Rolls razor which has broken. Could you please try to find him a replacement?'

Roy searched London's shops, wondering if he was going to be looking for razors for all the archbishops in the Anglican Communion for the next nine months. Eventually he was successful and passed his first test.

During Roy's time as study assistant another tradition was established. John, then in his mid-fifties, had grown concerned that young Christians could easily become over-familiar and lacking in healthy respect towards their seniors, pastors and teachers. During a meeting of student Christian Union leaders chaired by John Wyatt, a member of All Souls, a young student whom he had not previously met addressed John Stott as 'John'.

Courteously but firmly, John made it clear that he felt such familiarity was not warranted.

'I am sure no disrespect was intended,' John Wyatt said. 'How would you prefer to be addressed?'

A few suggestions were made but they didn't make any headway until someone suggested 'Uncle John'. John Stott warmed to this.

'Oh, yes!' he said, brightening. 'If you want to call me Uncle John, I won't protest at that.'

After that an ever-widening circle of people at home and abroad began to use this name, including all the study assistants, as a combination of family intimacy and due respect.

John had a reputation for his extreme punctuality, his early rising, his high standards and attention to detail. Successive study assistants tried hard to live up to these ideals. Roy McCloughry, thinking he was going to be late for one appointment with John, took a very expensive taxi across London to drop him in Devonshire Street outside Bridford Mews. He waited there for thirty seconds then, turning round, walked down the Mews (because John could see everybody who came down the Mews from his window) and rang the bell at precisely the right second.

Roy imagined that he was the only one who had ever done this but later found that nearly all the study assistants had done similar things in their early days working for such a punctilious boss. Most study assistants, too, shared Roy's experience of leaping out of bed at eight a.m. to answer the phone, trying to rid their voice of slumber and, in response to John's apologies, sound as if they had long been at their desk.

John established a range of study groups to help him write the books he produced in the 1970s and 80s. He asked his assistants to help him run these groups. One group first read and then came together to discuss John Fowles' novel, *The Magus*. As the group was going round the circle saying what they thought of it, one of the members of the group expressed surprise that he had been asked to read the book.

'I found the book very unhelpful to me as a Christian,' he said. 'There's far too much sex in it. I am going to leave the meeting as I have nothing to contribute.'

With that, he got up and left the room. John sat there, let him leave, and then looked up over his glasses.

'Oh, I think that was most unfortunate,' he said. 'I thought the book was erotic, but not pornographic!'

For years afterwards, people who had been in the group used to say to one another, in a John Stott type of voice, 'It's erotic, but not pornographic!' They felt much comforted by the distinction between these two things which had not previously dawned on them.

In June 1976 John made one of three visits to Bathurst Inlet on the northern shore of Canada's North West Territory, just inside the Arctic Circle. While some of his party started to fish, he and others set off from

Bathurst Inlet Lodge and walked upstream to a spectacular gorge and waterfall. Their walk back, still in hot sunshine though now with a cool breeze, was relaxed and invigorating. They reached the lake in good spirits and were totally unprepared for the news which greeted them.

'Jacob has drowned.'

Jacob Avadluk was a nineteen-year-old boy, whose sister and half-sister both belonged to the Inuit community at Bathurst Inlet. Jacob, together with three younger Inuit boys, had set off to swim across to a sandbar. Halfway over, Jacob had suddenly disappeared. He resurfaced once calling for help, but after that no one saw him again.

When the news reached the Lodge, John's friend, Glen Warner, set to work with the nearest Royal Canadian Mounted Policeman to find the body, first dragging with an improvised grapnel, and then by diving in flippers and mask. But night was approaching, the weather turned against them, and they had to give up. In the evening John visited Jacob's half sister who was disconsolate.

On Sunday morning they resumed the search. While both boats started dragging again, John felt it was his turn to help. Being older at fifty-five, and not in good training, he was nervous. He had never worn underwater goggles before. Although he found that he soon got used to the cold water, he only had enough energy to take him ten or twelve feet along the bottom before having to push himself hard up to the surface again. He covered the whole distance between two markers without finding the body and, after six or eight dives, he was too out of breath to continue. So he came out and resumed his other role of trying to comfort the sad and distraught relatives.

At last, late in the afternoon, they recovered the body. A doctor examined it before the mounted police stowed it in a canvas body bag. After several men had dug a grave, they assembled for the funeral in one of the Inuit houses and found someone who agreed to interpret for John.

'I tried,' John recorded, 'to comfort the stricken community with the gospel of God's love, Christ's defeat of death and the hope of new life and resurrection.'

Only the men went to the graveside, about eight pallbearers carrying Jacob's body, still in the bag for a coffin, laid on a ladder for a stretcher.

As he was lowered into the grave, John read words from 1 Corinthians 15. The Inuit men picked up the spades and shovelled back the earth. Then a dozen or so people stood round in the twilight of an Arctic evening reflecting in sorrowful silence on life's tragedies.

19. MEETING FANTASY WITH REALITY

At last the All Souls congregation was able to abandon its temporary home in St Peter's, Vere Street, and move back into the splendidly refurbished church, with the new Waldegrave Hall beneath offering the improved accommodation for which so many had prayed and worked.

The doors opened again on 2 November 1976, All Souls Day. Attendance at the re-opening service strained the accommodation to its limits, filling every conceivable space in the church, with hundreds more participating downstairs in the Waldegrave Hall watching the TV relay. The queue of people waiting to get in stretched up Langham Place into Mortimer Street. Noël Tredinnick had composed an anthem for the occasion, allowing the organ, orchestra and choir to mark the great day at full volume.

John preached the first sermon from the new pulpit on the pre-eminence of Christ. On the old pulpit there had been a brass plaque to catch the preacher's eye, 'Sir, we would see Jesus', and this reminder was retained in the new pulpit with this inscription added:

Many friends of John Stott combined to give this pulpit and communion table out of deep gratitude for his dedicated ministry as evangelist, teacher and pastor during 25 years as Rector of All Souls (1950–1975). He taught us to make God's Word our rule, God's Spirit our teacher and God's Glory our supreme concern.

To deliver the 1976 London Lectures, a series which John had established, the committee chose the writer and broadcaster Malcolm Muggeridge. In 1967 Malcolm had received a vivid 'moment of illumination' while filming in the Church of the Nativity in Bethlehem, though he preferred to think more of 'a series of happenings than one dramatic one'. He told the world of his personal commitment to Christ in his *Jesus Rediscovered* in 1969. He and John had stood together on the platform in Trafalgar Square for the Nationwide Festival of Light rally in September 1971. He had made an unforgettable impression when he had spoken at the 1974 Lausanne Congress.

The committee invited him to give three lectures in All Souls on 'Christ and the Media'. This was a subject on which he had characteristically provocative views since he had come to see the kingdom of God, as proclaimed in the New Testament, as our true habitat, and the media, in which he had spent his life, as getting things the wrong way round: 'their light was darkness, their facts were fantasy, their documentation was myth'.

On three Monday evenings that November, All Souls was packed to capacity. The chairman for the first evening was Sir Charles Curran, Director General of the BBC, and many other broadcasting luminaries, including Sir Michael Swann, chairman of the BBC governors, were present. Malcolm didn't let this deter him in the least.

'It is a truism to say,' he began, 'that the media in general, and TV in particular, and BBC television especially, are incomparably the greatest single influence in our society today.' So far so good and uncontroversial. But he lost no time in warming to his theme.

'The influence, I should add, is, in my opinion, largely exerted irresponsibly, arbitrarily, and without reference to any moral or intellectual, still less spiritual, guidelines whatsoever.' John glanced anxiously across to see how the BBC top brass was reacting.

'Furthermore,' Malcolm continued, 'if it is the case, as I believe, that what we call western civilisation is fast disintegrating, then the media are playing a major role in the process by carrying out, albeit for the most part unconsciously, a mighty brainwashing operation, whereby all traditional standards and values are being denigrated to the point of disappearing, leaving a moral vacuum in which the very concepts of good and evil have ceased to have any validity . . .

'The only antidote to the media world's fantasy is the reality of Christ's kingdom proclaimed in the New Testament. This is why I am particularly glad to have been asked to deliver these lectures by John Stott, for whom I have so great a regard and affection, and to deliver them here, in this church, where his and his successor's ministries have been so outstandingly effective, and which has now been so excellently reconstructed by their congregation's own efforts, rather than in some secular hall or lecture theatre.

'The prevailing impression I have come to have of the contemporary scene is of an ever-widening chasm between the fantasy in terms of which the media induce us to live, and the reality of our existence as made in the image of God, as sojourners in time whose true habitat is eternity. The fantasy is all-encompassing; awareness of reality requires the seeing eye which comes to those born again in Christ. It is like coming to after an anaesthetic; the mists lift, consciousness returns, everything in the world is more beautiful than ever it was, because related to the reality beyond this world . . .

'When the Roman Empire finally disintegrated, it provided the basis for a new great civilisation – Christendom, whose legatees we are. All the greatest artists, poets, musicians dedicated their genius to celebrating it, and majestic cathedrals were built to enshrine it and religious orders founded to serve it.'

John thought that Malcolm had gone too far in his attacks on the media in general, and the BBC in particular. He wrote to Malcolm in his own hand a few days after the first lecture describing it as 'characteristically brilliant' and saying 'you certainly held us in your hand'. But he went on:

Shall I stop there? Or dare I add something on the other side? Because of your hatred of hypocrisy, you don't want to surround yourself with toadies; and Christian friendship means little if it does not involve a high degree of openness. So here goes!

179

I fear you tended to indulge in the kind of blanket condemnation I'd begged you not to. Of course with your main thrust (that the media feed more on fantasy than on reality) I'm in wholehearted agreement . . . But . . .

The letter goes on to list four points concerning inconsistency, distortion, imbalance and overemphasising the negative. 'Dear Malcolm,' John finished, 'it's unfair to write after only one lecture and it's probably impertinent. But you have two more Mondays in which to redress the balance . . . '

John also wrote to the Director General of the BBC, feeling he might have taken personally some of Malcolm's poisoned darts. Charles Curran replied reassuringly, adding that he hoped John would succeed in his efforts 'to persuade Malcolm to come nearer the heart of the matter in his next two lectures instead of spending all his energy in a kind of pyrotechnic display'.

The second lecture was chaired by Sir Brian Young, Director-General of the Independent Broadcasting Authority. Although there is no record of any reply from Malcolm to John's note, there is evidence that it had had some effect.

'I am conscious,' Malcolm said on the second Monday evening, 'of having perhaps dwelt too intensively in my first lecture on the sinister aspects of the media, and on the hopelessness of expecting any good in Christian terms to come out of them. So let me add that Christianity is, and always has been, and always will be, not just a religion of hope, but in itself, the most stupendous hope the world has ever known.

'It is as ridiculous to talk about the beneficent influence of the media in widening people's horizons, opening windows on to the world, and all that sort of humbug, as it is to blame the media for all our present ills – an error, I admit, I am prone to fall into myself.'

He returned then to his overriding theme.

'I have a longing past conveying to stay, during such time as remains to me in this world, with the reality of Christ, and to use whatever gifts of persuasion I may have to induce others to see that they must at all costs hold on to that reality. Good and evil provide the basic theme of the drama of our mortal existence. The transposition of good and evil in the world of fantasy created by the media leaves us with no sense of any moral order in the universe, and without this, no order whatsoever, social, political, economic or any other, is ultimately attainable. There is only chaos. To break out of the fantasy, to rediscover the reality of good and evil, and therefore the order which informs all creation – this is the freedom that the incarnation made available.'

At Malcolm's request, John himself chaired the last of the three lectures. Malcolm drew attention to the special danger represented by television documentaries which were liable to pass for being objective and authentic, whereas actually they too (because of the editor's ability to select material at will) belonged to the realm of fantasy. Eventually Malcolm came to his inspiring conclusion:

> It is precisely when every earthly hope has been explored and found wanting, when every possibility of help from earthly sources has been sought and is not forthcoming, when every recourse this world offers, moral as well as material, has been explored to no effect, when in the shivering cold the last faggot has been thrown on the fire and in the gathering darkness every glimmer of light has finally flickered out – it is then that Christ's hand reaches out, sure and firm, that Christ's words bring their inexpressible comfort, that his light shines brightest, abolishing the darkness for ever. So, finding in everything only deception and nothingness, the soul is constrained to have recourse to God himself and to rest content in him.

In his closing remarks at the end of the third lecture, bringing the series to a close, John suggested that we should regard Malcolm Muggeridge as a true prophet of the twentieth century.

'He has courage,' John said. 'While Christian civilisation seems to be crumbling around us in the West, and there is an urgent need for Christian leadership, Malcolm Muggeridge again and again is a voice crying in the wilderness.

'I shall never in all my life forget the contrast Malcolm has been drawing between fantasy and reality, and I hope the thing I'm going to take with me is his words in the lecture last week: stay with the reality of Christ. Lash yourself to the reality of Christ, like sailors in a stormy sea. I leave these lectures with a fresh determination to do even that in this fantasy world in which we live. So Malcolm, we thank you very much indeed, and even more we thank Jesus Christ, whose reality shines, if we may say so, very brightly in yourself.'

'What John Stott said after the third lecture,' Malcolm wrote later, 'though undeserved, will always be for me a precious memory.'

20. WHAT IS AN EVANGELICAL?

In 1974 the Church of England Evangelical Council (CEEC) set up a planning committee, with John as chairman, to plan for another National Evangelical Anglican Congress on the tenth anniversary of the Keele Congress. John also acted as general editor of a series of three paperbacks with the overall title *Obeying Christ in a Changing World* which were written as preparatory papers.

NEAC '77, like its predecessor at Keele, chose to meet at a university, this time at Nottingham on its impressive campus three miles from the city centre, from 14 to 18 April. The 1,900 delegates who made firm bookings were invited to meet in parish study groups and to prepare and submit their own views as written responses to the published papers. From these, a preliminary draft statement was hammered out, to be reshaped in its entirety as the Congress developed. Both archbishops addressed the Congress.

John approached the Congress with some anxiety, afraid that the different emphases of what was now seen as an 'evangelical coalition' might lead to disarray.

On the second day a leading article in the *Church Times*, under the headline 'Evangelicals in the ascendant', observed that probably 'no other section of the Church of England has the strength to organise such an assembly . . . The Evangelical theological colleges are fuller than the others, and the Evangelical lay associations are far more vigorous. In the universities and colleges Christian or Evangelical Unions flourish where the branches of the liberal (or in recent years Leftist) Student Christian Movement have withered away . . . The religion of the Evangelicals feeds the souls of men and women because all the time it draws very directly on the inexhaustible power of the risen Christ.'

At a press conference before the Congress ended, a journalist had a key question for John: 'What is an evangelical?'

John King reported in the *Church of England Newspaper* that John looked 'slightly dazed' at the question. John King added that hundreds of delegates would go home happier if they could answer that question without using incomprehensible jargon. He repeated the question, 'What is an evangelical? Tell us somebody please!'

Anxious that the delegates should leave the Congress happy, John answered the question in his final address to them on the Saturday.

'We do not retain our separate identity,' he said, 'because we live in the past and cannot face this exciting new situation in which we are no longer, thank God, a beleaguered minority. On the contrary I suggest we retain the designation because there are certain distinctive convictions that we cherish which we must on no account surrender, and to which we must bear faithful witness so long as there is anybody left who does not share them with us.

'Evangelicals share two major distinctive convictions. We are Bible people and must go on learning how to learn from Scripture. And we are gospel people. If the first hallmark of the evangelical is biblical supremacy, the second is the centrality of the gospel.'

He expanded on this in a booklet (*What is an Evangelical?*) based on his closing address at Nottingham: 'In the end what matters most of all to an evangelical is not a label, nor an epithet. It is not a party ticket; it is not even in the end the Bible and the gospel. It is the honour and glory of Jesus Christ which are bound up in the Bible and the gospel.'

But not everyone's verdict on the Congress was positive. Jim Packer, although a key contributor, hadn't wanted it to be held, feeling it would distract from the continuing study in many local churches which began at

Keele. In his view some of the methodology, some of the stress on experience in charismatic groups, some of the poverty of historical understanding
of evangelical roots, turned the Congress into 'something of a dud'. It
helped to convince him that the time had come for him to leave England
for Canada.

Alister McGrath saw the most important long-term achievement of the
Congress as the highlighting of the importance of hermeneutics: this had
been a buzz word at the Congress, referring to everything involved in the
process of interpreting and understanding the Bible – not just issues
involving the written text, but everything in the interpretative process. But
Alister, like others, saw that hermeneutics could become a tool for mischief
as well as for good. Despite the value of hermeneutics rightly applied,
the idea spread that the teaching of the Bible was expressed in terms
of the culture of its times to such an extent that it could not be related to
life today as confidently as it had been. It became less acceptable, as Oliver
Barclay remarked, to say 'the Bible says'.

In Australia, the Archbishop of Sydney, Sir Marcus Loane, heard glowing
reports of the Congress and wrote to his friend John to congratulate him
on his 'tremendous contribution'. But his letter went on to speak of some
aspects of those reports which disturbed him and he begged 'my dear
John' to use his influence to persuade the younger generation 'to capture
the Church of England, not to fracture it'.

Replying, John admitted that he saw at Nottingham 'disturbing signs of
. . . the beginnings of a new "liberal evangelicalism" . . . With you I want to
see evangelicals capturing the Church of England for the truth of God. I
also agree that in our new concerns for social ethics (owing to some past
neglect) we must not lose, or in any way underplay, the central themes of
salvation, justification, personal holiness . . . I will try to say this more often.'

In summer 1977 John paid a second and longer visit to Latin America,
travelling again with René Padilla, speaking at pastors' conferences and
working among students. Some 150 years after achieving their independence from Spanish and Portuguese colonial rule, he found that Latin
Americans were looking for other kinds of liberation – from economic
dependence on North America, from the oppressive regimes of right-wing

dictatorships, and from grinding poverty. Against this background the 'theology of liberation' had grown up.

John was happy to agree with the goal of 'liberation' since the God who made (and makes) human beings in his own image was obviously opposed to everything which dehumanises them. But he did wonder about what he saw as some of the dubious arguments Latin Americans used to buttress their position, and certainly disagreed with those theologians who were outspoken advocates of violent revolution.

A highlight of the trip was a week's bird-watching in the Galapagos Islands, made famous by Charles Darwin's visit in 1833 and the part the islands played in developing his theory of evolution by natural selection. On arrival on the islands, however, John fell ill with food poisoning. They stayed first in the island Presbytery of a young and welcoming Roman Catholic priest. Here two nuns fed them, cared for them and restored John to health. The priest helped John and René hire a local boat, the *Cristo Rey*, which took them round the islands of the Galapagos group.

They landed on the beach of an idyllic green lagoon and carefully picked their way through a huge colony of sea lions. As they travelled round the coast, John took pictures of bright red crabs on the black basaltic rocks and marine iguanas up to three feet in length, black with dark red markings on their backs, clambering skilfully up the rocks.

Besides iguanas, of course, they saw the giant tortoises ('Galapagos' in Spanish) from which the islands take their name, and innumerable birds. Some of the birds, as Charles Darwin had noted, were endemic species, found nowhere else in the world, including the thirteen varieties of finch which bear Darwin's name.

Five years earlier, in his popular and successful book *Understanding the Bible*, John had given his view on Darwin's theory. 'Speaking for myself,' he had written, 'I cannot see that at least some forms of the theory of evolution contradict or are contradicted by the Genesis revelation. Scripture reveals religious truths about God, that he created all things by his word, that his creation was "good", and that his creative programme culminated in man; science suggests that "evolution" may have been the mode which God employed in creating. To suggest this tentatively need not in any way detract from man's uniqueness.'

More generally, asking himself at the end of his second visit to Latin America whether there was any solution to the continent's problems, he remained convinced that there was more hope in evangelisation than in any other single Christian option. 'Nothing,' he reflected, 'is more human-ising than the gospel. Through it men and women begin to be remade in the image of God. Moreover, the gospel of God's love supplies the most powerful of all incentives to rescue people from everything that dehuman-ises them.'

He had seen for himself how, in Latin America as elsewhere, the young with their strong loathing for the inauthentic quickly detected any dichotomy between the church and its founder. Jesus had never ceased to attract them. They saw him as the radical he was, impatient with the traditions of the elders and the conventions of society, a merciless critic of the religious establishment.

If the church in Latin America could regain an authentic contemporary preaching-and-teaching ministry rooted in Scripture, a warm and caring fellowship, worship that expressed the reality of the living God, and an imaginative, sensitive and compassionate outreach into the community, then young people would be less tempted to vote with their feet by aban-doning the church altogether.

Less seriously, Latin America had taught him three lessons: to appreciate a long afternoon siesta, to renounce that peculiarly English vice called 'punctuality', and to enjoy the liberty of kissing everybody within reach! He appears to have kept this lesson in mind nearly twenty years later at a summer school in Vancouver when he put on a party for the students, and it was reported that he greeted all the girls with a kiss on the cheek.

'We were careful when washing our faces,' one of the girls said later, 'to leave untouched the spot John had kissed. We called it our "Stott spot". It was awful not to have one!'

Following the colloquium in Pasadena, John's Theology and Education Group undertook a study of 'the Gospel and Culture' and this was the theme of their next meeting in January 1978 at Willowbank, Bermuda.

The venue was a Christian guest house well situated on a cliff top with a spectacular outlook over the ocean, and the location gave its name to their 'Willowbank Report'. The large group of over thirty theologians, anthropologists, linguists, missionaries and pastors from all six continents included about half from the developing world. Coming from different cultures and academic disciplines, communication wasn't easy. John found that all his skills were needed.

He was playfully accused, as chairman, of English imperialism for trying to impose 'Westminster parliamentary procedure' on Africans, Asians and Latin Americans whose cultural ways of discussion and reaching consensus were more leisurely and more emotional. 'Wordiness and gesticulation come naturally to them,' he wrote in his diary. 'English economy of words, precision and "sweet reasonableness" do not appeal to them at all! So we had a lively time.'

After a day or two, Bishop Stephen Neill took John aside.

'If you don't stop the South American delegate from dominating the discussion by his verbosity, then I shall catch the next plane back to London!'

The key issue at the meeting was the interplay between the three cultures which are involved in every attempt to communicate the gospel. First, there is the cultural situation in the Bible. Second, there is the cultural background of the missionary or evangelist. And third, there is the culture of those to whom he goes. How then can a missionary from one culture take a message from another to people who live in a third?

After six days of discussion, they produced the Willowbank Report. 'Many of us evangelical Christians,' the report said, 'have in the past been too negative towards culture. We do not forget the human fallenness and lostness which call for salvation in Christ. Yet we wish to begin this report with a positive affirmation of human dignity and human cultural achievement. Wherever human beings develop their social organisation, art and science, agriculture and technology, their creativity reflects that of their Creator.' One missiologist believed it was the most important document on gospel and culture to appear in the twentieth century. (You can read it at www.lausanne.org.)

John flew home from Bermuda via New York. At Kennedy airport the attendant at the check-in desk studied John's ticket and passport.

'Are you any relation to John Stott?' she asked.

'Yes, that's my name.'

'But I mean the other John Stott, the Christian apologist who recently died.'

'Well,' John replied, feeling his way, 'I suppose you might describe me as a Christian apologist, but, as you can see, I haven't died yet.'

'There must be some mistake,' the attendant persisted. 'I'm a graduate of Wheaton College, where I heard John Stott speak several times, but I understand he is dead.'

Only with some difficulty, and to her increasing embarrassment, was John able to set the record straight.

Back in England, John chaired the National Evangelical Conference for Social Ethics, at High Leigh. Vacating the chair for a while he sat in the back row and listened as a young curate expounded Psalm 85. Seeing John out of the corner of his eye, he spoke with some trepidation.

The curate's name was Christopher Wright and the conference organisers had asked him to speak amid the growing evangelical ferment over social ethics and their relation to evangelism, the kingdom of God, and creation. Chris was feeling the rising excitement in the post-Lausanne years of the challenge of engaging with culture in ways which had been discussed at Willowbank. To him and many other young people, John Stott was a hero.

Chris had heard John many times before, especially during his years in the CICCU in Cambridge, and as a theological student. But they had never met in person. So he was nervous to be expounding Scripture in John's presence.

When Chris finished his talk, John approached him.

'Well done!' he said. 'If I may say so, I appreciated the balanced and thorough way in which you handled the text. Perhaps we may have lunch together?'

It was the beginning of a long friendship.

One of John's study assistants later told Chris that John had noted him from that time as a BWW.

'BWW?' asked Chris, looking blank.

'Bloke Worth Watching!' replied the study assistant.

21. INTIMATE ENCOUNTERS

On 19 December 1978 John visited Dr Martyn Lloyd-Jones at his home. He wanted to build bridges after their public disagreement in the 1960s and repair their friendship. Lloyd-Jones was affable and welcomed John into his roomy ground-floor study. Mrs Lloyd-Jones brought in coffee and chocolate biscuits. The conversation turned to Lloyd-Jones's outspoken criticism of evangelical Anglicans.

'Dr Lloyd-Jones,' John said, 'you give the impression that you think we evangelical Anglicans are unprincipled in our commitment to the Church of England. You use expressions like "mixed denomination" and "comprehensive church" as if we gloried in this. Speaking for myself, I'm first and foremost an evangelical.'

'I find that hard to believe.'

'But I am . . . '

Later, Lloyd-Jones asked, 'Would you ever leave the Church of England?'

'Yes indeed. I could envisage such a situation, if the church itself compromised officially one of the central doctrines of the faith. I'm not committed to the Church of England irrevocably.'

Three times in their conversation, Lloyd-Jones spoke of his desire that the two of them could work together. 'I wish we could be together, you and I. We belong together. Together we could make a terrific impact on the church and the country.'

'But, Dr Lloyd-Jones, we are together,' John replied, 'theologically, though not structurally.'

'But we ought to *be* together. If God spares me, and we could be together, I'd say like Simeon, "Lord, now lettest thou thy servant depart in peace".'

They never met again. When Lloyd-Jones died in 1981 John contributed to a symposium published in his honour. 'The doctor,' he wrote, 'always distinguished between principles and personalities, and was at heart a man of love and peace, a spiritual father to many of us.'

Addressing Guildford Diocesan Evangelical Fellowship a few years later, John made clear where his loyalties lay as between evangelicalism and Anglicanism.

'First and foremost,' he said, 'by God's sheer mercy, I am a Christian seeking to follow Jesus Christ. Next, I am an evangelical Christian because of my conviction that evangelical principles (especially *sola scriptura* [Scripture alone] and *sola gratia* [by grace alone]) are integral to authentic Christianity, and that to be an evangelical Christian is to be a New Testament Christian, and vice versa. Thirdly, I am an Anglican evangelical Christian, since the Church of England is the particular historical tradition or denomination to which I belong. But I am not an Anglican first, since denominationalism is hard to defend. It seems to me correct to call oneself an Anglican evangelical (in which evangelical is the noun and Anglican the descriptive adjective) rather than an evangelical Anglican (in which Anglican is the noun and evangelical the adjective).'

John's sister, Joy, cared for both Arnold and Lily in their old age, and then for 'Auntie Babe'. After Lily died, Joy seemed to lose her way, finding it difficult to settle down. Increasingly she began to think of herself as a failure and struggled with a lack of self-worth. For a while she had become a Roman Catholic.

'I am not strong enough or stern enough to belong to your Evangelicalness,' she told John. 'You see, all the things you hate so much, like candles and saints and genuflecting are big aids to me – and in a Catholic church one is sure that *God is there*. I've popped in and out of these churches since during the war – and more and more I find a sweetness and endeavour towards holiness there which I have never found anywhere else. All these things which you find so odd, not to say wrong, are for me absolutely understandable.'

She moved to a small house in Chapel-en-le-Frith, not far from her sister Joanna, where she enjoyed the Derbyshire dales which she explored in her car. Her Roman Catholicism did not last and she had long conversations with the local Anglican priest in Chapel-en-le-Frith.

When she began to hear voices in her head, she was diagnosed as suffering from schizophrenia. Medication did little to help.

Then one day in 1979 while John was in America she swallowed all the pills she had and rang her sister to tell her what she had done. They rushed her to hospital critically ill. Joanna rang John who caught the next plane home. In the hospital, Joy recognised her brother but was unable to sustain a rational conversation. She died the next day.

The coroner returned an open verdict. Having seen many cases like this where people with mental troubles took overdoses to call attention to their problems, he was reluctant to call it suicide.

The Anglican vicar told John that Joy had spoken to him of the shattering experience when her faith had become meaningless to her.

As he recovered from the shock of Joy's death, John began to recall with pleasure their shared childhood, her war service, her teaching and lecturing, and the way she had nursed their parents at the end. She had 'a rare and colourful spirit' and an unusual blend of 'fun, mischievousness and eccentricity'.

John used his share of the money Joy left to build a first-floor extension at The Hookses, with two more bedrooms and an extra bathroom. He called the bigger bedroom 'Joy's room' in her memory, and the smaller 'Fanny's room' since that was the name of Joy's much-loved but totally undisciplined beagle.

In April and May 1980 John visited Eastern Europe. After many engagements and some bird-watching he arrived in the small town of Benatky, in the central Bohemian region of what is now the Czech Republic, where he preached for the young pastor, Pavel ('Paul') Cerny.

In the vestry John was giving a final briefing to his interpreter when a tall and rather burly man, well-dressed and smiling, was ushered in.

'This is the Secretary for Church Affairs of the District Council,' the interpreter explained to John.

The pastor had been obliged to report John's visit, and the secretary had decided to attend, only his third visit in five years. John found him 'affable, almost obsequious'.

'We are honoured to have you visit our community,' the communist official said. 'In the present climate of world affairs it is important for England and Czechoslovakia to come closer together. Our relations should be developed.'

John thanked him, and the service began. The Secretary for Church Affairs sat in a pew with the rest of the congregation. Being a party member and therefore an atheist, he declined the offer of a hymnbook and took no part in the service. John began his sermon by risking a joke.

'We are honoured to have the Church Affairs Secretary with us today,' he said. 'There have been close links between Czechoslovakia and England since John Hus read John Wycliffe's books. The secretary mentioned to me that our relations should be developed and I therefore hope that when you all apply for a passport to visit the UK, the secretary will help you to get it!'

The joke worked and there were smiles all round. The government official seemed to listen carefully as John spoke from the Sermon on the Mount on the distinction between Christians and non-Christians, as seen in Christ's 'salt' and 'light' metaphors, on the influence which Christians should have on their community, and on the inadequacy of materialism. When he described the decay of secular society, he thought it more prudent to refer to the condition of England than of the Czechoslovak Soviet Socialist Republic.

The secretary, first to leave when the service was over, uttered conventional pleasantries as he shook hands with the preacher, making no reference to what John had said. Pavel Cerny apparently did himself no harm by inviting John to his church since he later became President of the Brethren Church in the Czech Republic.

Mark Labberton succeeded Tom Cooper as study assistant in 1980. In his late twenties, Mark had studied at Fuller Theological Seminary. He and

John had met briefly at Urbana four years earlier and during a summer school at Regent College, Vancouver. John liked American study assistants because he knew they were pushy enough to get things done.

On arrival in Frances Whitehead's old-fashioned office at the back of the Weymouth Street Rectory, Mark suggested to John and Frances that she might have a chair which ran on castors, a new filing cabinet and better lighting.

John and Frances discussed in Mark's presence whether this was a worthwhile and justifiable expenditure. They decided it was and the investment was made. Later, Mark persuaded an at first reluctant Frances to move into computing. She quickly mastered her first 'Apple Mac' and became a fan.

Still in his early weeks as study assistant, when Mark was driving him to Heathrow, John mentioned something about his sister Joanna. Mark decided to probe a little deeper.

'Describe your relationship to your sister to me,' Mark said. 'How do you get along?'

There was silence for a moment as John perhaps reflected on the ways of brash young Americans.

'What is this inquisition to which you are subjecting me?' John replied.

'I'm not trying to be intrusive,' Mark replied. 'I will try not to be. I just didn't know.'

Then, to Mark's surprise, John went on to answer the question in much greater detail and more candidly than he had been expecting. He was to find that intimacies like these didn't come often, but at unexpected moments of relaxation.

Early in 1981 John travelled with Mark to India and Bangladesh. John received a note from a Tamil bishop they had met in Burma to go and visit his mother who lived in a very poor area of Dhaka. All they were given was a name and a district where the woman lived. The streets didn't have names and it was hard to work out where they were. It took John and Mark a couple of hours of searching to locate the right street before arriving in the dark inner courtyard of a very dilapidated building.

John explained through an interpreter why he was there and who they were looking for. There was an animated response and a group of people disappeared into the building. Then out came a tiny, almost toothless, lady who was thrilled to see John. After greetings were exchanged she had a request to make.

'Would you share with us the gospel?' she asked.

When John agreed, they produced a tiny carpet square and asked him to stand on it. Mark then listened as through an interpreter 'in a most elegantly simple, wonderfully expressed way, John shared the love of God for about five minutes'. Then the woman and friends stepped forward and everyone in the house knelt in front of John.

'Pray for us,' they said.

John prayed for each of them and then he and Mark were on their way. Mark reflected that John saw all preaching as of equal value, whether to seminarians, to experienced missionaries, or to a poor family in a dark Dhaka courtyard. 'This is one of the most interesting things about John: how a particular gospel in one culture and hemisphere becomes in him a global gospel. He made a journey across the boundaries.'

On the same visit to Dhaka, John and Mark met Mother Teresa. The meeting came about almost by chance at very short notice. Mother Teresa was dressed in a slightly soiled white sari edged in blue, and a dark grey cardigan. John never forgot how frail she looked but he felt that the light of Christ shone through the creases of her wrinkled face.

'I am a friend of Malcolm Muggeridge,' John said.

Mother Teresa's face lit up.

'He has really come to know Jesus for himself,' she said.

John presented her with a copy of his book *Focus on Christ* which had recently been published. On the cover it had a reproduction of Richard Westall's painting *Ecce Homo* which hangs in All Souls.

'How beautiful,' she murmured. 'But his hands are tied. Isn't this what we always do with Jesus' hands?'

John told her about the pages in the book which were about her. Then they talked about her Missionaries of Charity, what it meant for her to minister in a setting where a Roman Catholic orphanage was caring for Muslim children.

'Here are children who need loving,' she said, 'and we are going to love them.'

Mark always remembered the way that John and Mother Teresa engaged with each other in conversation.

'Pray for us,' she requested as they parted, 'that we may not spoil God's work, and that it may remain his work.'

John and Mark returned to Calcutta. It was Mark's first visit and he thought it unlike any other place on earth. At the airport, Mark had a question for John.

'Do you honestly think you could live here in Calcutta?' he asked.

'Well,' John replied, 'one would count it an honour if one were called, wouldn't one?'

'Well,' Mark replied, matching the formal style John had adopted, 'one would like to think one would count it an honour, but one is not sure that one would especially if that one were me!'

'But,' John said, 'doesn't meeting Mother Teresa make you want to join her army?'

'Yes,' replied Mark, 'meeting Mother Teresa does make me want to join her army but the problem is that would involve taking a full vow of poverty or I could never actually do this.'

They had a conversation about the implications of solemnly taking such vows. In their case, in time of need, they could make a call to the West and help would come. This was not an option for the poor in Calcutta or for those like Mother Teresa's Missionaries of Charity who had taken a vow of poverty.

The visit to Calcutta affected John deeply. On 16 February 1981 he climbed into the pulpit at All Souls and preached a sermon which he entitled, 'Is God on the side of the poor?' He offered two complementary approaches.

'One could answer this question rationally,' he said, 'with the cool detachment of statistics. There are now over 4,000 million inhabitants of planet Earth, and one-fifth of them (800 million) are destitute. Every day, 10,000 give up the struggle for survival, succumb to starvation, and die. Meanwhile, more than another one-fifth live in affluence, consume four-fifths of the world's income, and contribute to Third World development the derisory annual sum of £20,000 million, while spending twenty-one times that amount on armaments.

'Or one could approach the question emotionally with the hot-blooded indignation aroused by the sights, sounds and smells of poverty. Arriving in Calcutta last month, I found the city enveloped in a malodorous pall of smoke from a myriad fires fuelled with cow dung. An emaciated woman clutching an emaciated baby stretched out an emaciated hand for *baksheesh*. Between a quarter and a half million homeless people sleep on the city's pavements at night, and human beings are reduced to foraging like dogs in its garbage dumps.'

The All Souls congregation went to their homes that evening agreeing with John that God *was* on the side of the poor, and that they were under an obligation to consider what they could do to demonstrate that they had genuine love for their global neighbours in need.

A woman in America, slightly younger than John, made a surprising revelation to Mark Labberton. 'Many years ago,' she said, 'my friend was nearly engaged to John Stott!' She told Mark the name of the woman.

'I've never heard about this,' said Mark.

'It's true,' the woman insisted.

When Mark was next with John he plucked up all the courage he could muster and raised the matter.

'I understand that you had an important relationship with this lady?'

'How do you know about this?' John asked.

'One of my friends told me in a non-gossipy way that you had really been important to this person.' Mark couldn't bring himself to refer to it as a near engagement.

'It is true,' John said, 'but I just came to feel that it wasn't God's calling for us to get married.'

Mark felt that they had gone far enough and dropped the subject.

John Wyatt, who first met John in 1972 when he started attending All Souls as a first-year medical student, and who later took on the role as his informal medical adviser, was always surprised by John's lack of enthusiasm for the single state. As a young man, if John Wyatt hinted that he would follow his example of singleness, John Stott nearly always pointed out its disadvantages and limitations. He was touchingly pleased when John Wyatt told him he was planning to get married, and preached at his wedding.

John Wyatt asked John to give a talk at the London University Christian Union.

'What do you want me to talk about?' John asked.

'Actually we would like you to talk about sex,' John Wyatt replied.

'You mean from my vast personal experience?' said John.

Once in conversation John announced to John Wyatt that he was about to travel to an exotic destination which would include two or three days bird-watching in an idyllic setting.

'It's all right for you as a single man to get away like that,' John Wyatt teased him. 'There's no chance that a married person with children like me could ever do such a thing!'

'Yes,' replied John plaintively. 'Bird-watching is my wife substitute – and a very bad substitute too!'

22. PREACHING FIT FOR A QUEEN

John celebrated his sixtieth birthday on 27 April 1981 at The Hookses with his friends Dick and Rosemary Bird. They gave him a present of aubrietias and primroses from the local nursery for his wild Welsh garden. Rosemary baked a chocolate cake, furnished with six candles, one for each decade.

In the afternoon John sat in his favourite nook on the Pembrokeshire cliffs and read the exhortation in Hebrews 12:1 to 'run with perseverance the race marked out for us'. He prayed for grace to persevere in Christian faith, life and service.

Over the years John became a friend to successive vicars at St James's church in the village of Dale, close to The Hookses, and a familiar figure to the congregation. Donald English, President of the Methodist Conference, always remembered an occasion when, sharing a holiday with John and a number of others at The Hookses, he attended an evening service in a barn where John, in pullover and cords, played the accordion to accompany the hymns.

In 1980 and much of 1981, John worked on his book, *I Believe in Preaching*. He painted preaching as 'bridge-building', crossing the cultural divide between the revealed Word and the contemporary world. 'Such preaching,' he wrote, 'will be authoritative in expounding biblical principles, but tentative in applying them to the complex issues of the day. This combination of the authoritative and the tentative, the dogmatic and the agnostic, conviction and open-mindedness, teaching the people and leaving them free to make up their own minds, is exceedingly difficult to maintain. But it seems to me to be the only way.'

The book was full of practical and engaging advice on sermon preparation. He told the story of a young American Presbyterian minister who frequently boasted in public that all the time he needed to prepare his Sunday sermon was the few minutes it took him to walk to the church from his manse next door. What did the elders in his church do? They bought him a new manse five miles away!

'Without doubt the best sermons we ever preach are those we have first preached to ourselves,' John wrote. 'When God himself speaks to us through a text of Scripture, and it becomes luminous or phosphorescent to us, it is then that it continues to glow with divine glory when we seek to open it up to others.' Of course not every sermon has to be preached out of personal experience. Bachelor John wrote, 'Some of us have to preach on marriage while remaining unmarried, and all of us have to preach on death before we have died. Yet sermons which emerge from deep personal conviction have a rich self-authenticating quality.'

For this reason most preachers find it necessary to have handy at all times a notebook. 'I wonder if your experience resembles mine. My mind is usually enveloped in a fairly thick fog, so that I do not see things at all plainly. Occasionally, however, the fog lifts, the light breaks through, and I see with limpid clarity. These fleeting moments of illumination need to be seized. We have to learn to surrender ourselves to them, before the fog descends again. Such times often come at awkward moments, in the middle of the night, when somebody else is preaching or lecturing, while we are reading a book, even during a conversation. However inconvenient the time, we cannot afford to lose it. In order to take fullest advantage of it, we may need to write fast and furiously.'

He advised choosing Sunday's text by the preceding Monday so that an 'incubation process' can go on. Then read the text, re-read it and read it again. Turn it over and over in your mind, like Mary the mother of Jesus who 'pondered things in her heart'. 'Probe your text, like a bee with a spring blossom, or like a humming bird probing a hibiscus flower for its nectar. Worry at it like a dog with a bone. Suck it as a child sucks an orange. Chew it as a cow chews the cud.'

What the preacher, John wrote, is actually doing is addressing two groups of questions: *What does the text mean?* What did it mean when first written or spoken? A text means what its author meant. *What does it say?* What is its contemporary message? How does it speak to us today?

John stressed the importance of *isolating the dominant thought* of a sermon. 'As we meditate by prayer and study, and jot down a miscellany of ideas, we should be looking for our text's dominant thought. We should persevere in meditation until it emerges and clarifies. Why? Every passage has a main theme. God speaks through what he has spoken and it is essential to ask what he is saying. Where does his emphasis lie? We need to resist the temptation to give the passage a twist or stress of our own.' A sermon differs from a lecture in that it aims to convey only one major message. 'A sermon is a living word from God to his people and it should make an impact on them then and there. They won't remember the details, we shouldn't expect them to. But they should remember the dominant thought.'

On illustrations, he said that like windows *they let in light*. He quoted Spurgeon: a building without windows would be 'a prison rather than a house . . . and in the same way a discourse without a parable [a sermon without illustrations] is prosy and dull, and involves a grievous weariness of the flesh . . . even the little children open their eyes and ears, and a smile brightens up their faces when we tell a story . . . We dare say that they often wish that the sermon were all illustration, even as the boy desired to have a cake made all of plums.' But of course a cake cannot be all plums any more than a house can be all windows. We need the happy medium.

A sermon's introduction is essential to arouse interest, stimulate curiosity, and whet the appetite for more. It genuinely introduces the theme by leading the hearers into it. Of course interest can readily be aroused by telling a joke or an arresting story, but if these don't lead naturally into the subject the interest gained will be as quickly lost. On the other hand you can introduce a subject in such a way as to lose people's attention before you have even won it. The right but hard way is to introduce the topic and arouse interest simultaneously and so dispose people's minds and hearts towards the message.

Conclusions are more difficult than introductions. 'Some preachers seem to be constitutionally incapable of concluding anything, let alone their sermons. They circle round and round, like a plane on a foggy day without instruments, unable to land. Their sermons "are nothing less than a tragedy of aimlessness". Others stop too abruptly. Their sermons are like a play without a finale, like music which has neither crescendo nor climax.'

He quoted the well-known and successful black preacher in the southern States of America: '"First I tell what I'm going to tell 'em. Then I tell 'em. Then I tell 'em what I've told 'em!" Some deft carpenters can drive a nail home with one mighty blow; most find it safer to hammer it in with a series. Truth needs to be driven home by the hammer blows of repetition.'

You must know, John insisted, what your overriding objective is in your sermon. What you want people to do about what you have said – how you want them to respond. Archbishop Whately said of some preacher, 'He aimed at nothing and hit it!'

After constructing the outline comes the praying. 'Of course we prayed before we began to prepare, and we have tried to continue throughout our preparation in an attitude of prayer. But now that the sermon is finished and written, we need to pray over it . . . It is on our knees before the Lord that we can make the message our own, possess or re-possess it until it possesses us. Then, when we preach it, it will come neither from our notes, nor from our memory, but out of the depths of our personal conviction, as an authentic utterance of our heart . . . Every preacher knows the difference between a heavy sermon which trundles away on the runway like an overloaded jumbo jet and never gets airborne, and a sermon which has what a bird has, a sense of direction and wings. Which kind any sermon will be is usually settled as we pray over it beforehand. We need to pray until our text comes freshly alive to us, the glory shines forth from it, the fire burns in our heart, and we begin to experience the explosive power of God's Word within us.'

Donald Coggan, who had recently retired as Archbishop of Canterbury, wrote an enthusiastic review of the book for the *Church of England Newspaper* under the heading 'This is what preaching is really about'. In

February 1982, the publishers, Hodder and Stoughton, sent a copy of this review, with a copy of the book, to every diocesan bishop in England. Dr Coggan urged parochial church councils to give their clergy a copy of the book.

In January 1983, the Queen invited John to preach at Sandringham and to join the royal family as her weekend guest at the home where she normally spent the early weeks of the year. He hired a dinner suit from Moss Bros. When he arrived at Kings Lynn station on the Saturday, Her Majesty's equerry was there to meet him.

'You are to be a guest at a barbecue,' he said.

After he had settled into his room at Sandringham House, the Queen's staff led John through a part of the 8,000-acre estate to a hut which the Queen had been given as a wedding present. It was Prince Andrew's last night before rejoining his unit.

In front of the hut was a platform, at one end of which the Duke of Edinburgh was cooking with Princess Anne at the other. About twenty people sat down to a meal including most of the royal family and the young princes. The Duke and the Princess produced hunks of barbécued beef, half-ducks, sausages and baked potatoes. John found himself sitting between the Queen Mother and Lady Abel Smith, the lady in waiting. When the conversation turned to Malcolm Muggeridge, John discovered that the Queen Mother didn't have a copy of Malcolm's book, *Jesus Rediscovered*.

'Do I have your permission to send you a copy when I return to London?' John asked.

'I should be most grateful,' the Queen Mother replied.

After the first course the Duke of Edinburgh went out to collect the dessert – a large dish of stewed fruit. When he passed behind John, the Duke tripped and spilt some of the dessert.

'It's alright, the floor's quite clean,' Prince Charles said, 'we can still eat the fruit.'

So they scooped the spilt fruit salad back into its bowl and heartily enjoyed it. After the meal was over the Queen went to a cupboard from which she took a mop and began to clean up the remnants of the spilled fruit.

'Ma'am I wish you'd allow me to do this for you,' John said.

'No,' the Queen replied, 'I love it. I really do.'

At breakfast on the Sunday morning, John sat next to the Prince of Wales.

'Last night we watched a film on Gandhi,' Prince Charles said to John. 'During a discussion about the film, I commented that I think we should know more about other religions.'

'We should indeed know more,' John responded, 'and the more we know, the more convinced we become of the uniqueness of Jesus Christ.'

Charles seemed anxious for John to enlarge on this, and he was just about to do so when the door opened and in walked the Queen accompanied by her four corgis. Unfortunately, after the disruption caused by Her Majesty's arrival, John was unable to steer the conversation back to Christianity in a multi-faith world.

The weather was sunny, though chilly, and the Queen walked the few hundred yards from Sandringham House to the church to hear John preach on salvation understood as freedom – freedom from guilt, self-centredness and fear. The Queen walked back to the house for lunch, at which John sat next to her and they discussed his sermon in some detail.

On Monday morning the Duke of Edinburgh, a well-known ornithologist who knew of John's lifetime's hobby, arranged for him to be taken for some early bird-watching.

A few days later, through the window of John's flat his study assistant Toby Howarth saw a police motorcycle turn into Bridford Mews. When it stopped outside the flat Toby wondered what John had been up to.

The policeman rang the doorbell.

'Is this the residence of the Revd Dr John Stott?'

'It is,' Toby admitted.

The policeman returned to his motorbike, opened one of the panniers, and lifted out a brace of pheasants.

'With the compliments of Her Majesty the Queen,' he said. She had clearly enjoyed John's sermon.

On 4 April 1982, Eric Nash, 'Bash', died aged nearly 89. When John conducted his memorial service at All Souls in June the church was packed with former Iwerne campers and camp leaders. In the book which was produced in Bash's honour, John tackled head on the subject for which Bash has been most severely criticised, namely his attitude to marriage.

'He was accused of grave imbalance,' John wrote, 'of an unhealthy policy of dissuading his officers from marrying, and even (it was sometimes darkly hinted) of latent homosexual tendencies. Since I worked with him closely for about seven years, both as a personal friend and as camp's secretary-treasurer, I am able to say with complete confidence that Bash was heterosexual. His own singleness, and his advocacy of the single state, was entirely due to his zeal for God's work.'

'I think that what appealed to people about Bash,' John told me, 'was the extraordinary degree of simplicity and directness with which he expounded especially the cross – he was very cross-centred – and the simplicity of his invitation to open the door to Christ. He had a consummate skill in presenting the gospel to fifteen- to seventeen-year-old boys – a great gift for story-telling and illustrations.'

23. INSTITUTE AND ISSUES

After Michael Baughen was promoted to become Bishop of Chester in the summer of 1982, a seven-month interregnum followed, during which Andrew Cornes presided. Richard Bewes arrived as the new Rector of All Souls on 12 January 1983. On his desk he found a Staffordshire pottery figure of Spurgeon with a note of welcome from John.

It was daunting for Richard to be Rector of All Souls. Until then, John had been a father figure to him. He first knew him when he was thirteen, and John drove him and his brother Michael to camp at Iwerne Minster in the back of his jeep and he made his decision for Christ. From then on John never forgot who Richard was. If he ever bumped into him, John instantly recognised him.

Now it hit him: 'I'm next door now to John Stott! He's my next-door neighbour!'

'John, I feel rather overawed by all this,' Richard told John.

'You mustn't feel that,' John replied, 'because you've no need to.'

At the first full staff meeting, following an opening prayer, Richard introduced the meeting.

'Right,' he said, 'what shall we all do *now*?'

John and Richard began the practice, every Saturday evening when John was in England, of meeting in the Rectory for coffee and prayer. They found that prayer kept the relationship sweet. John would say to Richard, 'You're my boss.' On Sunday evenings, John joined Richard and his wife Liz for John's favourite supper – scrambled egg. Sometimes John joined the Bewes family for breakfast. One morning Richard's teenage daughter, in her dressing gown, put her head around the door. She had dyed her hair an incandescent red.

'Wendy,' John greeted her, 'you look marvellous!'

Richard was to remain as Rector of All Souls for nearly twenty-two years. He remembered how visiting preachers, or members of the preaching team, would flounder if John walked into the vestry. If he wasn't quite happy with a sermon, you could see John's fingers begin to drum on his knee. But he wouldn't say anything. 'He put us all on our mettle,' Richard told me. 'Knowing that he would be there made you a little bit extra careful when preparing your notes: is that really what the passage says?'

New members of the preaching team at All Souls had to be established preachers in the tradition of biblical exposition, but with a populist touch because All Souls had an international congregation. At one point in Richard's time there were nearly eighty different nationalities at All Souls. 'John was a wonderful preacher – his command of language was superb. The words were simple Anglo-Saxon and easily translatable. There was a little place for humour but not too much. Humour doesn't always translate to other languages. Not everyone understood English humour and to some it was offensive.'

In the early 1980s, if John was preaching, they had to open an overflow downstairs to accommodate the extra crowds because of his international following. 'Some Americans arrived at All Souls with their video cameras already running!' Richard joked.

Frances sometimes said to Richard, 'John is coming back from a foreign tour. There are hundreds of letters for him to deal with and he's off again in three days' time.' Then she would drive him to the airport in her little blue car. On arrival abroad he would be fêted. 'They would throw garlands around his neck and give him lavish presents. Then he would return and there would be Frances in the little car waiting to drive him back to his flat.'

There were times when foreign visitors to All Souls thought that Richard Bewes was John Stott.

'I heard you preach in Sydney in 1958,' one Australian lady said to Richard. 'Thank you so much!'

'Bless you!' said Richard, not daring to disabuse her.

Early in 1977 John had arranged for a study group he had convened to discuss the need for contemporary Christian thinking in public affairs. Over the next few years he discussed with key contacts how a new body he was proposing would relate to existing organisations such as the Shaftesbury Project or the Nationwide Festival of Light. He was thinking of establishing an Institute for Contemporary Christian Studies which would be dedicated to the integration of Christian faith, life and mission.

The goal of the Institute would be to help students become more complete Christians in their personal and home life, and more effective Christians in their professional and public life. In the forefront of John's thinking as he pursued his proposal to establish the new institute was the whole idea of 'double listening' – that Christians, and preachers and teachers in particular, should devote their energies to understanding both God's Word and God's world if they were to be effective.

By no means all evangelicals were happy about the establishment of the Institute. Some were suspicious of the whole idea of double listening. 'What do you mean, double listening?' they asked. 'We shouldn't be listening to the world – we should be proclaiming the truth.' John resisted these criticisms.

Who should be the director of the new Institute? John was already sixty. He couldn't take on a vast new task without giving up other commitments. When, after prayer, it was agreed that he would be the Institute's first director, he relinquished, or prepared to lay down, his work for Lausanne, his work as honorary general secretary of the Evangelical Fellowship of the Anglican Communion and joint chairmanship of the Church of England Evangelical Council and Anglican Evangelical Assembly, and his chairmanship of Care and Counsel. He agreed to reduce his overseas travel at least in the immediate future.

In deciding to be the Institute's first director, John stipulated that the appointment would be for five years only and that there would be an administrative manager. Martyn Eden was then teaching politics. He wasn't on John's personal radar but when his name was suggested, John approached Martyn with honesty, directness and clarity and persuaded him to become the founding 'Administrative Dean' of the Institute though it would mean a drop in salary and a lower profile than other possibilities which were open to him.

John launched what came to be called the London Institute for Contemporary Christianity (LICC) at a press conference in mid-January 1982, and the first ten-week course with twenty-seven students from fourteen different countries opened in April. The institute's first home was at a newly-built St Paul's Church complex in Robert Adam Street, London.

'The London Institute is for me,' John told an interviewer, 'a culmination of these last fifteen years in which I have begun to struggle with contemporary issues and preach about them, and have seen the need to encourage other people to do the same thing.'

Michael Baughen had invited John to preach a number of occasional sermons at All Souls under the title 'Issues Facing Britain Today', and from these grew his book *Issues Facing Christians Today*. Several times in the course of writing this ambitious book, John confessed, he was tempted to give up. The complexity of each topic had attracted an extensive literature which he needed to absorb. He persevered as someone who was trying to think Christianly, and apply the biblical revelation to pressing issues of the day. In preparing the book he was anxious to do justice to the arguments on both sides of an issue.

Both the London Institute and the *Issues* book were the inevitable outcome of one of the resolutions in the Keele statement way back in 1967 which admitted that 'we have not thought sufficiently deeply or radically about the problems of our society', and resolved to do better.

In preparation for each issue, John got Tom Cooper, his study assistant at the time, to bring together a small research group of about eight people. So for the one on work and unemployment, they enlisted a trade union leader, two unemployed younger people, an employer and an economist. After doing some preliminary reading, John gave them their brief.

'These are my questions,' he told them, 'these are my problems; can you throw light on them for me from your point of view and from your expertise? I've studied the biblical aspect: I want you to give me the practical.' Then when they came together, he would listen to them talk for two hours, taking notes. He found it fascinating.

At the end of September 1983 Paul Weston, recently graduated and soon to begin ordination training, visited The Hookses. He found that John had been there for the whole month working on the *Issues* book in his study overlooking West Dale Bay with his binoculars at his side. He had been rising early, spending long hours at his desk in the morning. Then he would take his famous 'horizontal half-hour' after lunch before working in The Hookses grounds each afternoon. John's evenings were flexible. When under pressure he worked until ten p.m., but, if things were going well he spent it in the house with other guests.

'We persuaded him to read a Saki short story to us,' Paul remembered. 'We had two readings in the end – the "Lumber Room" and the "Stalled Ox" during which John was reduced to tears of laughter . . . Off came the half-moon glasses and he rubbed his eyes in laughter.' John had been introduced at Rugby to the Saki stories by H. H. Munro, and he was especially fond of 'The Lumber Room'.

Next day, instead of Saki, John read from the draft of the chapter in *Issues* on Industrial Relations. It took over half an hour and he abridged much of the final section because he thought he was boring his impromptu audience. Though the writing was a model of clarity and read well, it was very long.

'Why don't you make the book two volumes?' Frances Whitehead suggested. John didn't think that would work.

He made remarkable progress considering the complexity of the book, completing five chapters in a week and sometimes one a day.

One of the most frequently cited parts of *Issues* is John's chapter on homosexual partnerships which was later to be both revised and reprinted in periodicals, symposia and in booklet form. His approach was to begin with God's creation ordinance of marriage and working from that to conclude that 'the only "one flesh" experience which God intends and Scripture contemplates is the sexual union of a man with his wife, whom he recognises as "flesh of his flesh".' He stated unequivocally that the only alternative to heterosexual marriage is sexual abstinence. As a bachelor he wrote, 'I think I know the pain of this.'

He was well aware of a widespread view in the secular world that sex was essential to human fulfilment, and that to expect homosexual people to abstain from homosexual practice was to condemn them to frustration and to drive them to neurosis, despair and even suicide. Was it not cruel to ask anyone to deny himself what to him was a normal and natural mode of sexual expression?

However John argued that, while certainly sex was a good gift of God, sexual experience was not essential to human fulfilment. If God calls us to celibacy, abstinence is not only good but also possible for homosexual as well as heterosexual people. 'To be sure,' he wrote, 'all unmarried people experience the pain of struggle and loneliness ... And we make it harder for ourselves if we listen to the world's plausible arguments, or lapse into self-pity, or feed our imagination with pornographic material and inhabit a fantasy world in which Christ is not Lord.'

Having written all this, he acknowledged with shame that the church had failed to show love to homosexual people, the great majority of whom, as he saw it, were not responsible for their disposition though they were for their conduct.

John believed that at the heart of homosexual disposition was 'a deep loneliness, the natural human hunger for mutual love, a search for identity, and a longing for completeness'. If homosexual people couldn't find these things in the local 'church family' then Christians had no business using that expression. The alternative, he wrote, 'is not between the warm physical relationship of homosexual intercourse and the pain of isolation in the cold. There is a third option, namely a Christian environment of love, understanding, acceptance and support.'

John didn't think it was either necessary or helpful to encourage homosexual people to disclose their sexual disposition to everybody. 'But they do need at least one confidante to whom they can unburden themselves, who will not despise or reject them, but will support them with friendship and prayer ... Same-sex friendships are to be encouraged, like those in the Bible between Ruth and Naomi, David and Jonathan, and Paul and Timothy. There is no hint that any of these was homosexual in the erotic sense; yet they were evidently affectionate and (at least in the case of David and Jonathan) even demonstrative. Of course sensible safeguards will be important. But in African and Asian cultures it is common to see two men walking down the street hand in hand, without embarrassment. It is sad when our Western culture inhibits the development of rich same-sex friendships by engendering the fear of being ridiculed or rejected.'

In the 1950s and again in the 1970s, John allowed his name go forward for bishoprics in Australia, but in the event declined specific invitations. He also discouraged influential friends who wished to put forward his name through appropriate channels for a number of English dioceses including Liverpool and Rochester.

When John V. Taylor retired from the diocese of Winchester in 1985, Michael Baughen, then Bishop of Chester, felt strongly that if John could be appointed it would very considerably strengthen the cause of evangelical theology within the House of Bishops. So Michael consulted Archbishop Robert Runcie who would act as Chairman of the Crown Appointments Commission – the body charged with nominating the new bishop. Two years earlier Runcie had invited John to accept a doctorate of Divinity 'as a recognition of the long and positive service you have given in leadership of the evangelicals in the Church of England'. The degree was conferred on him at a ceremony at Lambeth Palace on 18 July 1983, the official citation speaking of 'your services to the Church as Theologian and Author'. Lambeth made it clear to John that the degree had been *earned* on account of his many writings and was not 'honorary'.

'I would be willing to lend my support to John Stott's name,' Runcie replied to Michael Baughen, 'should it come up for discussion and if John himself is ready to let his name go forward and would accept the appointment if it were offered.'

Michael then put this idea, and the thinking behind it, to John at a private meeting at 12 Weymouth Street. 'I should like a weekend,' John said, 'to ponder the proposal and for your permission to consult one or two close advisers.'

He duly consulted and his friends advised against it.

'I felt I could not now change the whole direction of my ministry,' John reflected later, 'without acknowledging that I'd made a mistake. In declining other approaches I believed I'd made the right decision, and I had no liberty to change direction now.'

However, some years later John confessed that in many ways he would have rather liked to have been a bishop. 'Not,' he said, 'for the self-gratifying quest for privilege, or the gas-and-gaiters comfort of high office: rather, for the sheer, naked power. Bishops still have a lot of influence, and I would have loved the opportunity to use that influence to serve the people of God and to defend and preach the gospel.'

Steve Beck first met John early in 1983 when he visited Menlo Park Presbyterian Church (MPPC), California, where Steve was a member and had started dating Dot Culver, an English woman who was working with the University Ministries at MPPC. Dot knew John well as she had been on the staff of All Souls for a number of years prior to coming to MPPC.

'This is Steve,' Dot said to John.

John eyed Steve up and down, and evidently approved of Dot's choice of boyfriend. He handed Steve a brochure for the upcoming Summer School at the London Institute.

'I really do encourage you to come,' he said.

So Steve did, but without Dot who had US visa trouble. Steve attended LICC's 1983 Summer School and listened to John teaching on hermeneutics, Os Guinness on apologetics, and Jim Houston on spirituality. When John invited him to breakfast at the flat, Steve turned up with an agenda. He put a long list of questions about 'simple lifestyle', having read Ron Sider's *Rich Christians in an Age of Hunger*. John patiently listened to his searching questions and responded with some helpful practical principles. After forty-five minutes or so on this topic, John caught Steve off guard with a characteristically pointed question: 'What are your intentions towards Dot?'

Steve didn't quite know how to handle the question.

'Marriage is a good thing, Steve,' he said, 'and Dot is a lovely girl.'

John proceeded to pray that the relationship between Steve and Dot would 'come to fruition'. Steve bowed his head but didn't pray quite the same prayer since he and Dot had only been seeing each other for a few months.

However, after this Steve's single days were numbered. He got engaged to Dot four months later, moved to London with her in September 1984 and they both attended the ten-week full-time 'Christian in the Modern World' course at the institute. John was teaching throughout that course and got to know Steve better.

During an evening of light-hearted entertainment, Steve persuaded Frances Whitehead to smuggle him John's cardigan and half-moon glasses. Equipped with these, he imitated John and his familiar mannerisms – such as his habit of putting his hand up to the side of his face with one finger under his nose, the other on top – in a sketch.

In the audience, John was first embarrassed and then joined the laughter. When it was all over he approached Steve.

'You rogue!' he said. 'I don't really do that, do I?'

Later, when he caught himself doing it, he looked at Steve and said, 'I *do* do that!'

When the London Institute celebrated its twenty-fifth anniversary with a video, Steve went on record with his assessment.

'LICC ruined my life!' he said. 'It so expanded my understanding of Christ's Lordship and so increased my expectations of what it meant to be a disciple that I couldn't just sit happily in church Sunday by Sunday, singing, praying and giving. I had to find out how God wanted me to get involved in the contemporary world.'

Another recruit to the London Institute from MPPC was Ken Perez. An admirer of John's books, Ken had become an early student at the institute. He had thoroughly enjoyed listening to verbal sword fights between Os Guinness (an Oxford graduate) and John from Cambridge. He had never heard anything so quick-witted yet polite and friendly. John had tapped Ken on the shoulder and introduced himself.

Ken wanted to develop a Christian mind – a Christian view of what it means to be a businessman. He arrived in London in 1984 to work at LICC as library supervisor. 'Some people are impressive in public,' Ken remembered, 'but disappointing in private. John is the opposite. He is even more impressive in private than in public. His Christ-likeness, gentleness, personal kindness and authenticity are unforgettable.'

When John invited groups of LICC students to his flat for breakfast, Ken cooked and John acted as host. Ken remembered John's gentle answers to those who tried to trap him at question times. To widespread surprise, John had developed a taste for James Bond films and Ken accompanied him. They gave him the LICC identification card number '007'. Perhaps it was because John watched too many Bond car chases that Ken (like many others) experienced John's alarming behaviour at the wheel of his Mini Clubman.

As a result of travelling in the developing world, and talking to author Ron Sider, John was practising the simpler lifestyle he had championed at Lausanne. He had maintained friendly relationships with Ron Sider when some people in the evangelical world had dismissed what Ron was saying as 'social gospel'. John agreed with Ron that right beliefs had to be matched by right action. Instead of seeing him as a threat or as heretical, he had embraced him. Ron spoke at LICC while Ken was there, as did Tony Campolo. Rather than dismissing these two as too liberal or left wing, John had welcomed the challenge they represented.

John had given away clothes and adopted a basic wardrobe. Many people became familiar with the blue sports jacket he wore for years. He diverted the substantial royalties from his books to a variety of Christian causes.

As LICC librarian, Ken received many books from John's personal library. John's use of his royalties as an economic engine in the cause of Christ had inspired others, notably Rick Warren. When John preached at Saddleback Church in southern California, Rick put his hand on John's shoulder and said, 'This guy is one of my heroes.'

24. CLIMBING THE HILL CALLED CALVARY

When I asked John which of his books he saw as his greatest achievement, he answered (as I expected) that it was *The Cross of Christ*.

'More of my own heart and mind went into it than into anything else I have written.'

John believes that the cross transforms everything: 'It gives us a new, worshipping relationship to God, a new and balanced understanding of ourselves, a new incentive to give ourselves in mission, a new love for our enemies, and new courage to face the perplexities of suffering.' In the book he tried to allow the Bible to say what it had to say rather than what he might want it to say. But he by no means confined himself to the Bible since, as he put it, 'to be disrespectful of tradition and historical theology was to be disrespectful of the Holy Spirit who has been enlightening the church in every century'.

John argues that the cross of Christ is the only ground on which God can forgive, but readily admits that this bewilders many people. 'Why,' they ask, 'should our forgiveness depend on Christ's death? Why doesn't God simply forgive us without the need of the cross? After all, if we sin against one another, we are required to forgive one another. Why can't God practise what he preaches and be equally generous? Surely this is a primitive superstition which modern men and women should abandon.'

John notes that the first answer to this was supplied by the medieval Archbishop of Canterbury Anselm (c. 1033–1109), in his book *Cur Deus Homo?* According to Anselm, if anyone imagined that God could simply forgive us as we forgive others, that person has considered neither the seriousness of sin nor the majesty of God: when our perception of God and humanity, or of holiness and sin, is askew then our understanding of the atonement is bound to be faulty.

Considering the Old Testament material in detail and reflecting on its New Testament application to the death of Christ, John comes to his conclusion: notwithstanding fashionable thinking in the academic strongholds of liberal theology, the biblical doctrine of atonement is substitutionary from beginning to end. Christ died for us. Christ died instead of us. 'While we were still sinners, Christ died for us' (Romans 5:8).

He admits, however, that advocates of substitution have often been guilty of crudities of thought and expression which bring the truth of the doctrine into disrepute. Jesus did indeed bear the penalty for our sins, but God was active in and through Christ doing it, and Christ was freely playing his part. We must never make Christ the object of God's punishment or God the object of Christ's persuasion. We must never characterise the Father as judge and Son as saviour.

The substitute who took our place and died our death on the cross was neither Christ alone, nor God alone, but *God in Christ*. View it this way, says John, and objections to a substitutionary atonement evaporate. There's nothing remotely immoral here. What is achieved through the cross is no merely external change of legal status, since those who see God's love there, and are united to Christ by his Spirit, *become radically transformed in outlook and character.*

The Christian community is a community of celebration. Whenever Christian people come together it's impossible to stop them singing. The whole life of the Christian community should be conceived as a festival in which, with love, joy and boldness, we celebrate what God has done for us through Christ.

John tells us that the cross in fact helps us understand who we are. How should we think of ourselves? What attitude should we adopt towards ourselves? We can't answer these questions satisfactorily without reference to the cross.

A low self-image is common today. Many people have crippling inferiority feelings. Partly this may be because they have come to think that we are 'nothing but' animals or 'nothing but' machines. An over-reaction to a low self-image is an exaggerated quest to develop our 'human potential': 'Be yourself, express yourself, fulfil yourself!'

How can we renounce the two extremes of self-hatred and self-love, and neither despise nor flatter ourselves? The cross of Christ supplies the answer, for it calls us both to self-denial and self-affirmation. First, the call to self-denial: 'If anyone would come after me, he must deny himself and take up his cross and follow me' (Mark 8:34). Our 'cross' is not an irritable husband or a cantankerous wife. It is the symbol of death to self. Self-denial is not denying to ourselves luxuries such as chocolates, cakes, cigarettes and cocktails (though it may include these); it is actually denying or disowning ourselves, renouncing our supposed right to go our own way.

But all this is only one side of the truth. Alongside Jesus' explicit call to self-denial is his implicit call to self-affirmation. He spoke of the value of human beings in God's sight – 'much more valuable than birds or beasts' (Matthew 6:26; 12:12). Our divine image gives us our distinctive value.

What we are is partly the result of creation (the image of God) and partly the result of the fall (the image defaced). The self we are to deny, disown and crucify is our fallen self, everything within us that is incompatible with Jesus Christ. The self we are to affirm and value is our created self, everything within us that is compatible with Jesus Christ. True self-denial (the denial of our false, fallen self) is not the road to self-destruction but the road to self-discovery.

Since the cross is a revelation of God's justice as well as of his love, the community of the cross should concern itself with social justice as well as with loving philanthropy. It's never enough to have pity on the victims of injustice, if we do nothing to change the unjust situation itself. Good Samaritans will always be needed to help those who are assaulted and robbed. Yet it would be even better to rid the Jerusalem–Jericho road of brigands. Injustice should bring pain to God's people as it does to God himself.

It's not only the justice of God which seems incompatible with the prevailing injustices of the world, but also his love. But here John admits the problem. In our lives we are confronted with personal tragedies and global disasters. When we reflect on the sum total of the misery of the centuries, we ask how these horrors can be reconciled with a God of love. Why does God allow them?

The fact of suffering constitutes the single greatest challenge to the Christian faith, and has been in every generation. John offers no glib answers to these agonised questions. But he reminds us that Christianity does offer evidence of God's love, just as historical and objective as the evidence which seems to deny it, in the light of which the world's calamities can be viewed. This evidence is the cross. If we are looking for a definition of love, we shouldn't look in a dictionary, but at Calvary.

According to the Bible, suffering is an alien intrusion into God's good world, and will have no part in his new universe. It is a Satanic and destructive onslaught against the Creator. How does the cross speak to us in our pain? In his book John offers some suggestions explaining in tender detail why he sees the cross as a stimulus to patient endurance, the path to mature holiness, the symbol of suffering service, the hope of final glory and the proof of God's personal, loving solidarity with us in our pain.

We have to learn, says John, to climb the hill called Calvary, and from that vantage-ground survey all life's tragedies. The cross doesn't solve the problem of suffering, but it supplies the essential perspective from which to look at it.

'I could never myself believe in God,' he writes, 'if it were not for the cross. The only God I believe in is the One Nietzsche ridiculed as "God on the cross". In the real world of pain, how could one worship a God who was immune to it? He laid aside his immunity to pain. He entered our world of flesh and blood, tears and death. He suffered for us. Our sufferings become more manageable in the light of his.'

The publishers had to reprint *The Cross of Christ* within a week of publication in 1986. It has been translated into over twenty languages. Commendations over the years have been fulsome. Jim Packer spoke for many when he concluded that 'John Stott rises grandly to the challenge of the greatest of all themes. All the qualities that we expect of him – biblical precision, thoughtfulness and thoroughness, order and method, moral alertness and the measured tread, balanced judgment and practical passion – are here in fullest evidence. This, more than any book he has written, is his masterpiece.'

25. WINCING UNDER ATTACK

Early in 1987, John met David Edwards for lunch. David was then Provost of Southwark, a prolific church historian, writer and editor. They discussed and eventually agreed a proposal that David should write a book which would involve a dialogue between liberals and evangelicals, as represented by David and John. David prepared a synopsis immediately after their lunch together, and by that summer had completed his part of the book.

John took the manuscript to The Hookses in August to prepare his response. He told Bob Wismer, his former study assistant, about the task which he had landed himself with: 'It's a book which David Edwards has written about what he calls my "published works". It's a pretty devastating critique – once he's through with the flattery!'

In the book which emerged, *Essentials: A Liberal-Evangelical Dialogue*, David described John as 'apart from William Temple [Archbishop of Canterbury who died in 1944] the most influential clergyman in the Church of England during the twentieth century', and described All Souls as 'the shop window of the conservative evangelical revival'. John, said David, was a man of God who was able to draw others into God's presence and had a vision of the church as it should be. He invited people to think, not merely to 'tremble or glow'.

He noted that, as well as being born into a privileged family and possessing an able mind, John had the incalculable asset of a 'calm and sunny temperament', confidence in his mission and the courtesy of a diplomat. His brand of evangelicalism attracted not only simple 'Bible believers' but also 'literate, educated and sensitive people, uneasily aware that they live amid many revolutions and many anxieties yet need to build the house of life on rock'. He had reminded people of their God-given responsibility to use their minds Christianly. Whereas some preachers who were sincere, earnest and courageous were also arrogant, John was characterised by humility.

David went on to describe the sense in which he himself was, by conviction, a 'liberal': he accepted such science as he knew; he was indebted to critical scholars for his understanding of the Bible; he didn't believe the Bible provided a complete system of theology which all Christians ought to accept, or a comprehensive guide to how all Christians ought to believe and behave; he believed that Christians were given freedom to make up their own minds on many matters in the light of the vision or principle taught by the Bible – and were given reason and conscience to help them. He thought that God had given many good gifts to all (not only to Christians) in order that everyone might choose to know his love, do his will and enter the joy of his salvation. God's light shines on everyone in the world.

'Yes, I question and I criticise,' said David, 'but I, too, believe in basic Christianity. I, too, have been converted and in my weakness I have received the Holy Spirit . . . I confess my sins. I thank Christ for dying for me and all sinners. I accept him as my Lord and Saviour and ask him to rule my life.'

David said he admired John's dedication and skill as an expositor of the Bible. He noted that John had laid down principles of hermeneutics some of which would (he asserted) be passionately rejected by American fundamentalists who supported institutions such as Bob Jones University, the Moody Bible Institute and Dallas Theological Seminary, who suspected Billy Graham was a liberal and who ignored the magazine *Christianity Today* in the conviction that it had sold out to the liberals.

However, David's sole purpose was not to pay compliments! He wanted to offer a critical commentary on the key themes in John's teaching. He argued that conservative evangelicals do not monopolise the understanding of the Christian gospel and that there are some conservative evangelical ideas which, whether or not they are valid, are *not* essential if one is to believe the gospel revealed in the Bible.

David had reservations about John's overall account of the authority of Scripture. He didn't think John's explanation of the phrase 'verbal inspiration' took enough account of the human or cultural element in Scripture. He accused John of having a 'lingering inclination towards fundamentalism' and still had a great deal of ground in common with those who affirmed without qualification that the Bible is 'infallible' or 'inerrant' leaving the impression on 'unsophisticated minds' that it is believed to be flawless.

Most modern scholars, David told John, thought that the Bible included errors. He pointed to a whole series of contradictions, inconsistencies, errors in various parts of the Bible and parts which were not accepted by historians. He gave examples of parts of the Bible that he didn't think could be God-breathed; and went into great detail in setting out what really was God's purpose in 'inspiring the composition of the Bible', and what God was actually aiming to achieve in allowing the preservation of these passages in the Bible.

John began his reply by speaking of his opponent's combination of gifts – his breadth of learning, his ability to recall earlier views and events, his tolerant and appreciative spirit (not least in relation to evangelicals) and his sharp critical judgement. 'Often,' John told David, 'I find myself in agreement with your comments. But now you turn your great intellectual powers on me! I tremble, even wince! The prospect of having my published works scrutinised by your penetrating mind alarms me.'

John pointed out that his writing (in 1988) had spanned more than thirty years and that during that period his mind had not stood still. No one person could represent the full spectrum of evangelical thought and life. Many evangelical Anglicans wouldn't be pleased that he had been appointed as their voice. Some on the 'right wing' dismissed him as a quasi-liberal, while others to the left of him regarded him as much too conservative for their liking. He often found himself caught in the crossfire between these groupings. David had given his readers his selections and summaries of his (John's) writings and had not always done full justice to what he had written.

In suggesting some reasons for the success of evangelicalism, David had failed to refer to the *attractiveness of Jesus Christ himself*. Self-conscious human needs couldn't account for conversions to Christ unless he was clearly and persuasively presented as the fulfilment of all human aspirations. He had begun *Basic Christianity* by referring to those who were 'hostile to the church (but) friendly to Jesus Christ'. He still thought there were many in this category. He had spoken to hundreds of university students, and encountered severe, even bitter, criticism of the church but he had yet to hear any criticism of Christ.

John insisted that the evangelical faith was 'historic, mainline, Trinitarian Christianity, not an eccentric deviation from it' and that evangelicals were 'recalling the Church to original Christianity'. He wouldn't think of giving up any of these truths (as David had suggested) because they 'communicate powerfully to men and women who are conscious of their alienation'.

Turning to David's points about the authority and inspiration of the Bible, John agreed that reason had a vital role in the understanding and application of revelation, but it could never be a substitute for it. Without revelation, reason groped in the dark and foundered in the deep.

John suggested to David that, since they both believed that God said and did something through Jesus Christ which was unique in itself and decisive for the salvation of the world, it was surely inconceivable that God should first have spoken and acted in Christ and then have allowed his saving word and deed to be lost in the mists of antiquity. John suggested that if God's good news was for everybody, which it was, then he must have made provision for its reliable preservation, so that all people in all places at all times could have beneficial access to it. This is an *a priori* deduction from our basic Christian beliefs about God, Christ and salvation.

John insisted that submission to Scripture was, for evangelicals, a sign of submission to Christ. He argued that, in his debates with the Pharisees and the Sadducees, Jesus went *beyond* the Old Testament but he did not go *against* it. Jesus was conservative in his attitude to Scripture and radical in his interpretations of it, which challenged the accepted wisdom of his day. He argued that the disciples of Jesus today are called to a similar radical conservatism. If submission to Scripture was right for him, as it was, it must be right for us also. '*Not* a wooden conformity to its letter, however, but a profound penetration into its demanding implications for the life of the kingdom.' He told David that he didn't like the label 'conservative evangelical': 'it conjures up the wrong image, an image of stubborn resistance to challenge and change. "Evangelical" should be enough on its own; but if you insist on the addition of a qualification, then make it "radical conservative evangelical".'

Turning to what would become the most talked-about aspect of the exchanges between the two men, David expressed his deep regret that the Lausanne Covenant seemed to support (without clearly stating) the old belief that all those who did not accept Jesus Christ as Lord and Saviour before they died were 'lost' or 'perishing' because doomed to hell.

David asked whether both the Lausanne Covenant, and John's commentary on it, amounted to 'a comprehensively just verdict on all non-Christian religion, a subject on which the Bible offers many more generous views'. His answer to his own question was that it was 'an insulting travesty of much sincere seeking, devotion and holiness to be found among Muslims, Hindus, Buddhists and other non-Christians. And to deny that God can save those countless millions through their response to the religious traditions into which they were born is, I think, to deny either God's power or his love.'

David asked John whether he believed that the wicked were ultimately annihilated – the doctrine known as 'conditional immortality'. For himself, David believed that the idea of annihilation was the only alternative to heaven which was compatible with the belief that God is love.

John responded by saying that he was drawn by David's passion: 'You think. You ask the questions which many of us prefer to sweep under the carpet. And you feel. Your heart goes out to human beings in all their need and pain. I wish the same could be said of all of us evangelicals. Some of us neither think nor feel. We go on defending our pet convictions without either facing or feeling their implications. Our mouth is larger than our head or heart.'

With great reluctance and 'with a heavy heart' John turned to the subject of judgement and hell which David had raised. His response was to prove

225

controversial, to make him deeply unpopular in some eyes and to cause some, especially in America, to disown him as an evangelical.

He began by vigorously distancing himself from the glibness and almost glee, the *Schadenfreude*, with which some evangelicals spoke about hell. 'It is a horrible sickness of mind and spirit.'

Asking the question, 'What is hell?' John noted that he and David agreed that the imagery which Jesus and his apostles used (the lake of fire, the outer darkness, the second death) was not meant to be interpreted literally. In any case it could not be, since fire and darkness exclude each other. David was right to say that he (John) had never declared publicly whether he thought hell, in addition to being real, terrible and eternal, would involve the experience of everlasting suffering.

John surveyed the biblical material afresh 'to open our minds (not just our hearts) to the possibility that Scripture points in the direction of annihilation, and that "eternal conscious torment" was a tradition which had to yield to the supreme authority of Scripture'. He had to agree that the eternal existence of the impenitent in hell would certainly be hard to reconcile with the promises of God's final victory over evil, or with the apparently universalistic texts which speak of Christ drawing all men to himself, and of God uniting all things under Christ's headship, reconciling all things to himself through Christ, and bringing every knee to bow to Christ and every tongue to confess his lordship, so that in the end God would be 'all in all' or 'everything to everybody' (1 Corinthians 15:28). 'I do not dogmatise about the position to which I have come. I hold it tentatively. But I do plead for frank dialogue among evangelicals on the basis of Scripture. I also believe that the ultimate annihilation of the wicked should at least be accepted as a legitimate, biblically founded alternative to their eternal conscious torment.'

Who will go to hell? John pointed out to David that neither the Lausanne Covenant nor the Keele Statement which preceded it, said anything about the final destiny of those who had never heard of Christ, never received a 'worthy presentation of him' and so never had a reasonable opportunity to respond to him. What will be their fate? What does the New Testament authorise us to say about them? 'If we grant,' he wrote, 'that human beings left to themselves are perishing, and that they cannot save themselves, and that Jesus is the only qualified Saviour – which are the three truths which evangelicals are at all costs anxious to safeguard – what condition has to be fulfilled in order that they may be saved? How much knowledge of Jesus do people have to have before they can believe in him? How much faith do they have to exercise?'

John discussed a variety of answers which had been given to these questions, including Norman Anderson's suggestion that some people who had never heard of Christ might be brought, by a sense of sin, guilt and inability to save themselves, to cry for mercy to the God they dimly perceived; that God did have mercy on them; and that he saved them on the basis of Christ's atoning work, through faith, even though they had never heard of him. 'Although,' John wrote, 'I am attracted by Sir Norman Anderson's concept, and although there may be truth in it and even some of the other suggestions, I believe the most Christian stance is to remain agnostic on this question.'

John said that he was, like David, imbued with hope. 'I have never been able to conjure up (as some great evangelical missionaries have) the appalling vision of the millions who are not only perishing but will inevitably perish. On the other hand, as I have said, I am not and cannot be a universalist. Between these extremes I cherish the hope that the majority of the human race will be saved . . . even while I remain agnostic about how God will bring it to pass.'

The book was launched at a press conference in April 1988. Reviewing the book in the *Church Times*, Richard Holloway said: 'David Edwards wants to make us think: John Stott wants to make us holy. We need to hear both challenges but John Stott's challenge is the primary one . . . my verdict would be a draw.'

The part of the book which attracted most attention from North American reviewers was where John had responded to David on the fate of the lost and his discussion of whether hell, in Scripture, points in the direction of eternal conscious torment or of annihilation.

Christianity Today was quick to notice that John had moved 'into positions that are not shared by all evangelicals'. One American, John Gerstner, wrote, 'If there is anything sadder than seeing Philip Hughes fall into the terrible error of denying God's eternal punishment of the impenitent wicked, it is seeing the one sometimes called the "pope of the evangelicals", John Stott, do the same.' One critic referred to John as 'that erstwhile evangelical'.

Some years later when conservative American Christians heard that study assistant John Yates was working for John, they said to him, 'John Stott doesn't believe in hell.'

'Where did you read that?' John Yates would ask.

'Well, I've heard about it from others,' they would admit. 'You see, I don't read John Stott because he doesn't believe in hell!'

'Many people went into print,' John said in an interview, 'without even having bothered to read what I had written.' The experience caused him a lot of pain.

The truth was that John didn't think there was any 'knockdown' argument on either side which effectively settled the debate as to whether the 'lost' would be annihilated rather than eternally punished. 'I am disturbed,' he said, 'by the excessive dogmatism of those who claim that only one view is biblical. I plead for greater humility of judgment. We evangelical people need to give one another liberty in areas in which Scripture is not absolutely plain. F. F. Bruce wrote to me in 1989 that "annihilation is certainly an acceptable interpretation of the relevant New Testament passages". He added, "For myself, I remain agnostic." My position is similar.'

Much of this comment on what John had written in the book was to be expected. More disturbing to John was the reaction from his old friend Jim Packer. Packer suggested that those prepared to consider the possibility of conditional immortality (as opposed to unending conscious torment) were wilfully (or at least emotionally) rejecting 'the obvious meaning of Scripture'. While the disagreement was painful to both men, it did not prevent each continuing to commend the other's writings with enthusiasm, nor lead to any lasting break in their friendship.

26. LOST IN THE JUNGLE

All Souls Orchestra and Choir under Noël Tredinnick arranged a series of Christian concerts, 'Prom Praise', first at the Barbican and later at the Royal Albert Hall. More than once, Prime Minister Margaret Thatcher came to these with a party of friends. On 13 February 1988 she took her seat in the Albert Hall and listened as John gave the closing address at Prom Praise.

'Fifty years ago today,' he said, 'on 13 February 1938 a young man knelt at his bedside and opened the door of his heart – or personality – and invited Christ to come in. I was that young man. I have now had fifty years in which to test the reality of Jesus Christ. Tonight, on my fiftieth spiritual birthday, I want to bear witness to him, and to the length, depth, breadth and height of his love.'

Margaret Thatcher remembered her visit to Prom Praise as 'a joyous and uplifting evening'. After the event, she wrote to Richard Bewes to thank him and record how it was 'an inspiration to hear the words of testimony and hope in Jesus Christ'.

The time had come for another National Evangelical Anglican Congress in succession to those at Keele in 1967 and Nottingham in 1977. The Church of England Evangelical Council (CEEC) made preparations.

The growth in the Charismatic Movement was reflected in the planners' decision that this time they would call it a 'celebration' not a congress.

They also decided that NEAC III would be held at a holiday camp rather than on a university campus, and eventually Caister-on-Sea, Norfolk, was booked for 28 April to 2 May 1988. The planners further decided not to frame or publish any final statement, encapsulating what had been agreed and achieved.

John told the Caister planners that the decision not to produce some kind of statement was unwise, since the event would be ignored and forgotten, and selfish since its fruits would be enjoyed solely by the participants. The organisers took no notice.

Although twice as many people turned up at Caister than had gone to Nottingham eleven years earlier, the event made little lasting impact. Addressing the celebration, Archbishop Robert Runcie challenged his audience to take their doctrine of the church more seriously by producing a 'developed evangelical ecclesiology'. John responded to Runcie's challenge by affirming evangelical loyalty to the Church of England but admitting that their tendency had been to focus on 'the concepts of an invisible mystical body' and 'local independent congregations' at 'the expense of an organised and visible society united by baptism and Eucharist'.

Michael Green, by then a Professor at Regent College, Vancouver, wrote to John after Caister: 'the [evangelical] movement is now so disparate and so multiform that it is hard to see it holding together, especially after the day of your own presidency . . . There is no individual who looks capable of replacing you.'

The work of the Lausanne continuing committees and consultations, involving for John much travel, correspondence and preparation, paved the way for Lausanne II, the second International Congress on World Evangelization, convened at Manila in the Philippines for nine days in July 1989.

Manila was primarily an elaboration and expansion of Lausanne I, with some 3,000 participants from 170 countries. Todd Shy, John's current study assistant, accompanied him to Manila, sharing in a four-day bird-watching holiday before the Congress began.

Against his will, John eventually allowed himself to be persuaded yet again to chair the drafting committee. Before travelling to Manila he had read the sixty or seventy plenary papers, and had prepared from them the first draft of the declaration which the delegates would debate and revise. As the Congress developed, his draft declaration met with a rough ride. Some delegates put forward proposals that the draft be abandoned entirely, and replaced with more 'pithy statements'. The draft was criticised as too long, too wordy, too vague and too tired. Others wanted to drop the idea of a manifesto and rename the document a 'memorandum', or to send it out, not with the authority of the Congress, but simply over the names of the drafting committee.

John was hurt by these criticisms and dismayed at the prospect of having to begin again. He began to suffer from a severe headache and was unable to go on. 'I felt confused and burdened,' he wrote in his diary, 'but found relief in prayer, especially when I was brought by God's grace both to repent of my wounded pride and to surrender the document to God . . . I no longer had a stake in it which I could not relinquish.'

Rest brought renewed strength, and eventually an overwhelming majority of the delegates agreed the text of the Manila Manifesto. Only a tiny handful voted against it.

'I was particularly thankful,' John recorded, 'that afterwards participants of both the "left" and "right" expressed their satisfaction and even gratitude. The radicals could see that the Manila Manifesto went considerably further than the Lausanne Covenant in declaring the indispensability of social action, "good works" making the "good news" visible. But conservatives were pleased too, especially (I suspect) with the strong theological state-ments on the human predicament and the uniqueness of Christ.'

The Manila Manifesto was primarily a continuing commitment to the Lausanne Covenant, and a renewed call for 'the whole church to take the whole gospel to the whole world'.

'What does the Manila Manifesto add to the Covenant or the process of Lausanne?' an interviewer asked John.

'It clarifies it,' John replied. 'It tries to bring evangelism and social action together rather than considering them as separate topics. It disarms an impression which has grown up in the intervening years that the Lausanne

Covenant was a kind of social gospel. In the Manifesto we thought it necessary to repeat that evangelism is primary.'

The Lausanne Movement is now under the leadership of Doug Birdsall as Executive Chairman and Lindsay Brown as International Director. Doug Birdsall first heard John speak at the Urbana Missions Convention while a student at Wheaton College. As a seminarian and then as a young missionary in Japan, he was profoundly influenced by the model of John's life, and by his writing. Lindsay Brown was introduced to John's writing as a student in Oxford, and their paths crossed frequently from then onwards as Lindsay went on to work with the Universities and Colleges Christian Fellowship (UCCF), and from 1991 until 2007 as General Secretary of the International Fellowship of Evangelical Students (IFES).

Doug Birdsall was appointed Chairman of the Lausanne Movement in 2004, and within a year plans were put in place for The Third Lausanne Congress: Cape Town 2010, which would press digital technology into wide service, hosting a global conversation on major challenges to world evangelisation on its website, using live links to the event in seminaries and churches across the continents.

As lifelong Honorary Chairman of The Lausanne Movement, John kept in close touch with news of the planning for Cape Town 2010. He was pleased at Doug's and Lindsay's appointments. Lausanne embodied so much of what he has sought to live for and pass on to others.

A few weeks after Lausanne II, John returned to South America, flying to Brazil, meeting old friends and speaking at two seminaries. In Rio de Janeiro he preached in the Presbyterian Cathedral, processing with five other pastors in white Geneva gowns among the church's marble columns. He delivered six addresses to a conference of some 1,500 pastors, devoting three or four hours to personal interviews each day.

The conference finished, he joined a party of seventeen people who sailed up the Amazon in a large boat to the Islas Anavilhanas National Park. The party included crew, cook, scientists and friends. The boat's cabins were small, with bunks, but wood-panelled, and his had its own tiny shower room.

From time to time the scientists put ashore in canoes to erect a mist-net of fine black nylon in which birds entangled themselves. Every half-hour or so they examined the net, recorded the birds, banded and then released them.

One day, after examining the birds, John wandered off on his own. Taking his bearings from the sun, he followed whatever movements he saw and songs he heard. After an hour or so, he decided to retrace his steps. But he couldn't find his way back to the scientists' net.

He shouted loudly but there was no response. After trying unsuccessfully to take his bearings again, he walked steadily in what he believed to be the right direction. As the undergrowth grew thicker, his arms got scratched and torn by innumerable spikes and thorns. He was lost in the Amazon jungle!

After struggling slowly and painfully through more dense and twisted vegetation, he heard a cock crow – a sure sign of civilisation. He guessed he was near a clearing he'd seen on the other side of an inlet, on which a house had been built. Hearing the sounds of children's voices ahead, he persevered through the thick, unfriendly undergrowth till he could see the water. But it was down a steep bank and the trees overhung the water so far and so thickly that he could see neither house nor people on the far shore.

'Oi!' (Portuguese for 'hi!') he shouted.

A woman's voice replied in Portuguese.

'No comprehendo, perdido!' John shouted.

At last he heard the plop of a paddle. Then a very large lady in a very small canoe manoeuvred herself through the screen of trees to the bank on which he was standing. With considerable trepidation John stepped into the canoe. It was already awash under her ample dimensions and, with their combined weight, John was afraid it would sink without trace. However, the indomitable lady paddled away with no apparent misgivings. John kept feverishly baling out the water they were taking in.

At last the lady safely steered the canoe to the bank of the river and allowed John to disembark. Eventually he found his way back to the rest of his party and lived to entertain his friends with the tale many times.

When, on 1 November 1988, John was in Edinburgh for a pastors' conference on preaching, he discovered that John Wimber, charismatic American pastor and one of the founders of the Vineyard Movement, was also in the city. John telephoned and invited him to breakfast.

He had read both John Wimber's books, *Power Evangelism* and *Power Healing*, in which Wimber asserted that signs and wonders were everyday occurrences in New Testament times and should therefore characterise the normal Christian life. This wasn't how John understood either the New Testament or contemporary Christian experience. His position was to try to avoid the extremes of asserting that miracles 'don't' or 'can't' happen on the one hand, and of seeing them as everyday normality on the other. He believed that God could and did perform miracles today, but not with the same frequency as they occurred in the ministry of Jesus and his apostles. He was curious to know where Wimber stood on this matter. The main topic of their conversation over breakfast was healing.

'All I am asking,' Wimber told John, 'is that people be open for God to do unique things occasionally, in confirmation of his word. An ever-increasing number of people in our church (the Vineyard Church in Anaheim, California) are *not* healed. I myself am sick in my own body and on daily medication. More than four hundred people have come to me saying that the Lord has told them that if they lay hands on me, I will be healed. I have said to them "OK, go ahead", but I haven't been healed.'

The two Johns agreed that it was difficult both to define what a miracle was and to prove that one had occurred in a documentable way.

'I think,' Wimber told John, 'that roughly thirty per cent are healed, thirty per cent are blessed but not healed, and thirty per cent receive nothing. I've never seen major deformities of the body healed, although thousands *say* they have been cured of conditions which can't be seen.'

'Perhaps,' said John to Wimber towards the end of their conversation, 'a part of the difference in our viewpoints can be accounted for by the tension between the "already" and the "not yet", "Kingdom come and Kingdom coming", "the new age inaugurated and the new age consummated".'

John Wimber died nine years later in 1997.

On 19 April 1991 the All Souls orchestra performed at the enthronement of George Carey as the 103rd Archbishop of Canterbury. Five days later

Dr Carey hosted a reception at Lambeth Palace to mark John's seventieth birthday.

In a speech George Carey described John as 'one of the greatest Christian leaders of the twentieth century'. According to the Archbishop, John was 'a first-class teacher and scholar whose ministry has influenced men and women of all traditions. His many writings express the notable gift he has to make the Bible live and convince many people of the reality of God.'

To mark John's seventieth, his sister Joanna, with her three daughters and their families, made him a birthday present of a TV. 'They are determined,' John told friends, 'to drag me back into the modern world, from which I slipped about ten years ago when my first set went *kaput* and I decided not to have it replaced!'

Two books were published in John's honour. Vinay Samuel and Chris Sugden edited *A.D. 2000 and Beyond – A Mission Agenda, A Festschrift for John Stott's 70th Birthday*, while Martyn Eden and David Wells edited *The Gospel in the Modern World – A Tribute to John Stott*.

For her part, the Queen appointed John as an 'Extra Chaplain', an honour only exceptionally given to a few of her chaplains once they reached retirement age.

27. AN URGENT PLEA

For more than twenty years John had been haunted by a conversation he had had with two brothers. They were university students who told him they had repudiated the faith of their parents in which they had been brought up. One was now an agnostic, the other an atheist.

'Do you no longer believe in the truth of Christianity?' John asked them.

'No, that is not our problem,' they replied. 'Our dilemma isn't whether Christianity is true, but whether it's relevant. How could it be? Christianity is a primitive, Palestinian religion. It arose in a primitive culture. What on earth does it have to offer us? We live in world of space travel, transplant surgery and genetic engineering. Christianity is irrelevant.'

John knew that this feeling of the remoteness, obsolescence and irrelevance of Christianity was widespread. The world had changed dramatically since Jesus' day, and continued to change at bewildering speed. People were rejecting the gospel, not necessarily because they thought it false, but because it no longer resonated with them.

In response, he was convinced of the need to re-state the fundamental Christian conviction that God continued to speak through what he had spoken. His Word was not a prehistoric fossil but a living message for the contemporary world. But could the gospel really be modernised?

John was determined to present the gospel in such a way as to speak to modern dilemmas, fears and frustrations, but equally determined not to compromise the biblical gospel in order to do so. Christians had to apply the Word, but not manipulate it. They must do their utmost to ensure that it spoke to the times, not edit it in order to secure a fake relevance. Their calling was to be faithful and relevant, not merely trendy. How could they be both conservative and radical simultaneously, conservative in guarding God's revelation and radical in their thorough-going application of it?

It was to try to answer some of these questions that he wrote one of his most ambitious and influential books, *The Contemporary Christian: An Urgent Plea for Double Listening*, first published in 1992. In arguing that Christians were called to listen both to the Word and to the world, he stressed that he wasn't suggesting that Christians should listen to God and to their fellow human beings in the same way or with the same degree of deference. 'We listen,' he wrote in the introduction to the book, 'to the Word with humble reverence, anxious to understand it, and determined to believe and obey what we come to understand. We listen to the world with critical alertness, anxious to understand it too, and determined not necessarily to believe and obey it, but to sympathise with it and to seek grace to discover how the gospel relates to it.'

Double listening was indispensable to Christian discipleship. It was only through the discipline of double listening that it is possible to become a 'Contemporary Christian'.

Not every critic liked the book. The *Church Times* reviewer Peter Forster (who went on to become Bishop of Chester) felt that in the book, 'Stott remains open to a charge of neo-fundamentalism' and that 'it contains far too many half-grasped nettles', giving as an example the relationship between the author's discussion of the quest for community and love, 'and the actual experience many have of evangelical Christianity as moralistic and judgmental'.

Jim Packer, on the other hand, reviewing the book for *Christianity Today*, described it as 'vintage Stott', 'a pastoral essay, a sermon on paper aimed at changing people . . . In it, as usual, we find him digesting and deploying a wide range of material with a symmetry matching that of Mozart, a didactic force like that of J. C. Ryle, and a down-to-earth common sense that reminds one of G. K. Chesterton. So the book is an expository treat.'

In the summer of 1993 John agreed to take part in a major debate on Christian sexual ethics with John Shelby Spong, who was Bishop of the Episcopal Diocese of Newark for twenty-four years before his retirement in 2001. Spong's current (2009) website describes him as 'a committed Christian who has spent a lifetime studying the Bible and whose life has been deeply shaped by it'. In his book *Rescuing the Bible from Fundamentalism* he described his upbringing in a devoutly Christian home, and himself as one who, brought up as a biblical fundamentalist, had enjoyed 'a lifetime love affair' with the Bible.

Bishop Spong, however, became 'disillusioned with the literal Bible', and his 'rethinking of the meaning of Scripture' led him to some speculations and conclusions seriously at variance with an orthodox, let alone an evangelical, view. In his book, *Living in Sin?* he asserted that 'the Bible presents us with ambiguous, contradictory, and sometimes absolutely unacceptable standards for making sexual judgments today'; and urged his readers to abandon 'the prejudice of Holy Scripture'.

On the evening of 7 July 1993 between 1,300 and 1,600 people crowded into Christ Church Cathedral, Vancouver, while a further 300 were turned away at the door. Stewards escorted John to a table in the nave where he took his seat, facing a battery of microphones and lighting for TV and video recording. Sitting on his right was the moderator of the debate, Dr Maxine Hancock, an English scholar and Canadian TV personality. On her right sat Bishop Spong.

Although John thought that the local homosexual community might turn up in force and perhaps disrupt the meeting, he was in fact given an attentive hearing.

John began his introductory remarks by listing his 'five disabilities' – he was a Brit, male, single, seventy-two years old and a church member. He went on to speak of the joy of celebrating human sexuality and love-making, drawing on the Song of Songs and the New Testament. Then he turned from 'celebration' to 'limitation'.

'The same God,' he said, 'who created sex, also established the context of sex, namely marriage. And marriage, defined in Genesis 2:24, in words later endorsed by Jesus himself, is monogamous and heterosexual, the loving union of one man and one woman.'

John spoke of the gospel as good news of a new beginning. 'For a humanity fallen short of God's standard for human sexuality, rest, freedom and joy are to be found, not in discarding the yoke of Christ, but in submitting to it. And the gospel speaks not only of good news for individuals but of a new community, and at the last, a new world. This new community is characterised by love.'

John didn't seek to defend the church's record on human sexuality. 'Do I hear someone beginning to snigger,' he asked, 'because you say the church as you know it is far from being a community of love? You have found it unsympathetic, judgmental, dismissive, homophobic. I know. It's true. Some churches *are* like that. And we need deeply to repent that any church of Jesus Christ could be like that. But there are other churches, you know, that are authentic communities of love – welcoming, caring, compassionate and supportive.

'Again, as the Church of England bishops say, homosexual people are in every way as valuable to and valued by God as heterosexual people, and should find the church to be a community of love. Now that doesn't mean that the church should give its approval to the homosexual lifestyle. If we genuinely love people we will want to help them to attain God's standards and to obey God's will and we shall not want to encourage them to break these standards or defy his will. So the church is the community of righteousness as well as love, called both to a prophetic witness to monogamous, heterosexual marriage and also to a ministry of pastoral compassion towards those who cannot attain these standards.'

Bishop Spong began his talk in light-hearted vein. 'John, I'm sorry you come with so many liabilities. I do want you to know that I am married to a Brit and it is wonderful!'

Once into his stride, the Bishop took up the theme of the oppression of women and how the Bible, in his view, supported that oppression. 'But I also come before this audience,' he said, 'as a committed Christian. I come as one who cherishes the Bible. I come as one who has made the study of the Bible the primary work of my entire life. Every book I have written, including even my book on sexual ethics, is in the final analysis nothing but a book about the Bible. I speak also as one who loves the Bible so much I am not willing to stand by idly while the Bible is used as a weapon to defend the sexist definitions and stereotypes of yesterday, and to justify a blatant homophobia toward gay and lesbian people.

'A Bible that reflects tribal, racial, nationalistic, and sexual prejudices needs to be confronted. I do not hesitate to say of part of Paul's first letter to Timothy, "This is not the word of the Lord. These are the words of a first century man locked inside the cultural definitions of his day, and trying to support his prejudices by an appeal to God" . . .

'Let me be quite specific. I regard homosexuality as a given, not a chosen; as a minority but perfectly normal position on the human sexual scale, not as an abnormality; and as an enriching part of the human experience . . . '

As John listened, he recognised the Bishop's skill in advocacy and his powers of passionate communication. But it was difficult to pin down the main areas of disagreement in such a wide-ranging, fast-talking and passionate presentation.

For his five-minute response he decided to focus on three points. 'First,' said John, 'I want to stress that although the world's view on ethical issues may have changed, Christians are not bound to agree with it. Second, I believe that in his treatment of Scripture Bishop Spong has been guilty of a great deal of selectivity. And finally, if we genuinely want to be submissive to our Lord Jesus Christ, we cannot treat his teaching in the cavalier way in which I fear that Bishop Spong has done.'

For his five-minute response, Bishop Spong returned to his attack on parts of the biblical record before coming to his conclusion. 'John Stott talked about monogamous marriage. I favour monogamous marriage with every part of my being. I understand and I appreciate the phrase, "what God has joined together, let no one put asunder". I intend to be monogamously married to the most wonderful woman in the world, and I covet that relationship of faithful monogamy for all of God's people, including God's gay and lesbian children.'

A time of questions to both speakers followed, before both of them were allowed a further five minutes for their closing remarks. John used his to share his anxiety about what the audience had heard during the evening of the treatment of Scripture. 'If you are scrupulous in your use of proper principles of biblical interpretation, far from manipulating and controlling Scripture, you'll find that Christ as Lord controls you, your thinking and your living, through the Scriptures. That is, I think, the area that we need to develop.'

Bishop Spong used his final five minutes to read from a powerful prepared statement. John took the view that the Bishop's unexpected use of this statement, in the course of which he had introduced new arguments, placed him at a disadvantage. When the editor of the magazine *Crux* proposed to carry a transcript of the debate, John wrote and asked to be allowed to make a brief further response in writing. This was agreed.

Bishop Spong was irritated by John's printed postscript to the debate's transcript, and went into print complaining about his poor treatment at the hands of evangelicals. The two men's basic presuppositions on the use of Scripture were so different that the debate in Christ Church Cathedral on that July evening made little progress towards any form of agreement. Writing to the Dean after his return to England, John urged that the next such debate should be on the authority and interpretation of Scripture. Maxine Hancock, who had acted as Moderator, also believed that a way forward should be based on agreed hermeneutical principles. That was indeed the crux of the matter.

In 1993 the group *Reform* was founded to bring together those who thought the Church of England had lost confidence in the truth and power of the gospel. John attended their first conference at Swanwick as a mark of solidarity. However, his misgivings about the movement are clear from a letter he wrote in July which said, 'I do not agree with the dogmatic statements which have been made about the ordination of women, namely that it is "plainly contrary to Scripture". It is nothing of the kind. The issues are much more subtle and complex, and involve the whole area of cultural transposition. I find myself personally in reaction against excessive evangelical dogmatism, and therefore against what I hear *Reform* people saying.'

John did regret that the founders of *Reform* had not talked in detail with the Church of England Evangelical Council before launching a new movement which was, in his opinion, likely to weaken the evangelical cause by further division.

In January 1994 participants at conferences and meetings at the Toronto Airport Christian Fellowship began to report dramatic healings, 'holy laughter', 'falling' or 'resting' in the Spirit and 'shaking' as well as incidents of personal transformation and a claimed greater awareness of God's love. British churches coined the phrase 'Toronto Blessing' to refer to these phenomena. Some visitors to Toronto attempted to carry the influence of what they had seen and heard back to their home churches and fellowships.

When a friend of John's in Africa toyed with the idea of visiting Toronto to meet 'the blessing' at first hand, John wrote to him regretting 'the wrong-headed lust for the spectacular and the physical'. He added that 'the idea of travelling to Toronto in order to "get the blessing" is very strange . . . We believe that the Holy Spirit has universalised the presence of Jesus, and that God has pledged himself to his people, wherever they are, not to places or buildings.'

John had four personal hesitations about what he had been hearing from Toronto. First he was concerned that it was an avowedly anti-intellectual movement. One of the first promoters had said, 'Don't analyse. Don't ask questions. Simply receive.' John thought that advice was both foolish and dangerous. Second, he was dismayed that, so far as he knew, charismatic leaders had not disassociated themselves from the animal noises which some Toronto people had been making, roaring like lions and barking like dogs. The whole Bible told us not to behave like animals. Third, there was no biblical basis for uncontrollable laughter – the main characteristic of true revival was weeping rather than laughing. And finally, although there were a few examples in Scripture of people falling down, they had invariably fallen on their faces after a vision of the majesty and holiness of God. This was quite different from all that he understood to be going on in Toronto.

John wrote to his old friend Billy Graham in December 1995, noting that 'though there is much to thank God for in the current scene, there is also much which seriously troubles Richard [Bewes] and me, and others of our perspective – not least the rapid spread of anti-intellectual "charis-mania", focused at the moment on the Toronto phenomena'.

All these new phenomena raised controversial issues which had the potential to divide Christians. John reflected on his own approach to controversy. In theological debate he thought it was important not to push people to the opposite extreme to the one he occupied himself, unless the facts warranted it. He believed that we should always beware of caricaturing our opponents' positions – of building a straw man and then demolishing it. We should always engage and answer their best arguments, not their worst ones.

He had developed four principles as a personal guide to dealing with controversy. First, he never initiated a conversation or correspondence on a controversial matter, but only responded to somebody else's specific questions. Second, he didn't speak about such matters publicly, from platform or pulpit, but only in private and in confidence. Third, he avoided saying behind anybody's back anything he hadn't said to his or her face. And fourth, he didn't speak negatively about anybody without first affirming what he could say positively.

In November 1995, the British people were riveted by an interview broadcast on the BBC television programme *Panorama* in which Martin Bashir interviewed Princess Diana.

'Do you think Mrs Parker-Bowles was a factor in the breakdown of your marriage?' Bashir asked.

'Well,' Diana replied, 'there were three of us in this marriage, so it was a bit crowded.'

Using his position as Extra Chaplain, and having been a Chaplain to the Queen for thirty-five years, John wrote personally to both Charles and Diana that November urging 'a new possibility – not for divorce but for reconciliation. For reconciliation,' he assured them, 'is at the heart of the gospel of Christ.' Sadly, neither party took his advice.

On a number of visits to the Arctic Circle over a period of twenty-five years John had caught fleeting glimpses of the snowy owl. On a visit to Canada in July 1996 to celebrate his seventy-fifth birthday, he made another attempt to achieve a good sighting of the owl. He arrived at Cambridge Bay, and with four friends took advantage of the midnight sun to drive into the wild in a ramshackle truck.

After three or four miles, the moment for which John had been waiting so many years at last arrived. In front of him a pair of snowy owls walked across the tundra to their eggs. John counted seven off-white shiny pear-shaped eggs and with them a newly hatched little chick. The 'nest' was just a scraping of bare earth situated on a rise in the ground at the foot of a small rock for protection. The site commanded a 360-degree view of any approaching enemy predators.

John and his friends managed to erect a hide. Because the Canadian Arctic is the land of the midnight sun, there was enough light to take photographs round the clock, including the early hours of the morning. And so here over the next few days John crouched, sometimes for six hours at a stretch, his camera at the ready. As he looked at the bird through his camera viewfinder, the owl's head and body filled the picture. 'She stared,' he recorded in his journal, 'even glared at me with her penetrating yellow eyes. Indeed, it was as if we stared unblinking at each other (though I realise she couldn't see me), eyeball to eyeball. I could even watch mosquitoes landing on her feathered face. They even walked on the surface of her eyes until she blinked and shook her head vigorously to dislodge them.' Every few hours the male would visit the nest with a freshly killed lemming. Ceremoniously the female took the lemming from the male and fed it to her chicks. John later reproduced the photographs in his book, *The Birds Our Teachers*.

28. THE LUCKIEST MAN ON EARTH

John Yates succeeded Nelson Gonzales as study assistant in 1996. He was the son of a family John Stott had known for many years, and whose father was Rector of Falls Church, Virginia.

'We can't have two Johns in the same office,' Frances Whitehead told him. 'What shall we call you?'

'Sometimes they call me JY,' John replied. So that is what they called him.

John was seventy-five and JY just twenty-two when he started working for him. On JY's first morning at work he walked into John's bedroom – his office during daylight hours – and found a ten-page handwritten manuscript on his desk. Attached was a brief note: 'This is an interview for a book written for single people in their 20s. Could you give me your feedback on what I've said, and suggest any changes to make it more interesting or relevant?'

JY read carefully through the manuscript and listed half a dozen suggestions for additions, deletions and modifications. Next morning, there again on JY's desk was a ten-page handwritten manuscript with a note: 'What do you think now?' John had rewritten the interview and taken some account of every suggestion JY had made.

For eighteen months, JY worked with John on a second revision of the book *Issues Facing Christians Today*. Each revised chapter had a designated expert for that particular theme and it was JY's job to liaise with the expert. The task of revision was gruelling and relentless. JY remembered working on it for ten hours a day for several weeks at The Hookses. Once they had a heated discussion, unable to agree how to approach an issue raised by the environment chapter. But John allowed JY to draft some of the revised sections himself.

At 11 o'clock on the evening of 17 January 1998 John Yates climbed into his bed at The Hookses and wrote up his diary: 'Today was our last long big go at *Issues*. It has been conquered and the end is in sight. Yesterday afternoon I finished my final read-through of the manuscript and today was Uncle John's day to go over it. He spent most of the day reading and we spent most of the evening talking, arguing, laughing, sighing and sorting through 18 separate folders and reams of papers.

'The fact that we have a relationship where I can disagree, debate and argue even to a fault speaks volumes about Uncle John's humility. He asks for my opinion, listens to it, sometimes questions it, usually clarifies it and often acts on it. You can only develop a relationship like this over time – time during which the older and wiser partner is consistently humble and patient with the younger, immature and often rash partner. I am given freedom to express every thought and opinion, am encouraged to feel my contributions are of genuine value and am as a result seriously challenged by the model of humility I am faced with set against my own pride, stubbornness and desire to be vindicated. Uncle John remains an incredibly stubborn individual, and yet it is his humility that leaves the deeper impression.'

Eventually they completed the task. JY was soon able to preserve for posterity a picture of how each day began for John. Each morning (usually at five a.m.) John swung his legs over the side of his bed and before placing a foot on the ground started the day (whenever possible) with a Trinitarian prayer.

'Good morning heavenly Father, good morning Lord Jesus, good morning Holy Spirit. Heavenly Father I worship you as the creator and sustainer of the universe. Lord Jesus, I worship you, Saviour and Lord of the world. Holy Spirit I worship you, sanctifier of the people of God. Glory to the Father, and to the Son and to the Holy Spirit. Heavenly Father

I pray that I may live this day in your presence and please you more and more. Lord Jesus, I pray that this day I may take up my cross and follow you. Holy Spirit, I pray that this day you will fill me with yourself and cause your fruit to ripen in my life: love, joy, peace, patience, kindness, goodness, faithfulness, gentleness and self-control. Holy, blessed and glorious Trinity, three persons in one God, have mercy upon me, Amen.'

It wasn't always possible for John to use this Trinitarian prayer, for instance when he was travelling, but he did when he could, and it provided a solid foundation for the day ahead.

Bible reading was the next item on the agenda of the daily quiet time. John was grateful that many years earlier Martyn Lloyd-Jones had introduced him to a Bible reading calendar produced by Robert Murray McCheyne for his congregation in Dundee which enabled them to read the whole Bible through every year: Old Testament once and New Testament twice. It was an exacting task as it meant reading four chapters a day: John's practice was to read two chapters every morning without stopping, to study a third, and keep the fourth for the evening, although he admitted he was by then often too tired to manage it. (Robert Murray McCheyne's method is now available as *More Precious than Gold*, published by the Lausanne Movement, in the *Didasko Files* series.)

Prayer came next, beginning with a responsive turning of the biblical text into praise and petition. At this point John would reach for a small leather notebook containing various folded papers and pamphlets. This notebook travelled the world with him as a companion to his Bible. He took off the strong rubber band and began to pray for friends, families, ministries and strangers – all listed in the notebook and constantly revised.

The Hookses served as a magnificent and unique venue for conferences, visitors, church weekends, holidays and as a writer's retreat. 'It is impossible,' John told a friend, 'to express my sense of gratitude to God for his providential gift of The Hookses. I sometimes say to myself that I'm the luckiest man on earth. The intoxicating Pembrokeshire air, the beauty of seascape and landscape, the stillness and seclusion, and the rich variety of bird life, together make a uniquely satisfying combination of blessings. My favourite nook is a turf ledge a few feet down from the top of a nearby cliff. Here, especially in the early evening, as the declining summer sun paints the sea silver and gold, I love to sit, either alone or with a friend, to read, to think, to dream and to pray. It would be hard to imagine a greater contrast between central London and coastal south west Wales, yet each has its own fascination and I enjoy them both to the full.'

John usually shared the task of cleaning out weeds and other unwanted vegetation from the small fish pond at The Hookses with his current study assistant and any willing volunteers who happened to be visiting. New arrivals at The Hookses were often surprised to see the internationally-known preacher and writer up to his knees in cold water, wearing grimy clothes, grinning with satisfaction as he repeatedly dipped his bare arms under water to grab handfuls of weed and throw them to the shore.

Because he made no contribution to the preparation of food at The Hookses, John always insisted on being allowed to do the accumulated dishes from the day after the evening meal. Although visitors were often reluctant to see him spending half-an-hour washing dishes, he always got his way. John Yates discovered that John washed dishes with a combination of a meticulous mind and the playfulness of a child. 'Each dish is vigorously scrubbed in the left-hand sink, and then summarily plopped into the right-hand sink filled with hot water for rinsing. The hapless volunteer who has assumed the job of drying receives a splash and a chuckle with every dish. By the end of the cycle the dryer is soaked, while Uncle John whisks off his plastic apron as dry as the moment he started.'

The Hookses is the only property John has ever owned, and in the late 1990s he passed it by Deed of Gift to the Langham Trust. The trustees accepted it on condition that the Hermitage (John's flat and study for him and office for Frances Whitehead) should be his to use during his lifetime. 'From my study window,' he wrote, 'I look out across West Dale Bay to the open ocean beyond. I sometimes claim to have an uninterrupted view of the South Pole!'

John Yates was fascinated by the relationship between John and Frances. 'The saving grace of Uncle John's life was Frances,' JY told me. 'Frances gave him the personal developmental advantages of being married without being married. I don't know another human being who could have kept up with John. She has felt that she has been a vital part of his ministry.'

Even the luckiest man on earth's good health didn't last for ever. In May 1998 John went bird-watching with friends in Lebanon. He found it difficult to see the birds he was watching, and it seemed at first as if one eye-piece of his binoculars was faulty. But on handing them to his companion, it was clear that the trouble was not with the binoculars but with his eye. Then he began to suffer acute abdominal pain which deferred his flight home by twenty-four hours. He arrived back at Heathrow in a wheelchair.

His friend and medical adviser, Professor John Wyatt, examined him. Tests revealed that John had suffered two embolisms which had permanently impaired the vision of his left eye, and were the probable cause both of the pain in his stomach and an irregular heartbeat which had developed.

After a few days in St Luke's Hospital, he was able to return home determined to continue with his future overseas engagements. Treatment with digoxin successfully returned his heart rhythm to normal but the loss of vision didn't improve. He was, however, still able to read, write and preach without difficulty, provided that he had good light. Occasionally he tripped over obstacles or bumped into people when walking in London and, tumbling from time to time, needed to take care when ascending and descending stairs. It was clear that he shouldn't drive again, though he retained his car so that Frances Whitehead or one of his study assistants could take him to his various engagements and to and from The Hookses.

John was well enough, over a period of a few months during 1998, to write what he eventually called *Evangelical Truth: A Personal Plea for Unity*. John Yates, during his last year as study assistant, helped John clarify in his mind what the main thrust of the book would be.

'As I approach the end of my life on earth,' he wrote, 'and as this year I complete sixty years of privileged Christian discipleship, I would like to leave behind me, as a kind of spiritual legacy, this little statement of evangelical faith, this personal appeal to the rising generation.'

Twenty years on from answering the question 'What is an evangelical?' at Nottingham in 1977, he chose a fresh approach to evangelical truth. But first he set out ten respects in which the authentic evangelical differed from the fundamentalist. Aiming to be as fair as he could to fundamentalists and desperately trying to avoid caricature, he set out as he saw it the differences between evangelicals and fundamentalists in the areas of human thought, the nature of the Bible, biblical inspiration and interpretation, the ecumenical movement, the church, the world, Christian mission, and the second coming of Christ.

John insisted that the supreme quality which the evangelical faith should engender was humility, readily admitting that this claim might well be met with a wry smile. He knew full well that evangelical people were often regarded as proud, vain, arrogant and cocksure. Evangelical Christianity was Trinitarian Christianity and, if this was correctly understood, it inevitably tended towards humility. Evangelicals held the three 'Rs' — revelation, redemption and regeneration, associating revelation with the Father, redemption with the Son, and regeneration with the Holy Spirit. Yet the more the three persons of the Trinity were glorified, the more completely human pride was excluded. To magnify the cross of Christ was to confess our utter lostness without it. To magnify the regenerating, indwelling and sanctifying role of the Holy Spirit was to confess our abiding self-centredness without it.

IVP, the publishers, launched the book at the IFES World Assembly at Seoul in 1999. The goal of the Fellowship, which John served as Vice-President for several terms and for which he is lifelong Ambassador-at-Large, is to make Christ known in every university in the world. At the assembly, Daniel Bourdanné introduced him as 'Papa Stott'.

'Papa John,' intervened John, correcting Daniel with a smile.

In November 1998 the broadcaster and sociologist Elaine Storkey retired after seven years as Director of the London Institute for Contemporary Christianity. In June 1999, Steve Beck became chairman of the LICC board. John, Steve, and Steve's predecessor Denis Osborne met Mark Greene, then Vice-Principal of the London Bible College, and appointed him as Elaine's successor in September 1999. After a difficult few years in the life of the Institute, Mark and Steve met John to discuss the future.

'The Institute will either rise like a Phoenix or go down in flames,' John said.

LICC needed some shaking up and could not be allowed merely to coast along. John remained fully engaged as the Institute went through several further financial crises, but turned a corner after 2003 and under Mark's leadership is thriving today.

In January and February 1999, John Yates accompanied John to China, Thailand, Taiwan and Hong Kong. At Chiang Kai Shek International Airport a ten-foot-wide bright red banner was furled across the arrivals hall reading, *WELCOME DR JOHN STOTT TO TAIWAN*. A personable Chinese woman presented John with a large bouquet of tiger lilies and roses before escorting him to a black Mercedes with curtained windows and leather seats which whisked him away to his first engagement in Taipei.

At the offices of the Campus Evangelical Fellowship, which published many of John's books in Chinese, he was led from department to department. Giggling young women peered round doorways and over cubicles as if a film star had arrived. 'Seventy-seven and he still gets girls to giggle!' John Yates commented. 'What a role model!'

JY may have been a little modest here since on several occasions Chinese people told him he looked like the *Titanic* actor Leonardo DiCaprio. Maybe that was at least part of the explanation for the giggles!

Giving an interview in Hong Kong, John was asked whether he had ever experienced great temptations or thought of giving up his ministry.

'Pastors are especially vulnerable to temptation,' he said in the course of his reply. 'Our chief problems are discouragement and loneliness. These can easily lead to burnout and so to giving up the struggle. I have never really been tempted to this because I have taken precautions. I have recognised that human beings are psychosomatic creatures, so that our bodily condition has a powerful influence on our spiritual life. I have tried to maintain a disciplined life, ensuring adequate sleep, food and exercise. I have known the great value of friends, to overcome loneliness. Birdwatching is an excellent recreation, for it takes you out into the wilderness with all the sights, sounds and smells of nature, and it is relaxing and absorbing to the mind. I don't think birdwatchers get nervous breakdowns!

I have found, however, that most important of all is a disciplined devotional life, with a determination to meet Christ every day.'

John suffered a chest infection towards the end of this stay in the Far East in February 1999, and later in the year became unwell when visiting Salisbury for the Diocesan Evangelical Fellowship. On his return to London he was admitted to hospital and found to be suffering from pneumonia. For a day or two there was serious concern for his health, even his life.

When he returned to the Rectory, there were times when Richard Bewes knocked on his bedroom door hoping he hadn't died. They installed an alarm so that if he felt ill, John could press a button – though he never used it. He invited Myra Chave Jones for lunch on her eightieth birthday. After the meal he had a bad turn and began to act strangely. His local doctor came quickly and they took him in a taxi to hospital. But he made a remarkable recovery and was soon back at work.

John, Frances and friends spent some weeks at The Hookses in June 1999. 'It is just glorious this week,' Frances Whitehead told their friend and biographer Timothy Dudley-Smith. 'We have had almost unbroken sunshine: we are revelling in the beauty and the peace. In the afternoons John has been humping damp pond-weed from there, up the steps and round to the compost heap – he counted twelve loads one day and thirteen the next! I don't know how his back survives!'

29. LAPS OF HONOUR

Corey Widmer succeeded John Yates as John's study assistant in 2000, aged twenty-two. After growing up in Chattanooga, Tennessee, he had attended the University of Virginia where he met John Yates. It was JY who recommended Corey to John as his successor. John and Corey met during a weekend when John was in Chicago for a meeting of the John Stott Ministries board. They got on well, and two months after graduating Corey left for London to begin three years working for John.

John, Corey and Frances spent Monday 31 January 2000 frantically taking care of last-minute details for a trip to Africa, sending faxes, dictating and typing letters, running errands, gathering information, and packing. They had to transport two large boxes of books to Africa, each weighing about thirty-five pounds. They decided the safest way of avoiding extra baggage costs was to distribute them throughout their cases. They managed to fit more than a hundred books into their luggage – but their cases far surpassed the weight limit.

They said goodbye to Frances, caught a taxi to Victoria Station and the train to Gatwick where, to their relief, the airline official checked their luggage, and sent them through without question. Aboard the plane, John slipped on an eye mask, put in some ear plugs, took a sleeping pill, and slept for six and a half hours without stirring. Corey managed a few minutes sleep only. They landed at Nairobi Airport around 9.30 a.m., after enjoying a beautiful view of the rounded white peak of Mt. Kenya.

'I couldn't sleep all night,' Corey said to John.

'It's a sign of a bad conscience,' John replied.

Would they be allowed through customs with hundreds of Christian books and Bibles? The official at passport control sent them through without a word. At customs, John shook hands with the official and greeted him in Swahili, 'Jambo!'

'Anything to declare?'

'Just some educational books,' said John.

The man smiled and waved them through.

'Bwana Asifiwe!' ('Praise the Lord') said John in Swahili.

The custom official's face broke into an enormous smile.

'Bwana Asifiwe! Amen!' he said, grasping John's hand.

'I prayed in the night, and this morning as we waited in line, that the Lord would grant us a Christian customs officer,' John told Corey.

A teacher at Nairobi Evangelical Graduate School of Theology (NEGST), met them at the airport and drove them to the School, set in a beautiful fifty-acre campus.

After Oscar and Beatrice Muriu welcomed the two men into their home, John's teaching programme began. It seemed to Corey that in Africa John took on a new vibrancy and life. His joy and sincerity attracted the Africans to him. When he finished his talks, his audience excitedly crowded around him with questions.

The Kenyans worked on a consistently lagging schedule – everything was assumed to start thirty to forty-five minutes behind the advertised time. On the second morning, the programme had stated that John would speak at 8 a.m., but he didn't actually stand at the podium until 9.15.

Oscar Muriu treated John and Corey to an authentic African meal. He bought a live goat, killed it himself, hung it upside down, cut the throat, drained the blood, and systematically cut it in pieces. The women spent hours in the kitchen cooking a feast for about thirty people.

On the final day of the NEGST conference Corey put a question to John.

'What initially sparked your interest in the developing world?'

'The Bible,' John replied. 'Its emphasis on love for the poor I take as an unavoidable call.'

John and Corey flew from Nairobi to Entebbe for a visit to Uganda. David Zac Niringiye, an old friend of John's and a former Langham Scholar, met them with his beaming face and infectious laugh. They stayed in the Namirembe guest-house to the Anglican Cathedral on one of Kampala's seven hills. The house overlooked the city and, as the sun rose in the morning, the birds and wildlife in the trees performed the sounds of the jungle.

John led a preaching workshop at the Kampala Evangelical School of Theology (KEST). About seventy pastors attended from five or six different denominations.

'Each of these men and women can influence hundreds of members of their congregations,' John said to Corey.

One afternoon, as they walked up the hill in Kampala to the Anglican Cathedral, John started singing to a young altar boy, 'Tuku tendereza Jesu' ('We are washed by the blood of the Lamb'). The boy couldn't believe John knew the song and joined in with him lustily.

On the Sunday morning, John, David Zac, Jeremy Lindsell and Corey attended an informal service in a shaded thatched gazebo by Lake Nabugabo, south-west of Kampala. John read the 'Gratitude' chapter from *The Birds Our Teachers*, and those present in turns said what they were grateful for.

'I am grateful for my parents,' said John, 'and most of all for my many friends all over the world, who I count as my world-wide family.'

They shared some needs for use in prayers of intercession.

'I should like to finish my race well,' said John, 'and to say with Paul, "I have fought the good fight, I have finished the race, I have kept the faith."'

'I think you have already finished the race well,' said Jeremy. 'Now you are just making laps of honour.'

It was 13 February. Sixty-two years earlier in 1938, John had become a Christian.

In their evening prayers, Corey thanked God for John's conversion and for sixty-two years of faithful service. John stood up and sighed.

'Where would I be without that day? Probably on some scrap-heap!'

John and Corey flew to Nanyuki, a market town in central Kenya, north-west of Mount Kenya. The town was founded in 1907 by British settlers, some of whose descendants still lived in and around the town. They were met by Jane Prettejon, an elegant older lady, but a relatively young Christian, who addressed everyone as 'darling'. She had arranged for a small party to visit some of her favourite places in this part of east Africa. They climbed aboard a small six-seater twin-engined plane and flew over scrubby plains, several large herds of zebra and a mountain range before landing on a small dirt strip.

Among the welcoming party was James, son of the chief of his Masai tribe. John, delighted to find that he knew every bird by sight and call, gave him a copy of *The Birds Our Teachers*. James led them to *Il Ngwesi*, a little group of thatched huts on the top of a small hill surrounded by hills covered with scrub on one side and long flat plains on the other. He showed John and Corey to a hut with a huge four-poster bed, a smaller single bed, two beautiful sturdy chairs, a desk, and a tall thatched roof. The west side was open, overlooking the mountains and a small watering hole visited by elephants, warthogs, leopards, bushbucks and giraffes. John and Corey fell asleep to the sound of playing, squealing elephants and woke to the chattering of a thousand birds. They had lunch by a pool, and breakfast and dinner in the shade of a cool veranda.

After this blissful break at *Il Ngwesi*, they took off again from the airstrip in a six-seater single-engine Cessna, arriving eventually at Sunshade Safari Camp – a cluster of green canvas tents with running water and showers. They were taken on a game drive and saw cape buffaloes, gazelles, zebras and birds of prey. When Steve, their driver, saw a distant lion through his binoculars, they made their way to it, and admired it in all its majesty. A male with a full mane, it lay lazily on a small hill, quite unimpressed by the presence of a group of admirers.

At a Masai village in Mara, an American, Jon Johnson, with his German wife and two daughters, had planted a little Bible church. John and Corey joined them on Sunday morning under an enormous acacia tree. About twenty Masai children sat in a circle in their Sunday school, flies swarming over their faces. Two little ones kept cuddling up to John and played with his white hand and forearm.

The adults, mainly from the Masai tribe, were joined by another American couple who were missionaries in the area. With them were two visiting American pastors from their supporting home church. Suddenly one of them looked hard at John.

'Are you *THE* John Stott?' he asked.

'Well, I am *A* John Stott,' John replied.

The Americans got excited.

'What a privilege! We will remember this day for the rest of our lives!'

They sang some English hymns with the words changed to Swahili. They asked John to give his testimony. John agreed but, after a few sentences, it was clear that his translator, one of the Masai men, was struggling. As a result Mustafa, a Muslim who was manager at the camp where John and Corey were staying, translated the whole testimony.

Back in England, John was thrilled when Archbishop George Carey conferred on Frances Whitehead an honorary MA degree at Lambeth Palace in June 2001. The citation read, 'In recognition of her energetic and enthusiastic ministry to God's Church through her dedicated support of Dr John Stott for over 40 years and for her visible Christian witness.' 'I felt a bit of a fraud receiving a degree without having had to pass an exam!' Frances said. But everyone who knew her recognised how much she deserved the honour.

In September 2001, John appointed Chris Wright as his successor to oversee the three strands of the work of Langham Partnership International. The Partnership's vision continued, as it remains, to see churches worldwide being equipped for mission and growing to maturity through the ministry of Christian leaders and pastors who 'sincerely believe, diligently study, faithfully expound and relevantly apply the Word of God'. The Langham Literature programme provides evangelical books for pastors, theological students and seminary libraries, and encourages evangelical writing and publishing in the developing world. The Langham Scholars programme offers scholarships to enable evangelical leaders to gain doctorates in biblical and theological studies, and return to their home countries as seminary teachers and church leaders. And the Langham Preaching programme develops networks and movements for the training of pastors and leaders in biblical expository preaching.

John maintained his avuncular oversight of all that Chris was doing in the Langham Partnership. Whenever they had their regular breakfasts together, Chris felt like Timothy reporting back to the Apostle Paul.

'I would come with a list of items to report,' Chris told me, 'and go away with another list of points he had made to me. And yet, although he took a detailed and daily prayerful interest in all that Langham has been doing, once I was appointed as International Director, he never "pulled rank" or insisted on any decision or policy, but very deliberately granted me freedom and affirmed my role in board meetings. I thrived on his support and prayer, and never felt overshadowed or constrained by his seniority or intrinsic authority.'

After many months of planning and anticipation, John and Corey Widmer waited on 2 February 2002 in the departure lounge at Heathrow, listening for their flight number to Madras to be called. John was just a few weeks away from his eighty-first birthday.

When they were called for boarding they were informed that they had been promoted to travel business class. They arrived at Chennai Airport at nearly 1.30 in the morning and were met by Roopy Carr, director of the SALT (Scripture Applied Leadership Training) Institute which he had founded, and who had been a member of All Souls in London in the 1960s. Roopy draped two elaborate Indian necklaces around John and Corey's necks. In the baggage hall they were joined by Roopy's son, Ravin.

After a relaxing break at a Scripture Union camp centre, John and Corey climbed into a large air-conditioned vehicle for a three-day bird-watching excursion. As they travelled to Tanjore, the 'rice bowl of Tamil Nadu', their driver constantly blew his horn, dodging and swerving around people, carts, goats, oxen, bicycles, motorbikes, minicabs, cows, trucks and buses. Roopy Carr, his son Ravin and wife Vasanthi went with them.

Eventually they arrived at the SALT Institute in Chennai, the new Tamil name for Madras, a polluted and noisy city with a population of six million, twelve per cent of whom were Christians in 2,000 churches. From John's and Corey's rooms on the third floor there was constant noise from the cars, trucks, bicycles, and mopeds on the busy road outside their windows. The house lay directly under the flight path of planes taking off and landing at Chennai Airport.

On Sunday morning John preached at a large Church of South India church, St Andrew's Kirk, established in 1821 by Scottish Presbyterians. The electricity shut off once or twice during the service, and the building looked as if it had been shipped out to India from Victorian Britain. The hymns were solemn and traditional. John preached powerfully, relieved at last to get this busy week of preaching off to a start.

On the Monday morning they returned to St Andrew's Church for a crowded event hosted by the SALT Institute. Over a thousand Indian Christians came from over a hundred different churches, representing many different denominations. John was visibly anxious and Roopy seemed haggard and on edge as the SALT workers tried to control a crowd of eager people congregating at the doors.

Just before the meeting started, John felt unwell and Corey rushed to a chemist shop for needed medicine. John seemed unstable and nervous as he waited to speak, but once he began he grew in confidence. The questions which followed reflected the concern of Indian Christians to present Jesus as unique Lord of all rather than another god to be absorbed into the Hindu pantheon.

Roopy took them to a small inlet on the coast, hoping to give John a short bird-watching break before his next appointment. When John spotted a blue-throated kingfisher, he dashed after it, hit a high kerb and fell heavily on to a polluted bank. He sustained a nasty cut on his leg about 3–4 cm long. Roopy and Ravin were gripped with remorse, blaming themselves for taking John there and for not seeing the kerb.

On the Monday morning John's injury looked more serious. The cut was bleeding and infected, and his ankle and foot had swollen to unnatural proportions. He was in continuous discomfort and pain. Ravin called a doctor.

'There is no need to amputate the leg,' the doctor said reassuringly. 'It already seems to be healing.'

They were forced to cancel personal interviews with John for the time being and return to the SALT Institute in the afternoons for rest. On

Wednesday John's foot returned to almost its normal size. At the preaching seminar John spoke from a sitting position with his leg propped up. But by the afternoon the ankle and foot had swelled to the same size as the night before. While John slept for his 'horizontal half-hour,' Corey called Frances Whitehead in London. She rang John Wyatt, who suspected that the swelling might be due to a blood clot or deep-vein thrombosis.

'I am concerned that he is in danger of a more serious coronary or stroke,' John Wyatt said. 'They should abort now and come home. But in the first instance they must send me a detailed report on John's condition so that I can make an informed decision.'

When John woke from his rest, Corey told him what John Wyatt had said. It seemed to Corey that John thought his death might be imminent. He began to sing a verse of the hymn he had chosen for his funeral:

Happy if with my latest breath,
    I may but gasp his Name:
Preach him to all, and cry in death,
    'Behold, behold the Lamb!'

'I am sure you're not approaching your "latest breath",' reassured Corey.

John smiled. 'I always want to be ready,' he said.

Sometime later Corey returned to John's room to find him in a contented state between sleep and consciousness. He showed no signs of anxiety and seemed peaceful. Corey read 1 Corinthians 1 to him, one of his favourite passages.

'It's amazing,' said John, 'how Paul could affirm both the sanctity and the dividedness of the church in Corinth. I wish the church today would be more willing to admit that same reality. Such an admission would prevent many conflicts.'

Then John began to speak to Corey about Paul's claim in 1 Corinthians 2:2 – 'I resolved to know nothing while I was with you except Jesus Christ and him crucified.'

'I have a prayer for you, Corey,' John said. 'It is that you will keep the cross as the centre of your ministry to the very end.'

'I will always try to do so,' Corey promised.

Then John prayed. 'Keep Corey faithful to the message of the cross,' he said. 'Bless his future ministry. Help him to hold more and more to the cross as the years go by, at Princeton and whatever comes beyond it. Bless Corey's wife Sarah and their marriage. Bless them with children. In the name of the Lord Jesus, Amen.'

On the Friday morning a 'Doppler Scan' on John's leg revealed that there was no clot or sign of thrombosis, and the swelling was a side effect from the cut. The Indian orthopaedic surgeon and the cardiologist in London agreed to let John continue with his programme as long as he was careful to keep his leg raised as much as possible.

From Chennai, where they commandeered a wheelchair for John, they flew to Manila in the Philippines for a 'Preach the Word' conference organised by the Philippine Council of Evangelical Churches. Over 2,000 pastors, preachers and teachers attended. John and Corey were led up to the stage in the shadow of a massive banner proclaiming, *PREACH THE WORD, WITH DR JOHN R. W. STOTT.* John was initially unnerved by the very charismatic worship as they entered the hall, led by a woman worship leader 'bouncing and leaping on the stage and waving her arms wildly'.

When the time of worship eventually came to an end, John began his talk to the crowded audience. He sat in a big wooden armchair with his left leg protruding forward onto another chair. At his back and sides pillows were silhouetted on the now-empty stage by powerful floodlights.

A Filipino surgeon, examining John, expressed concern about his leg and continuous preaching. This alarmed Corey more than it did John who insisted on carrying on with his planned visit to Hong Kong, where they flew on 24 February 2002. They were met at the airport by two Scripture Union board members, equipped with a cane and wheelchair. They drove John and Corey to the YMCA, a modern forty-five-storey building overlooking Hong Kong Harbour.

On the Saturday night, John spoke at the Hong Kong Scripture Union's fortieth anniversary in a Methodist church with nearly 1,000 people present. His subject was the 'The Lordship of Jesus Christ' and he used an interpreter. To John's surprise, when the interpreter translated several of his phrases, the audience erupted into laughter. The English original words were not intended to be funny.

John preached on the Sunday morning at St Andrew's, an English-speaking Anglican church with a mix of both expatriates and Chinese. His subject was 'The Authentic Jesus' but he struggled. He lost his place three or four times. The strain of the long Asian tour and his poor health were taking their toll.

After church John had invited some Chinese friends, including the three Hong Kong Langham Scholars, to a Langham Partnership promotional lunch. He said a few words after the lunch: 'I hope that a Hong Kong Branch of Langham Partnership International will come into being, especially with the vision to equip pastors and seminaries in mainland China.'

On 25 February, John and Corey arrived safely back in London. It was not quite his last visit to the Far East, but for now as he continued his recovery he set to work on his next books.

Way back in 1986, Richard Bewes had invited John to preach four sermons on *Why I Am a Christian*. Friends urged him to write these up into a book and to add a chapter or more. This John did, completing the task at the beginning of 2003.

In the book, for which he chose the same title as the sermon series, John referred to Francis Thompson's magnificent poem, 'The Hound of Heaven' and to the fact that it was Jesus Christ, the 'tremendous lover', who had pursued, pricked and prodded him until he surrendered to him. 'Why I am a Christian,' he wrote, 'is due ultimately neither to the influence of my parents and teachers, nor to my own personal decision for Christ, but to "the hound of heaven". That is, it is due to Jesus Christ himself, who pursued me relentlessly even when I was running away from him in order to go my own way. And if it were not for the gracious pursuit of the hound of heaven I would today be on the scrap-heap of wasted and discarded lives.'

John said that he was a Christian because only Jesus could fulfil the basic aspirations or longings which all human beings experience. This was a claim validated by millions of Christians, among whom he included himself. 'There is a hunger in the human heart which none but Christ can satisfy.

There is a thirst which none but he can quench. There is an inner emptiness which none but he can fill. As Augustine wrote at the very beginning of his *Confessions*, "You have made us for yourself, and our heart is restless until it rests in you." God's purpose it to build a new society, a new family, even a new human race, that lives a new life and a new lifestyle.'

30. SHAPING OUR WORLD

What does John Stott have in common with George W. Bush, Gordon Brown, Bill Clinton, Barack Obama, Cardinal Joseph Ratzinger, Clint Eastwood, Rupert Murdoch, the Dalai Lama, Bill Gates, Nelson Mandela and Oprah Winfrey? The answer is that on 10 April 2005 they were all named by *Time* magazine among the 100 most influential people in the world – people who shape our world.

To construct the list, the editor of *Time* magazine sought proposals from all his correspondents in the USA and overseas, and spoke to many experts outside the magazine for advice in their fields. Having made the selection, the magazine asked an appropriate person to make the case for the choice. In John's case they approached Billy Graham who said, 'I can't think of anyone who has been more effective in introducing so many people to a biblical world view. He represents a touchstone of authentic biblical scholarship that, in my opinion, has scarcely been paralleled since the days of the 16th-century European Reformers.'

The wisdom of *Time* magazine's selection should not be lightly dismissed since Gordon Brown went on to become British Prime Minister, Barack Obama was elected US President and Cardinal Ratzinger was chosen as Pope!

John had no idea that the magazine was going to publish the list. When he read the issue he 'literally burst out laughing' because he thought it 'utterly absurd'. He told Brian Draper of the London Institute that 'there must be hundreds of thousands of people whose influence is greater than mine'. Others felt that *Time* magazine was closer to the truth than John. And indeed a few months later the British Establishment awarded John a CBE (Commander of the Order of the British Empire) in the New Year Honours List, for 'services to Christian scholarship and the Christian world'. John was pleased with the citation but embarrassed by the continuing reference to the British Empire which long ago ceased to exist!

John's study assistant from 2002 to 2005 was Matthew Smith – his father had lived in the Weymouth Street Rectory in the 1960s. One of Matthew's key tasks was carefully to read, and to make many suggestions for improvement in the writing of one of John's most ambitious and attractive books. They finished the job in September 2005, handing the manuscript to Frances Whitehead shortly before she completed fifty years as John's secretary. With beautiful watercolour illustrations by Fred Apps, *Through the Bible Through the Year* is a daily devotional book covering the entire narrative of the Bible, the seasons of the church year and all key Christian themes. It is often a very personal book, such as where John ends his reflections on Psalm 130 – 'Out of the depths I cry to you, O Lord; O Lord, hear my voice' – with the words: 'Many times I have needed to make this penitential psalm my own, and many times its promises have brought me the assurance of God's forgiveness.'

It is also an honest and realistic book which doesn't avoid problems or duck uncomfortable questions. Commenting on Matthew 6 with its call to trust God and seek first his kingdom, John writes: 'We must not misunderstand Jesus' teaching. Firstly, trusting God does not exempt us from working to earn our own living. The birds teach us this lesson. For how does God feed the birds? The answer is that he doesn't! Jesus was a keen observer of nature. He knew perfectly well that birds feed themselves. It is only indirectly that God feeds them by providing the wherewithal with which they feed themselves. Secondly, trusting God does not exempt us from calamity. True, not a single sparrow falls to the ground without our

Father's permission. But sparrows do fall and get killed. So do human beings. So do aeroplanes.'

Weeks 18 to 34, where John takes us through the life of Christ, rank among the most beautiful passages he has ever written. He charmingly combines vivid recreations of scenes from the life of our Lord with often searching meditations. Going through week 31, where John reflects on the seven words from the cross, would transform Holy Week for any sensitive reader.

In January 2006 John made another visit to China accompanied by Chris Wright, Mark Hunt (at that time Chair of the Langham Partnership International Council), David Cansdale and the leaders of the Langham Foundation in Hong Kong. John is greatly respected in China, enjoys high standing with the Three Self Church, and many flocked to hear him speak. He met the top leadership of the China Christian Council, greeted them one last time, and officially handed over his leadership of the Langham Partnership to Chris Wright in their presence amid much Chinese protocol. He returned via Hong Kong where he spoke at a packed public meeting about the Langham Partnership. These were his last public words in Asia, and church, seminary and student leaders paid him many warm and grateful tributes.

On Sunday 20 August 2006, while Rector Hugh Palmer was at All Souls taking the 8 a.m. service, John was getting up in his Bridford Mews flat, preparing to preach at the 11.30 service. Among those looking forward to hearing him preach that morning was Tamara Dewdney (née Coates), his cousin, who had lived for extended periods with the Stott family eighty years earlier.

The service was to be followed by a lunch for visitors which John was to host in the Rectory basement dining room, after which he was to leave for several weeks at The Hookses together with Chris Jones (CJ), his new study assistant who had arrived from America just two weeks earlier.

Frances Whitehead was at her home in Bourne End for the weekend, preparing to leave early on the Sunday morning for The Hookses ahead of the other two. But back at Bridford Mews, while dressing in his bedroom, John tripped over a chair and fell heavily to the floor. He realised that he had damaged his hip and couldn't get up. Using the aid-call button round his neck which friends had insisted he should wear, he was able to buzz a call centre for help. Neighbours quickly arrived on the scene and summoned an ambulance to take him to hospital. Frances was about to leave for The Hookses when the phone rang.

'Don't drive to The Hookses. Please return to London as soon as possible,' the caller said.

She repacked and hurried to the Accident and Emergency department at University College Hospital where she found John lying in a cubicle awaiting admission to a ward with a suspected fractured hip. He seemed in good spirits, but concerned about Hugh Palmer.

'I'm so sorry that he will have to preach in my place at such short notice,' he said to Frances. 'And what shall we do about the people I have invited to lunch?'

In the event, Tamara Dewdney and the All Souls congregation listened as Hugh preached the sermon from notes which John had prepared. Hugh acted as host at the lunch, assisted by CJ, and by the time Frances arrived at the Rectory, the event was in full swing.

John had an operation on his hip the next day, and was in hospital for ten days before spending a month at a convalescent home out of London. Then he returned to his flat and tried to resume some kind of normality.

In October, *Christianity Today* recalled that the *New York Times* columnist David Brooks had written that 'if evangelicals chose a pope, they would likely select John Stott'. With this in mind, *Christianity Today* senior writer Tim Stafford asked John how he would evaluate the immense growth of the church worldwide during the sixty-one years since he had been ordained.

'The answer is "growth without depth",' John replied. 'None of us wants to dispute the extraordinary growth of the church. But it has been largely numerical and statistical growth. And there has not been sufficient growth in discipleship that is comparable to the growth in numbers.'

John spoke to Tim about the importance of preaching. 'When I enter the pulpit with the Bible in my hands and in my heart,' John said, 'my blood begins to flow and my eyes to sparkle for the sheer glory of having God's Word to expound. We need to emphasise the glory, the privilege, of sharing God's truth with people.'

'Where do we evangelicals need to go?' Tim asked. 'We've been through quite a trip in the last 50 years.'

'My immediate answer,' John replied, 'is that we need to go beyond evangelism. Evangelism is supposed to be evangelicals' specialty. Now, I am totally committed to world evangelisation. But we must look beyond evangelism to the transforming power of the gospel, both in individuals and in society. With regard to individuals, I'm noting in different expressions of the evangelical faith an absence of that quest for holiness that marked our forebears, who founded the Keswick movement, for example, and the quest for what they sometimes called scriptural holiness or practical holiness. Somehow *holiness* has a rather sanctimonious feel to it. People don't like to be described as holy. But the holiness of the New Testament is Christlikeness.'

John talked about the role of Christians in transforming society and the implications of the biblical metaphors of salt and light. 'My hope,' he concluded, 'is that in the future, evangelical leaders will ensure that their social agenda includes such vital but controversial topics as halting climate change, eradicating poverty, abolishing armouries of mass destruction, responding adequately to the AIDS pandemic, and asserting the human rights of women and children in all cultures. I hope our agenda doesn't remain too narrow.'

John had never forgotten Robert Runcie's words to the third National Evangelical Anglican Congress (NEAC), at Caister in 1987: 'If the current evangelical renewal in the Church of England is to have a lasting impact, then there must be more explicit attention given to the doctrine of the church.'

Runcie's words had divided evangelicals. Some had nodded their assent, fearful that his stricture was correct, but others protested that they had turned away from the stubborn individualism for which they used to be notorious. John had also noticed the recent proliferation of books about the church, and followed with interest the growth of 'seeker churches', 'purpose-driven churches', the 'emerging church' and 'fresh expressions' of church.

He read the writings of social analysts who were trying to summarise what was involved in the cultural shift from the modernism of the Enlightenment to the arrival of postmodernism. He recognised that both modernism and postmodernism were extremely varied phenomena. He applauded some characteristics of postmodernism, in its critique of modernism, believing that they offered new opportunities for the gospel, whereas other aspects were to be rejected.

John and his study assistant Tyler Wigg Stevenson (and Christopher Jones from August) spent 2006 reading widely and reflecting together on the subject of the church, including ideas and publications from the emerging church. In his book *The Living Church: Convictions of a Lifelong Pastor*, published in 2007, he asked: What were the marks of a church in a postmodern culture? What were advocates of the emergent church saying?

He concluded that what was evolving so far was more a conversation than a movement, and still modest enough not to claim too much, since the situation was continuing to develop. Characteristically he was convinced that traditional and emerging churches needed to listen attentively to one another, with a view to learning from one another. Traditionalists needed to recognise that much of what they recognised as traditional today was itself once revolutionary and even 'emerging', and therefore they needed to be open to today's creative thinking. Advocates of the emerging church should be wary of loving newness for newness' sake. Both sides could afford to be less suspicious, less dismissive of each other, and more respectful and open. He agreed with Archbishop Rowan Williams who had said that 'there are many ways in which the reality of "church" can exist'.

In his book he set out what he believed to be the essential marks which would always characterise an authentic and living church. He said that what was needed were churches which were 'conservative' in the sense that they conserved what Scripture plainly required, but 'radical' in relation to that combination of tradition and convention which characterised 'culture'. Scripture was unchangeable, culture was not.

Richard Bewes thought that John's book was a 'life-giving tonic'. 'From beginning to end – right through to his enthralling appendices – John Stott has given us gold on every page. *The Living Church* deserves to be read, discussed – yes, and re-preached – by pastors and Christian workers, ordained and lay, at every level and across every Christian denomination going. It ought to become required reading, not only in campuses and seminaries world-wide, but – because of its sheer readability – in everyday homes and fellowships where God's people are to be found.'

'This is a gem of a book,' said David Jackman, then President of the Proclamation Trust. 'Here is the heart-beat of a godly and faithful minister of Christ, whose influence for good has been, and continues to be, incalculable. Full of distilled biblical wisdom, refreshing candour and honesty, penetrating discernment and plans for practical action, it speaks with clarity and power to the confused and often demoralised contemporary church, with a message that is pure gold. This is a book which every committed Christian needs to read!'

At eighty-six, John hadn't lost the ability to produce a winner.

On Friday 8 June 2007, John moved into the College of St Barnabas, a residential community of retired Anglican clergy set in lovely countryside near Lingfield, Surrey, entering fully into the prayer and worship life at the college (even though its tradition of churchmanship is higher than his).

Six weeks later on 17 July he preached what would be his last sermon at the Keswick Convention. The warmth of his welcome and the long applause which greeted his appearance was a tribute to the love and affection for him among the regular convention goers. A few were even able to remember his first address to the convention forty-five years earlier. After a joke at his own expense he launched into his talk.

'I remember very vividly, some years ago,' he said, 'that the question which perplexed me as a younger Christian (and some of my friends as well) was this: what is God's purpose for his people? Granted that we have been converted, granted that we have been saved and received new life in Jesus Christ, what comes next? Of course, we knew the famous statement of the Westminster Shorter Catechism: that man's chief end is to glorify God and to enjoy him forever: we knew that, and we believed it. We also toyed with some briefer statements, like one of only five words – love God, love your neighbour. But somehow neither of these, nor some others that we could mention, seemed wholly satisfactory. So I want to share with you where my mind has come to rest as I approach the end of my pilgrimage on earth and it is – God wants his people to become like Christ. Christlikeness is the will of God for the people of God.'

He spoke about the biblical basis for the call to Christlikeness and suggested that we are to be like Christ in his incarnation, his service, his love, his patient endurance and his mission. 'Let me invite you,' John said, 'to come with me to the upper room where Jesus spent his last evening with his disciples, recorded in John's Gospel, chapter 13: "He took off his outer garments, he tied a towel round him, he poured water into a basin and washed his disciples' feet. When he had finished, he resumed his place and said, 'If then I, your Lord and Teacher, have washed your feet, you also ought to wash one another's feet, for I have given you an example'" – notice the word – "'that you should do as I have done to you.'" Just as Jesus performed what in his culture was the work of a slave, so we in our cultures must regard no task too menial or degrading to undertake for each other . . .

'God's purpose,' he concluded, 'is to make us like Christ. God's way to make us like Christ is to fill us with his Spirit. In other words, it is a Trinitarian conclusion, concerning the Father, the Son and the Holy Spirit.'

I visited John the following December. Frances Whitehead was there, armed with mince pies, while John had persuaded the chef to prepare us a beautiful lunch using some salmon that had been sent him by a friend. It was the first of a number of conversations I had with him over a period of eighteen months looking back on his remarkable life.

He told me about what he called his three renunciations. 'One was against an academic career when I was at Cambridge. My professors were urging me to stay in Cambridge, to get a fellowship at one of the colleges and to pursue an academic career. It was very attractive, but I was convinced that God had not called me to that but rather to a pastorate. Then of course there was marriage. I was expecting to marry. I went about with a weather eye, and in my twenties and early thirties was looking for a possible bride. I did have two girlfriends – not simultaneously but one after t'other!

But all I can say is that when the time came to decide whether to go forward in the relationship or not, I lacked the assurance that I should. That is the only way I can really explain it. And the third is the ecclesiastical hierarchy, whether to become a bishop or an archbishop – and once again, I believed that God had called me to the pastorate.'

In conversation with me and with others, John admitted that the third renunciation was not clear-cut. 'Occasionally I feel that I wish I were a bishop because it is extraordinary how people will listen to bishops as if they were angels or archangels. Being a bishop gives you a platform which I admit is a little enviable.'

We talked about Michael Ramsey and William Temple, two archbishops whom John had quoted in his summer sermon at Keswick. 'Glory was a key word in Ramsey's thinking,' John said. 'I have heard that it was the word on his lips on his deathbed. He kept whispering glory, glory, glory. I admire him because he was a man of God. He was first and foremost not an administrator but a man of God. Ramsey said that Luther had got it right on justification and that's very endearing. Ramsey excluded conservative evangelical churchmen from the criticism he had made of fundamentalists.

'William Temple was largely responsible for that remarkable report, *Towards the Conversion of England* (1945). When I get to heaven I want to discuss with him what happened to the report because I think the truth is it fizzled out. And there may be some reason why it fizzled out. I don't know why it fizzled out. But I love Temple's writings and preaching. He taught me that sin equals self.'

After lunch, while John lay down for his 'horizontal half-hour', I reminisced with Frances in St Barnabas library about the incredible fifty-five years during which she had known him.

'In the 1950s and 60s,' she told me, 'John was always so busy and so disciplined that he rarely had time for a relaxed conversation. He appeared aloof and many people were in awe of him. He kept himself to himself. He was old-fashioned and a stickler for formality. He's changed a lot over the years, but even here at St Barnabas a few days ago, a woman resident challenged him, "John why do you never have time to talk to me?" "I'll talk to you at ten o'clock on Monday!" he replied.

'He had tremendous presence,' Frances continued, 'and I was somewhat scared when I first worked for him, especially if I had to knock on his study door when the notice "Do not disturb" was hanging there!'

'Does John have a dark side?' I asked Frances.

'No,' she replied. 'He is thoroughly consistent. He is what he professes. He wants to please God and that's all he cares about – doing God's will, living for his glory, being faithful. I've never found any real flaws in him. Oh yes, he can be impatient. He got that from his father. He always said that he inherited his father's short temper. There have been occasions when I have roused his disapproval, which is devastating because you don't want to put a foot wrong. Like his father he doesn't suffer fools gladly – but he doesn't show it. Most of the time he's very patient. Once when I got some envelopes muddled up and sent an important letter to the wrong person, he couldn't have been more gracious. He was very kind about it – I was expecting a rebuke but it never came. He's a man of integrity who keeps his word. If he says he will do a thing he does it. Remember what he said in his last address at Keswick about the damage a messenger of Christ does if he doesn't bear the image of Christ.

'It's been very hard work,' Frances continued. 'I wouldn't have persevered for over fifty years if John hadn't been authentic. For years I didn't have a private life because I had to work so hard. But what he was saying was true, and I could see that the gospel he proclaimed was true – it changed people's lives.'

THANKING GOD FOR JOHN

In March 2008, I spent five days at The Hookses with John and a dozen of his friends. From my desk in the Langham Den where I wrote some of this book, I enjoyed a glorious view across the little stream next to which John had pitched his tent fifty-six years earlier, over a grassy slope to the sea with waves breaking on the shore in West Dale Bay.

I talked to John Smith about his days living in the Rectory from 1963 to 1968.

'I think of John as much as a pastor,' John Smith told me, 'as an international preacher and author.'

'Some people think there is a certain inscrutability about John,' I suggested, 'which makes him difficult to know.'

'He's not inscrutable at all,' John Smith assured me. 'He's very transparent. Thousands of people consider themselves to be a friend of his. That's because of his capacity for friendship and making you feel special. And he's full of table talk. Mind you, he was never at his best in the morning. I never joked with him in the morning!'

On Thursday 6 March, John felt unwell and was unable to join us for breakfast. His friends talked to me about why they thanked God for John.

Ted Schroder thanked God that John had believed in him, given him his first opportunity to serve at All Souls, instilled in him a love for truth, and had remained an inspiration over his long, productive life.

'I thank God,' said John Smith, 'that over some fifty-one years of friendship he's been an amazing person, an outstanding preacher, and a wonderful pastor. I thank God for John's Christlikeness, genuineness, integrity, discipline, gentleness, humour, and forgiving spirit which he has exercised in my favour many times.'

Sara, widow of former All Souls curate Miles Thomson, thanked God for John because he never made her feel a fool. 'I'm not a woman of intellect,' she said, 'while he is a man of intellect. But he always made Christ relevant in a way that I could understand, whether it was serving in the team at All Souls or before that when I was engaged to Miles. He never expected more from his colleagues than he was prepared to give himself.'

'I think if I were to sum it up for me personally,' Richard Bewes reflected, 'I would say that John has been, and is under God my insurance policy against so many things. I've always felt completely safe with John. When it came to the time of the growth of the Charismatic Movement I remember writing to John asking for his advice. He wrote back a terrific handwritten letter which I still keep in my file. The letter reassured me and gave me advice. I thought, "John, you're my insurance policy against anything which isn't quite right or is off-centre." He doesn't know it, but he held me around that time.

'Then began the friendship,' Richard continued. 'And it was a friendship between him, Liz and me. It was a real trusting friendship. And once again I had this strong feeling that he was my insurance policy. I used to feel at All Souls, as the morning service began, John would be there and I'd think, *Nothing can go wrong. John Stott is here!* He was an anchor figure to me.'

John felt better later in the day and joined us for the evening meal. In jovial mood he told us why people in various parts of the United Kingdom love the gospel. 'The English,' John said, 'love the gospel because it gives them something to talk about, the Welsh love it because it gives them something to sing about, the Irish because it gives them something to fight about, and the Scots love it because it's free!'

Then, egged on by John Smith, he told us one of the anecdotes he loves to tell against himself.

'I was invited to preach in a cathedral in Florida, and was introduced by a Dean,' John said switching to a southern drawl. '"When ah first read a book by John Stott", the dean said, "ah said to mahself I'll crawl one hundred miles on my hands and knees to hear this man speak. And now ladies and gentleman you are going to hear him for yourselves . . ."' Eventually he handed over to me and sat down prominently in the front row. I made a few appropriate remarks and then proceeded with my talk. After five minutes I glanced down to see how the Dean was taking it and noticed that he had fallen fast asleep. I could only assume that he was worn out after his crawl!'

Later that same month on a visit to Uganda, I called at Kampala Evangelical School of Theology (KEST) where John had led a preaching workshop in 2000. The church in Africa is growing rapidly, a situation that requires church leaders equipped to apply the gospel to contemporary Africa's spiritual, physical, political and socio-economic realities. KEST was established by Zac Niringiye and others to help develop visionary, creative leaders for the African church. Aggrey Mugisha talked to me about John and his impact on East Africa.

'There are Christians in Uganda,' Aggrey told me, 'who say "we have the Spirit and don't need theology!" This is where Uncle John's approach of balanced Bible-based Christianity is so valuable.'

Next day, returning from a visit to Jinja, I boarded a packed public minibus for the journey from Kampala town centre back to Bukoto where I was staying. Making my way to a seat at the back, I found myself sitting next to a Ugandan woman called Harriet. It turned out that she was a member of Kampala Baptist Church.

'In 1992,' she told me, 'I attended a Christian Impact course led by John Stott in London. I have read his book on bird-watching.'

What a remarkable demonstration of John's impact on Africa that I should quite by chance find myself sitting next to Harriet!

A week later I called at the offices of the Anglican diocese of Kampala to see John's friend David Zac Niringiye, now Bishop of Kampala. The Langham Partnership partly funded his MA at Wheaton College and a PhD at Edinburgh University.

'I first met John in Nairobi in 1980,' Zac remembered, 'at a national conference for Christian leaders at which John was the keynote speaker. I was a young man in my late twenties working as Director of the Fellowship of Christian Unions in Uganda. I was so drawn by the quality of John's preaching and teaching that I sought him out the morning after he finished speaking. I was surprised when I met him a week later at All Saints Cathedral in Kampala that he remembered me.

'It was the beginning of a life-transforming friendship. From then on, John became my mentor, through his books, his personal letters, and the many opportunities when we met, at conferences, and through bird-watching and praying together. He revealed his human, vulnerable side. The controversy following his musings about hell in the mid-80s, and some of the things which were said, hurt him deeply. But he doesn't easily take offence. John has a great gift for friendship and for bringing people together.'

'What are John's weaknesses?' I asked Zac. He thought for a moment.

'I think he has put too much emphasis on "reason",' Zac replied. 'He is too much a "child of the Enlightenment". In a postmodernist age, John is "the last modernist". And he is too afraid of being seen to be vulnerable in public. Perhaps it's the stiff-upper-lip, English public schoolboy in him. But I'm very interested in the way that he has changed over the years. I hope you will bring that out in your book!'

When I promised to try, I was rewarded with one of Zac's famous hugs.

In July 2008, I flew to Philadelphia to talk to John Yates, then serving on the staff of the Good Samaritan at Paoli to the west of the city. When we were joined by Steve Beck, who had just come to the end of long spell as chairman of the London Institute, he drew attention to elements of the entrepreneurial and innovative about John.

'He was an entrepreneur,' said Steve. 'Two things characterise an entrepreneur: first, extraordinary strength and clarity of vision – having the courage of your convictions. And second, the ability persuasively to communicate the vision – to get others on board to put the vision into practice. In John's case, to these qualities were added his integrity. The combination of John's thinking, writing and living was a rudder for the Christian church for half a century. He had the courage to defend the Lausanne vision of combining evangelism with social action. He had the courage to establish the London Institute in the face of those who didn't believe in "double listening".

'But added to John's vision, courage and integrity was his ability to get things done. His gifts are not just conceptual: he's a "wheeler dealer" who can spot talent and then gently, or not so gently, twist the right person's arm to get him or her involved in his projects. Spotting Frances Whitehead was an early example of this. He was forceful in getting things to move in the way that he wanted them to move organisationally. He was able to move from the level of theological abstraction to making things happen on the ground. His iron-will discipline went hand in hand with a pastoral heart. He got things done through people: the combination of gentleness, charm and firmness by which he invited people to get involved in projects meant that people responded.'

John Yates, Steve Beck and I agreed that alongside the humble follower and modeller of Jesus, there was the human John Stott: ambitious for himself as well as for the glory and honour of Christ. 'He found it hard to suffer fools,' said Steve. 'I've heard him on more than one occasion forcefully correct sloppy thinking or imprecise language. The offender would melt. But I've also heard him apologise for being too quick or too strong with his corrections. He set very high standards for himself and for those around him but he was also very self-aware.' Steve once asked him after a breakfast meeting with two dozen admiring international students how he managed to maintain his evident humility. He quoted a Scottish clergyman back to Steve: 'If you could see in my heart you would spit in my face.'

'He told me,' said John Yates, 'that humility is not another word for hypocrisy – it's another word for honesty.'

I flew to San Francisco and spoke to Ken Perez. A quarter of a century earlier Ken had been librarian at the London Institute. Now he was President of John Stott Ministries in Menlo Park. He talked to me about how they encourage American donors to support the work of Langham Partnership. 'If you are over forty there is a chance that you have read some John Stott books or heard him speak perhaps at Urbana. If you are under forty you haven't. Perhaps you are reading Rick Warren, Bill Hybels, John Ortberg or Tim Keller. All those people quote John Stott. We estimate that there are twenty to thirty million mission-minded evangelical Christians in America. A million of those will participate themselves, taking vacation time to get involved in the work of mission in some way. The challenge for us is to engage with a younger generation who don't know about John.'

From Menlo Park I drove across Dunbarton Bridge and north up the east side of San Francisco Bay where John's former study assistant Mark Labberton was now senior pastor at First Presbyterian Church of Berkeley. As well as working and travelling with John, Mark heard him preach at home and abroad, listened to many recordings of his sermons, and wrote a paper on John the preacher.

'John has many eccentricities,' Mark told me, 'but these don't take away from the core of who he is, his commitment, his convictions, his holiness. This is at the core of any explanation of the impact of his preaching. It is the story of a man who has sought faithfully to live the story of the One he proclaims. This has been true in places where the culture is very different from the one where he has lived most of his life.

'In his early days as a preacher he was very anxious to lay out a logical case: one early sermon had over fifty points in it! When I drew his attention to this he put his face in his hands and said, "Oh what was I ever thinking!" Later in his preaching, intuition came to play a greater role. He became more accepting and acknowledging of nuance and mystery, that "we see but we see through a glass darkly". This came out too in his later writings. So he has been on a journey. He has come a long way towards acknowledging that there are limits to our certainties even in the central presentation of the shape of the gospel. I once said to John, "You are actually less of a rationalist than you appear to be. You imply that you have a greater confidence in reason than I think you actually do." He did not dissent.'

Mark and I discussed the extent to which John could be described as 'creative'.

'I would put it this way,' said Mark. 'He's not imaginative in the sense of being interested in producing original thought. He's not driven in that way. But what he has done is to draw together a convergence of themes and issues in a way which can appropriately be called creative. He brings together things which in many people's minds are unrelated. Although this may not be exactly creative, it is ingenious, fascinating, enlarging. John can expand your thinking.

'John has been the initiator of institutions, alliances, relationships, partnerships in a highly creative way. These institutions wouldn't exist today were it not for John. He has made things happen.'

Way back in 1972, a young man from Londonderry came to London to study law at King's College and went along to All Souls. 'I will never forget,' he remembers, 'the visual impact of John in his scarlet Queen's Chaplain cassock and gleaming surplice (lovingly ironed by some of the admiring ladies of the congregation!) kneeling in the pulpit before he preached – as was then his practice. I had never heard preaching of such authority or clarity. I simply couldn't get enough of it!'

The young law student's name was David Turner and All Souls has been his church ever since. Now he is a circuit judge and a trustee of the Langham Partnership. After David had sung John's praises to me, I pressed him to tell me some of his weaknesses.

'Well,' he replied, 'these are the reverse of some of the strengths. He has a single mindedness which has tended at times to the inflexible. In earlier times he wasn't always a great listener, but responded well when Ted Schroder challenged him on this. He sometimes demonstrates a baffled incomprehension at times that people are in general neither as focused nor as disciplined as he is. He sometimes had a limited grasp of the real pressures and demands of family life placed on the people with whom he worked and of whom he had exceedingly high expectations.

'And then there was an occasional pedantry about ropey grammar and expression. He didn't hesitate to correct or challenge, irrespective of the feelings of the other party! He hasn't always been good at "chilling out". Social calls were brief, small talk limited, pastoral engagement time strictly limited and orderly, supper invitations terminated to ensure bed on time, and seconds rarely accepted! This at times felt like an austerity, though actually John was and is by no means austere. It was the "iron discipline" which he refused to compromise.

'But frankly,' David concluded, 'it is no exaggeration to say that John is the finest man I have ever known. No human being has overall influenced or inspired me more. My debt to him is incalculable. To be with him and to work with him were never entirely comfortable, but invariably profoundly uplifting and fulfilling.'

John Wyatt first attended All Souls (like David Turner) in 1972 as a medical student. Now, as a senior consultant in a London hospital, he has acted for some years as an informal medical adviser to John. He has found it a privilege to share the painful experiences of illness, major surgery, increasing disability and dependence with John.

'Self-disclosure is not easy for him,' John Wyatt told me. 'It's partly a generational and cultural factor, and partly his own personality. He is not naturally prone to excessive amounts of self-reflection or analysis. I think this is why, when people ask him to share from his own experiences, especially of weakness or depression, he often finds it difficult. He is much more interested in finding avenues for service and for engaging with others than in reflecting on his internal emotions.

'But in private over the last years we have on occasion been able to share together some of our deepest concerns, struggles and fears. He has often taught and preached about human frailty and weakness and our utter dependence on God. About the God who enters into our human experience of weakness in order to identify with us. But the practical experience of suffering, dependence and memory loss hasn't been easy for him to bear. As someone with a lifelong razor-sharp intellect he has found the memory lapses and occasional confusion of old age painful and at times humiliating. He has always defined himself in terms of Christian service, and perhaps the realisation that his public ministry was coming to an end was particularly painful for him. But he has accepted these losses with Christian fortitude and good humour.'

We have come to the end of our tale which began in 1921, five years before the invention of television when David Lloyd-George was British Prime Minister and King George V still had fifteen years to reign. I conclude with a bold claim: that John Stott's life has been unique in the history of the Christian church. Unique in his nearly ninety-year link with the same parish church, close on sixty-five of them either as curate, Rector or Rector Emeritus. Unique in working with the same secretary for over half a century. Unique in his skill in writing fifty books which have been translated into sixty-seven languages, as well as editing a series of expositions of the entire New Testament which succeeded in being loyal to the text, relevant to the modern world and readable. Who else has done this? Unique in his entrepreneurial ability to translate vision into reality, whether in the establishment of the London Lectures, the London Institute or the Langham Partnership. Unique in the legacy he has left in his programmes for providing finance and inspiring people to improve scholarship, literature and preaching in the developing world. Unique in his ability to persuade evangelicals globally to embrace a new balance between evangelism and social action. Unique in building a network of friends from all over the world who testify to his transparent integrity. Unique in his ability to relax, whether spotting his beloved birds through his trusty binoculars or lovingly cleaning out his pond at the idyllic Hookses retreat which he has delighted to share with so many. Unique in generating love through his endearing blend of humility and mischievous humour. Unique in his commitment to the cause of the gospel and ability to present Jesus Christ as the attractive Saviour of the world who gave himself for us on a cross.

Our story is over but John's is not. He looks back with gratitude to the gracious pursuit of the hound of heaven down the arches of the years through labyrinthine ways. And though frail he is still able quietly to work, to pray and to welcome, with his familiar twinkle, those who are privileged to know him as a modeller of Jesus, gentle pastor and treasured friend.

MORE INFORMATION

If you would like further information on initiatives founded by John Stott, or with which he has worked, you should visit the following websites:

http://www.langhampartnership.org/
http://www.johnstottministries.org/
http://www.lausanne.org/
http://www.capetown2010.com/
http://www.licc.org.uk/
http://www.allsouls.org
http://www.ifesworld.org/
http://www.tearfund.org/
http://www.scriptureunion.org.uk

If you would like to contact the publishers of this book you should visit:

http://www.ivpress.com

If you would like to contact the author you should visit:

http://www.rogersteer.com/

BIBLIOGRAPHY

Unpublished material
John Stott papers held at Lambeth Palace Library.

Biographical material

Brooks, David (2004), 'Who is John Stott?' in *New York Times*, 30 November.

Chapman, Alister (2004), *John R. W. Stott and English Evangelicalism, 1938–84*, PhD thesis submitted to the University of Cambridge.

Christianity Today (2001), 'Stott's Emerging Legacy', *Christianity Today*, April.

Draper, Brian (2007), *Interview with John Stott*. London Institute of Contemporary Christianity DVD.

Dudley-Smith, Timothy (1999), *John Stott: The Making of a Leader*, Leicester: IVP.

Dudley-Smith, Timothy (2001), *John Stott: A Global Ministry*, Leicester: IVP.

Kelly, Jim (2005), 'The Time 100', in Special Issue of *Time Magazine*, 10 April.

McCloughry, Roy (1996), 'Basic Stott', in *Christianity Today*, 8 January.

Stackhouse, John (2000), 'An Elder Statesman's Plea', in *Christianity Today*, 7 February.

Stafford, Tim (2006), 'Evangelism Plus', in *Christianity Today*, 13 October.

BIBLIOGRAPHY

Wells, David (1996), 'Guardian of God's Word', in *Christianity Today*, 16 September.

Contemporaries
Eddison, John (ed., 1982), *Bash: A Study in Spiritual Power*, Basingstoke: Marshall Morgan and Scott.
Gilchrist, Dr Rae (1958), 'Obituary of Sir Arnold Stott', *British Medical Journal*, 28 June.
Graham, Billy (1997), *Just As I am: The Autobiography of Billy Graham*, San Francisco: Harper/Zondervan.
Muggeridge, Malcolm (1977), *Christ and the Media*, London: Hodder and Stoughton.
Telegraph Media Group (2007), 'The Reverend Professor C. F. D. Moule' (Obituary), in *Daily Telegraph*, Telegraph Media Group Ltd, 2 October.

Evangelicalism, Scripture and authority
Barnes, Gary (2003), 'Why Don't They Listen: Interview with John Stott', in *Christianity Today*, 1 September.
Bebbington, David W. (1989), *Evangelicalism in Modern Britain*, London: Routledge.
Geldenhuys, J. Norval (1953), *Supreme Authority*, Grand Rapids: Eerdmans.
Harris, Harriet A. (1998), *Fundamentalism and Evangelicals*, Oxford: Clarendon Press.
Noll, Mark A. (2006), 'Truth from the Evangelical Viewpoint', in *Christianity Today*, 29 September.
Noll, Mark A. (2006), 'Where We Are and How We Got Here', in *Christianity Today*, 29 September.
Packer, J. I. (1958), *'Fundamentalism' and the Word of God*, London: IVF.
Packer, J. I. (ed., 1967), *Guidelines: Anglican Evangelicals Face the Future*, London: Falcon Books.
Steer, Roger (1998), *Church on Fire: The Story of Anglican Evangelicals*, London: Hodder and Stoughton.

285

Yeats, Charles (ed., 1995), *Has Keele Failed?*, London: Hodder and
Stoughton.

Works by John Stott
Men with a Message (1954), London: Longmans.
Basic Christianity (1958), London: IVF. Revised 1971.
The Preacher's Portrait (1961), London: Tyndale. Reissued Leicester: IVP,
1995.
The Baptism and Fullness of the Holy Spirit (1964), London: IVF. Revised
and enlarged 1975.
Christ the Controversialist (1970), London: Tyndale.
Understanding the Bible (1972), London: Scripture Union.
Your Mind Matters (1972), London: IVF.
Guard the Gospel: The Message of 2 Timothy (1973) London: IVP.
Walk in His Shoes (1975), London: IVP.
The Lausanne Covenant: An Exposition and Commentary (1975), Minneapolis:
World Wide Publications (now available at http://www.lausanne.org/).
Christian Counter-Culture: The Message of the Sermon on the Mount (1978),
Leicester: IVP.
I Believe in Preaching (1982), London: Hodder and Stoughton.
Issues Facing Christians Today (1984), Basingstoke: Marshalls. Revised and
updated with new chapter 2006, Grand Rapids: Zondervan.
The Authentic Jesus (1985), London: Marshall Pickering.
The Cross of Christ (1986), Leicester: IVP. Revised with study guide
Nottingham: IVP.
Essentials: A Liberal-Evangelical Dialogue (with David Edwards,1988),
London: Hodder and Stoughton.
The Contemporary Christian (1992), Leicester: IVP.
*Authentic Christianity: From the Writings of John Stott, Chosen and Introduced by
Timothy Dudley-Smith* (1995), Leicester: IVP.
The Birds Our Teachers (1999), London: Candle/Hudson.
The Incomparable Christ (2001), Leicester: IVP.
People my Teachers (2002), London: Candle/Hudson.
Evangelical Truth (2003), Leicester: IVP.
Through the Bible Through the Year (2006), Oxford: Candle Books.

The Living Church: Convictions of a Lifelong Pastor (2007), Nottingham: IVP.
BST New Testament CD-ROM (ed., 2007), Nottingham: IVP.
The Last Word: Reflections on a Lifetime of Preaching (2008), Milton Keynes, Authentic Media.
The Radical Disciple (2010), Nottingham: IVP.

ALSO BY ROGER STEER

George Müller: Delighted in God
A Living Reality
Admiring God
George Müller: Heroes of the Cross
Hudson Taylor: A Man in Christ
Love Will Find a Way
Dream of Reality: An Evangelical Encounters the Oxford Movement
Hudson Taylor: Lessons in Discipleship
Canvas Conversations
Church on Fire: The Story of Anglican Evangelicals
Letter to an Influential Atheist
Good News for the World: The Story of Bible Society
Radical Discipleship